HAVE WE ALL GONE MAD?

HAVE WE ALL GONE MAD?

WHY GROUPTHINK IS RISING AND HOW TO STOP IT

JEROME BOOTH

Biteback Publishing

First published in Great Britain in 2022 by
Biteback Publishing Ltd, London
Copyright © Jerome Booth 2022

ISBN 978-1-78590-772-2

10 9 8 7 6 5 4 3 2 1

A CIP catalogue record for this book is available from the British Library.

Set in Minion Pro and Trade Gothic

Printed and bound in Great Britain by
CPI Group (UK) Ltd, Croydon CR0 4YY

FSC
www.fsc.org
MIX
Paper | Supporting
responsible forestry
FSC® C171272

CONTENTS

INTRODUCTION

This is a book about mass groupthink, which is a type of mass moral thinking. It is about the impact new technology is having not only on how we communicate but on how we think and self-identify, on our mutual toleration and on our politics. It is a defence of reason and science and history. It is a wake-up call for us to protect our liberal democracy.

Even before Covid-19 and lockdown, it seemed that we were living in an increasingly irrational and anxious world in which mental illness was worsening. This is odd because it follows widespread peace and clear improvements in global health, well-being and economic prosperity. Global inequality has massively reduced in my lifetime and agricultural technology means we can now amply feed the world's projected population using less land than currently.

We have faced a series of crises which we have poorly prepared for and then dealt with badly on their arrival. Why? There seems to be some dysfunction in our politics and a lack of engagement with electorates. Our political elites and media sometimes appear to be in bubbles of their own, cut off from the majority of public opinion.

Have we all gone mad? Can we identify the patterns and causes of what is happening and try to stop it?

Why did the policy reaction to Covid-19 not take into account the side effects of lockdown? Why did the financial crisis of 2008 occur, and will another one happen? What is behind the recent surge in political correctness? Is net zero sensible or affordable? Why are people becoming disillusioned with democracy?

I have written this book as an attempt to explain what is going on. I argue that the less than satisfactory responses to these and other recent questions have at least one commonality. Mass group-think is on the rise. I argue that the current heightened confusion and dissatisfaction within society, including an alienation of many from the ideas and interpretations emanating from political elites and the mainstream media, can best be understood in the context of what we know about psychology and some vicious postmodern memes (a meme here meaning a sort of intellectual virus, a sticky idea which self-replicates across society). Also, recent changes in communication technology (especially the internet and social media) have had a profound impact on the way we communicate and interact with others. They have affected our networks and communities, our sense of identity, the groups we belong to, our values and moral systems and our tolerance for others. Our Stone-Age brains have not yet adjusted to all this, and our societies and political systems haven't either.

That our brains have evolved slowly compared to our technology is nothing new. Neither is great complexity in our environment and our need to depend on shortcuts in our thinking. Such shortcuts include norms of behaviour but also standard patterns of thought, association of ideas and concepts of right and wrong. Shortcuts in thinking are common and inevitable, and immensely useful, but can also get us into deep water. When we don't have the same ideas and values, they may be constructively challenged. When we do, the result can be collective irrationality. Our common ideas and shortcuts can seriously let us down when we face particularly marked changes in our environment. We may also find it difficult to cope if these shortcuts for whatever reason change rapidly. Yet they are fashioned by rapidly changing networks and interactions, and this is particularly worrying where such change is non-random but rather orchestrated by others for profit or control.

Of the various forms of collective irrationality, groupthink is particularly dangerous. It occurs where a partially or completely false set of beliefs is sustained through lack of effective challenge. It thrives unnoticed by those captured by it. At worst, groupthink becomes moral and binary, good versus evil; one either believes wholeheartedly or is a heretic, with no room for doubt. Transgressors can be bullied, ostracised, punished, and vigorous efforts are made to stop any challenge or debate.

Avoidance of criticism and refusal to consider alternatives, consciously or unconsciously, has led to momentous mistakes throughout history. Irving Janis, who popularised the term groupthink, which is deliberately resonant with Orwell's doublethink, used as an example the uncritical thinking in the John F. Kennedy Cabinet that led to the abortive 1961 US invasion of Cuba known as the Bay of Pigs disaster.[1] In considering the military strategy, they did not give sufficient attention to the flaws in the plan or its alternatives. Discussion was limited within unquestioned parameters. The group assumed the President backed the invasion and nobody publicly questioned the overall wisdom of it, only the details. Afterwards, Kennedy recognised the faulty planning and adopted an approach to avoid repeats. This was then successfully deployed in the 1962 Cuban Missile Crisis, when it seemed the world was on the brink of nuclear war. In responding to the threat posed by the deployment of Soviet nuclear weapons in Cuba, just off the US coast, Kennedy formed groups to consider different strategic options and stayed out of them so they would not be overly influenced by his preliminary views. There was a process of rigorous challenge and consideration of different policy options. Unlike with the Bay of Pigs fiasco, good choices were made and a successful result achieved.

Janis's concept of groupthink has been used by management consultants advising on how to make better board decisions ever since. He highlighted eight groupthink symptoms: (a) an illusion of invulnerability; (b) collective rationalisation; (c) belief in the inherent morality of the group; (d) the stereotyping of those disagreeing as being deliberately opposed to the group, as well as morally weak or evil; (e) exercise of pressure on dissenters within the group to conform or leave; (f) self-censorship; (g) illusions of unanimity; and (h) self-appointed mind guards to squash heretical thinking within the group.

Although Janis's emphasis was on small-group decision-making, groupthink can be society-wide. In large-scale groupthink, as fear of transgression builds, particularly amongst elites, so too does acquiescence. Self-censorship takes hold and public discourse suffers. The very sense of the improbability that so many people could be wrong in itself sustains the lie. Indeed, there is a term for this: the Big Lie.

THE STRUCTURE OF THE BOOK

In Chapter 1, I look at the psychology behind groupthink. We like to think of ourselves as rational, but human beings are irrational. Rationality is something we have evolved to justify our actions to ourselves and to others after the event. Moreover, the more intelligent, educated and erudite, the more convincing we are in this task. And so elite bubbles are formed, impervious to outside reality. Our politicians and media elites are often more collectively blind than those around them.

We have different moral foundations and different groups and identities. As patterns of thought are repeated within groups and are less challenged from outside, they become stronger and help define group cohesiveness, but this also creates intolerance for the beliefs of others. Loyalty to shared values and care for those inside the group helps explain how groupthink develops.

I also discuss risk and uncertainty and criticise the widespread adoption of the precautionary motive in place of more comprehensive cost–benefit analysis. By focusing on only one problem, the precautionary motive can lead to reckless disregard to side effects and other problems.

In Chapter 2, I explore the importance of how we behave in interactions with others and how we are networked. These patterns have an impact on both social capital formation and local communities, and our democratic engagement is also affected. New technology and the business strategies of Big Tech are also in the mix and have implications for the ancient struggle between democracy and authoritarianism.

In Chapter 3, I explore how new media, as with communication technology innovations of the past, are forcing major societal change. Our psychology has not changed much over many generations, but our technology has. The introduction of the printing press led to popular access to the Bible, followed by schism and the Thirty Years War. This led to the deaths of a third of the population in the central part of Europe. The new communication technologies of today bring huge opportunities but also dangers that we don't yet know how to cope with. More connectivity has brought new identities, incentives and values. New political voices are not just being heard but are becoming dominant.

New media holds the promise of ushering in a new era of enfranchisement and liberty – what I call the Great Enfranchisement. But it is also an incubator for progressions from tribalism and fear, through intolerance and anger to hate and suffering.

Values are our new tribal colours and the 'us versus them' mentality is growing. One person's virtue is another's bigotry. Where the sense of moral boundaries being crossed is strongest, those challenging the in-group values can be attacked viciously, often starting on social media. An innocent tweet can now be deliberately and anonymously misconstrued and so destroy a career. Fear of arbitrary and unjust attack is now widespread, creating timidity and self-censorship.

In this new world of greater expression, our selection of what we hear is far from random. This is largely due to our own choices, but it is also partly driven by companies who have harvested vast data on our behaviour and wish to profit by it. Surveillance capitalism has arrived, and it is not benign.

In the next two chapters I give examples of groupthink in finance and academia. I first became aware of mass irrationality in finance and economics. In Chapter 4, I explain some of the misunderstandings and missed signals which led to the global financial crisis in 2008/09 and why a repeat is possible. I also tell the story of the economics behind quantitative easing, make some preliminary remarks about the Covid-19 lockdowns and analyse the newish fad for cryptocurrencies. This chapter illustrates that irrationality and groupthink can occur well beyond the boardroom, in very large fora and where there is plenty of competition, including competition of ideas. It is a humbling thought that so many people can be wrong about something. Much of it is down to groupthink.

Toleration, liberalism, history, reason and science are under threat. In Chapter 5, I defend science and discuss current trends against reason. Freedom of thought and speech are under threat; political correctness is on the rise. Self-censorship is increasing. Postmodernism and other philosophical developments contrary to the idea of the existence of a single objective reality, and erosive to the approach established in the Enlightenment that progress in science is based on refutable hypotheses, have spread. The existence of objective reality has been superseded; we all now have our own 'truths'. History is no longer seen through the moral spectrum of those who made it and so is losing its meaning and usefulness, becoming propaganda to bolster existing morality rather than a means to understand humanity. The scientific method is under attack by those certain of their truths, and scepticism is no longer seen by some as the engine driving science forward.

In the last three chapters, I deal more explicitly with politics and the threat to democracy we currently face. Chapter 6 reviews historical ideas of liberty, democracy and governance. Some risks and patterns of authoritarianism and revolution are discussed. I then consider some of the features of politics in the age of social media, including the impact of the growth of group rights and the balance between theory and practice in politics. To have teeth, foreign policy should be in the national interest, and yet this is often not the case. We seem to have retrogressed to a pre-Machiavellian world in which ideals, not reality, drive the international agenda. Are we heading towards a dystopian future?

More and more absurd nonsense in public life and the media goes unchallenged. Many of us get the feeling we are being systematically misled by a biased media, and government and mainstream media have been fearmongering, spreading propaganda. In Chapter 7, I discuss how many in the media and politics have lost objectivity and impartiality, eroded by activism. Our elites have ended up in groupthink bubbles, not only spreading propaganda and 'dumbing down' communications with the public but 'dumbing up' themselves in the process.

Liberal democracy is under threat from this perfect storm. Our leaders have yet to respond appropriately. Instead of offering hope and showing courage, defending reason and sound policy, politicians have been less than transparent, resorted to technocratic policies and used fear to manipulate the public. Chapter 8 gives some hints as to how we can counter groupthink and reduce its impact in public life.

The purpose of this book is largely to help us learn quicker how best to cope with new communications technology and avoid losing time. The big concern is to resist an erosion of liberalism and reason and with it a decline into non-democratic politics.

CHAPTER 1

FOOLING OURSELVES
AND OTHERS

'The only true wisdom is in knowing you know nothing.'
Socrates

The classic 1957 movie *12 Angry Men* is set almost entirely in one room and depicts the deliberation of a jury on whether to find a young man guilty or not guilty of killing his father. A vote is taken early on and eleven out of the twelve find the accused guilty. A number of pieces of evidence seem compelling, including from two witnesses. An old man downstairs heard the accused tell his father he was going to kill him and heard a thud, and then saw the accused leaving the building. A lady across the street, woken in the night, saw the accused stabbing his father, albeit through the windows of the last two carriages of a passing train.

But juror eight (played by Henry Fonda) is not sure. He cannot say beyond reasonable doubt if he thinks the boy murdered his father or not, and he at least wants to spend some time discussing it. The judge has told them that a unanimous verdict is required. The majority puts pressure on juror eight to conform, so he says that if, after an hour discussing it, no one else has reasonable doubt, then he will also vote guilty. What then happens is a gradual recollection of key facts which the accused's lawyer has obviously neglected to pick up on, until finally there is a unanimous verdict of not guilty. Along the way are arguments and shouting but also reasoning from new angles and questioning of assumptions. One juror just wants a quick result so he can get to a ball game. Another is racially prejudiced and a third (the last to change his mind) has an estranged son, which clouds his judgement. A simple plot; a gripping film.

One of the reasons it is so gripping is because it resonates with our experience of how people actually think and talk. There is nothing unbelievable about the twelve characters, and yet eleven of them are initially so certain of the accused's guilt that they are willing to send a young man to his death. In the course of the discussion, and in remembering key facts and their implications, they all realise, one by one, that they were wrong. The old man turned out to be an unreliable witness – he could not have moved to the door in time to see what he said he did. He was possibly lonely, craving the attention of being a witness. Likewise, the lady woken from her sleep across the street did not have time to put her glasses on to see what she said she did – it must have been a blur.

INDIVIDUAL AND COLLECTIVE IRRATIONALITY

We are less rational than we believe. Being rational is difficult. Truth is the successful outcome of being able to think impersonally and inhumanely, as the Austrian modernist writer Robert Musil put it.[1] Yet without great effort our egos reign over our decisions. We think the more intelligent and educated know better because they are in theory, we believe, more capable of being rational. Yet it might be more accurate to say that education and intelligence are not good indicators either of better morals or of more rationality outside the limited spheres of thought where they have become habit. Indeed, as we shall see, when there is groupthink, the more educated and intelligent can be less wise than others not so advantaged.

At best we are logical only some of the time. Yet we even call some types of thinking rational which on closer inspection seem quite irrational. Cognitive scientist Keith Stanovich describes two different types of rationality: instrumental rationality describes how we use all available resources to get what we want; epistemic rationality reflects the degree to which one's thoughts map reality.[2] If the first is a rough approximation to cleverness, the second is closer to worldly wisdom, and the first without the second often leads to stupid conclusions and actions – best not to make judgements on people's rationality by this split into components. One could even go so far as to argue that instrumental rationality is in essence merely a measure of how ego drives thought. As *Moby-Dick*'s Captain Ahab says in his obsessive quest for his whale: 'All my means are sane, my motive and my object mad.'[3] I would not call Ahab's chasing of his whale either sane or even instrumentally rational (you can tell that I think the term jars) but quite simply the whole pattern of his behaviour and thought is crazy. More generally, just because someone is rational part of the time because it is in their strong interests to be so does not mean they can be trusted to be rational when it is not in their interests. For example, it is a common misconception that experts of various types can be trusted to be objective and rational outside the very specific areas

3

where they have strong motives for being so. They may be no more rational than anyone else. Indeed, quite often they have clear incentives not to question orthodoxy, not to think outside the box, and especially not to challenge ideas fundamental to their well-being.

THE RATIONALIST MYTH

The rationalist myth is the idea that humans are guided by reason and that our experts, institutions and political elite can for the most part be trusted to make rational decisions. This myth has a pedigree which goes back to ancient Greece and is linked to a fundamental difference between Plato and Socrates, between rule by the good leader and democracy. Plato highlighted the importance of choosing a wise leader, Socrates the folly in thinking that someone 'wise' placed in power without being held to account would not turn out to be a tyrant.

Though the rationalist myth is a powerful meme which has held sway for centuries, our philosophy has of course evolved over the past couple of millennia. Human psychology, in contrast, has developed very little, if at all, over such a short evolutionary period. As Benjamin Franklin observed, we are tool-making animals. Tribal and kin conformity was a winning strategy for much of human history, with it being more important to look right than be right. We have evolved many behaviours which are beneficial for our group but not for the individual. Self-sacrifice is common, but its non-rational basis is revealed by cases of what is called pathological altruism, when self-sacrifice also harms one's group (for example, supporting the harmful addiction of a loved one). This and many other behaviours can be seen at best as reflections of evolutionarily successful behaviour patterns, but they are not necessarily rational, let alone wise. Our societies have changed much faster than our behaviours, and this is the cause of much visible irrationality. This is not always without benefit – in their book *The Stupidity Paradox* Mats Alvesson and André Spicer have written about the benefits (such as not wasting time second guessing) as well as the pitfalls (such as avoidable collective short-sightedness) of what they call functional stupidity.[4]

As with other physical and behavioural traits, rationality is not necessarily and always useful in a new setting different to the one in which evolution took place. Also, competence is more valuable than comprehension, and certainly often comes first. This explains why so-called practical intelligence is verifiably useful. In studying firemen, psychologist Gary Klein noted how experienced crew leaders often have a feel for fires and how they might develop, but this understanding is not expressible in words.[5] Similarly, Michael Polanyi coined the term tacit knowledge to explain much the same phenomenon of useful knowledge which is incapable of being explained in detail or monitored.[6] And even when someone can explain their motivation, their espoused theories are often different from the mental models actually determining their behaviour.[*] We should not conceive conscious thought, let alone rational conscious thought, as the only or even principal factor driving our behaviour. Rather, we have acquired rationality and have then nurtured it in large part to help us explain the world and reduce our anxiety about uncertainty.

There are plenty of examples of our irrationality, often stemming from using assumptions we know to be false, or not examining

---

[*] Anthropologists focus on society-wide patterns in this type of gap.

justifications or wider meaning. Irrationality can be as simple as not listening to advice which we know to be sound, or invading a foreign country against overwhelming odds for little benefit. Behavioural studies have identified all sorts of biases. Even when we try to be rational, we frame decisions (i.e. we limit our thought within certain parameters – we think inside the box) and use short-cuts to help us. Many may be inappropriate for the situation. Our undeclared and unexamined assumptions are often the root cause of arguments between us, and this is compounded by the problem that we interpret the same words to mean different things.

We are lazy in our thinking, which makes us efficient: once we have found a credible explanation we seldom look further. Related to this is outcome bias, which is when we focus on actual outcomes but not on what might have been had circumstances been slightly different. The significance is that the information available (including expected probabilities) when a decision is made is often less or different than what we have after the event – a decision with a bad outcome may have been rational at the time even if it looks stupid with the benefit of hindsight. And this goes for moral assessments too. A decision may have been right at the time yet easy to judge later as morally wrong.

Also, many people can fall for the same bias, and knowing that others have a particular way of thinking can lead to copying. For example, if one person exaggerates a story or fact in a particular direction, the next person may likewise embellish further. Truth can become significantly distorted when each person in a network passes information on with accumulating prejudice. This phenomenon is known as bias cascade.

We also, quite literally, ignore evidence right before our eyes. In one of the most famous examples, Christopher Chabris and Daniel Simons made a film of two basketball teams wearing white and black shirts. Viewers were asked to count the number of passes made by white-shirted players, ignoring those made by black-shirted players. Watching this video is an absorbing task. Halfway through the film, a woman wearing a gorilla suit appears prominently for nine seconds, but when asked later if they saw anything unusual, half of the viewers said no. As Kahneman observes: 'The gorilla study illustrates two important facts about our minds: we can be blind to the obvious, and we are also blind to our blindness.'[7]

Indeed, the way we see is not commonly understood. We see what we are expecting: our optic nerves have more information flow into the eye than out, a reflection that our sight is largely a confirmation process.

Science writer David Robson identifies four forms of intelligence trap. We may: lack important knowledge, such as tacit knowledge or counterfactual thinking, which is significant in context; fail to identify flaws in our own reasoning; place too much confidence in our judgements; and have entrenched automatic behaviours which make us oblivious to warnings.[8] But one could build a whole library on the subject of flawed thinking.

For example, confirmation bias is where we search for and interpret evidence which confirms but does not challenge. Disconfirmation bias manifests as scepticism that tears down alternative arguments. By considering alternatives in a cursory and biased way and discounting their importance, one can erect barriers to future re-examination. And the smarter you are, the better at this you can become. Closely allied, and coined as a legal concept in the nineteenth century, is wilful blindness. This is a refusal to look at sources of information which might challenge group beliefs. The paradox is that you have to know where not to look in order not to see something – yet in order to know that you must have seen it.

We defend our prejudices fiercely. They are precious to us. Indeed, they help define our self-image. When challenged, even by a barrage of overwhelming evidence and argument, any excuse may be grabbed and elevated to discount all other factors. Hence prejudice is a lot more difficult to overcome than mere ignorance. Logical fallacies and the ignoring of contextual factors are also commonly employed methods to avoid reaching undesirable conclusions. Defence mechanisms and irrational beliefs are terms used by psychotherapists to describe similar patterns.

ACT FIRST, THINK LATER

Our egos and emotions typically come first, rational justification afterwards. Daniel Kahneman's *Thinking, Fast and Slow* describes two systems of thought. The first is fast, emotional and intuitive. The other is slower, interpretive, more reasoned and, potentially at least, more rational. But it often isn't. Human consciousness is not naturally rational but a social reason-giving system which seeks to legitimise our behaviour, personally and publicly.

Jonathan Haidt explains this further.[9] He describes our subconscious selves as elephants which go whichever way they want. Our conscious self sits atop our elephant with next to no control over the direction the elephant takes. Occasionally, we can give our elephant useful information about what is ahead, but we do not decide where it goes. Yet we, our conscious selves, convince ourselves that we are in control, telling our elephants where to go.

Highly significant is the fact that the more educated, intelligent and erudite we are, the better our elephant-sitting conscious selves are at fooling us, and others, that we are in control. The intelligent find it more difficult to accept facts contrary to their worldview precisely because they are, without psychological defences to prevent it, more capable and likely to think through the consequences and locate inconsistencies. It is for this very reason that our most intelligent and educated are often the most upset by and determined to resist contrary ideas.

The rider, let alone the elephant, is not naturally rational. However, by using emotional reasoning the rider can understand the elephant. As Haidt puts it: 'The rider acts like a lawyer or press secretary whose job is to rationalize and justify the elephant's preordained conclusions, rather than to inquire into – or even be curious about – what is really true.'

There is, however, some chance of rationality shining through thanks to emotional reasoning, but it is the exception. Haidt again:

> The rider has some ability to talk back to the elephant, particularly if he can learn the elephant's language, which is a language of intuition rather than logic. If the rider can reframe a situation so that the elephant sees it in a new way, then the elephant will feel new feelings, too, which will then motivate the elephant to move in a new direction.

But what is emotional reasoning? It appears to amount to empathy. There has been a good deal of work done on emotional intelligence, including emotional intelligence (EQ) tests, modelled on IQ tests. However, although some people are clearly better at these tests than others, the evidence that such intelligence is of much use, at least in the workplace, is disappointing. As Alvesson and Spicer summarise: 'In many cases people get caught up in a therapeutic mentality and overstress the importance of fine-tuning the adaptation to and manipulation of people's emotions.' This is in contrast to the practical intelligence or tacit knowledge already referred to. Emotional intelligence enables us to read ourselves and others better – it helps us communicate with our inner elephant and those of others – but it does not appear to lead to more rational decisions.

Most of us never even realise that we have an elephant to tame, so what chance have we of any control? None. As Kahneman says: 'Our comforting conviction that the world makes sense rests on a secure foundation: our almost unlimited ability to ignore our ignorance.'

WHAT DOES THE ELEPHANT WANT?

So, it appears that we are driven by our subconscious, with our conscious selves acting as little more than publicity agents. The next question is: where do the feelings come from which motivate our inner elephant? The answer is that we respond emotionally to biological and psychological stimuli and needs – our passions. These are both individual and collective, and they are also manipulable, as attested by advertising executives and politicians.

The passions have long been understood to drive behaviour, and philosophers have struggled with the consequences. In the political context, Machiavelli, the first modern political observer, broke with the Platonic distinction between ideal forms and reality and the idea that some rational, perfect leader knows best. Spinoza likewise supported the attack on those who would see men as they ought to be rather than as they are. But it was Vico who saw that the answer was to play one passion – that of monetary gain – to tame others. Bernard Mandeville and Adam Smith further promoted this idea that the private interests of individuals, albeit within what we might today call an appropriate governance framework, may work for the greater good. The term 'interest' was used to define a passion which countervailed other passions, but it later became more specifically identified with economic interests, and once this had happened its shine came off somewhat. Interest was, however, seen as the way forward between, on the one hand, passions which were destructive, and on the other hand, reason which was ineffectual.

This strand of thought became submerged by Adam Smith's focus on economic interest. As economist Albert Hirschman says: 'By holding that ambition, the lust for power, and the desire for respect can all be satisfied by economic improvement, Smith undercut the idea that passion can be pitted against passion, or the interests against the passions.'[10] Subsequent thinking has been more about the exceptions to this rule rather than a resuscitation of the idea that interests subdue passions, yet I believe, as did Hirschman, that the idea does help us understand the way in which passions are moderated through self-discipline and societal incentives. It is by consciously changing our habits and motivations that we can indirectly use reason to change our behaviour. Society can also provide inducements to build good habits. As we mature as individuals, and as institutions deepen, these habits, motivations and inducements strengthen. Their normal influence is demonstrated by what can happen during their occasional absences, when discipline fails, when interests are loosened and give way to more myopic and emotional impulses – for example incidences of individual drunkenness, but also mob violence.

Moreover, once we recognise that irrationality is the natural state for all of us, including our leaders, then our faith in 'rule by the wise' may be shaken. We are naturally sceptical of the wisdom of others who we suspect may have ulterior motives. We do not necessarily believe them or willingly do their bidding. Smart leadership consequently amounts to pandering to our tastes and altering our incentives gradually to change our habits, not appealing to rational argument. Indeed, leaders trying to change the views of an electorate through direct appeal to reason commonly become frustrated (frustration which for some may lead to a desire for less candidness and more autocracy). Put another way, remonstrating with elephant riders doesn't induce their elephants to alter course. In summary, pursuing our interests, individually and collectively, gives us the best chance of reaching rational decisions. Such outcomes are often unachievable through attempts by human brains to be rational or appeals to other human brains to be rational.

Unfortunately, people do not necessarily pursue their own interests or even know what they are. This is true for groups and even nations, not just individuals. Fortunately, individuals can be much better at understanding their own interests than governments. Nevertheless, there is still a struggle between interests and fear, which has the ability to eclipse everything else.

INCREASING ANXIETY

Freud saw fear as central to psychic life. He distinguished between fear, which relates to a specific object, and anxiety, which is without a single cause but relates to future unspecified uncertainty. In practice, increased anxiety reinforces concern about specific threats.

Expectant fear relates to worst-case thinking, and when this is habitual it leads to what Norwegian philosopher Lars Svendsen calls a low-intensity fear which taints our entire view of the world.[11]

Fear is perhaps the most important emotion disrupting rationality. If we see danger, our evolutionary response is to run, not to analyse first. We may not have to run away from the large predators of the African grasslands any more, but the group command to run is very much still with us. One of the triggers is the word 'emergency', calling for a knee-jerk reaction to danger and the suppression of thought and criticism in the face of a real or imagined common threat.

It may have been ever thus, but anxiety seems to be on the increase, and with it fast emotional thinking and less chance of rationality. Sociologist David Riesman, writing in the middle of the twentieth century, describes three types of character.[12] These also relate to stages as societies become more cosmopolitan. They are the tradition-directed person; the inner-directed person; and the other-directed person. The tradition-directed person is culturally constrained and cares about what a small group of people he or she meets daily thinks of them. Their behaviour is moderated by shame. The inner-directed person has 'early incorporated a psychic gyroscope which is set going by his parents and can receive signals later on from other authorities who resemble his parents'. The inner-directed have a solid moral foundation which guides them through life. Guilt mediates them. Other-directed people, in contrast, tune their children to respond to the action, especially the symbolic action, of others. With such freedom to be open to more influences, the other-directed child breaks free from traditional and family constraints and is open to many other influences – and is motivated much more by other children than by their parents.*

The tradition-directed and inner-directed have clear guidelines on how to behave, with avoidance of shame and guilt preventing any stepping out of line; the other-directed lack such clear guidelines, and though they may develop an internal locus of control, which helps them cope with uncertainty, they may suffer from constant anxiety. Without authoritative explanations which enable the processing of the unknown, anxiety becomes so dominant as to guide behaviour away from reason towards avoidance of even reasonable risks. We may, to quote Roosevelt, have 'nothing to fear but fear itself', but that is quite enough to exhaust many of us. We are increasingly other-directed, increasingly anxious. Even those confident of their inner-directedness or solid moral grounding are not immune. Riesman argues that in order to get on in society the inner-directed often mimic the other-directed, but in doing so they become what they mimic.

Anxiety is fundamentally linked to uncertainty about the future. Whether or not one thinks that anxiety is greater now than in the distant past, there were plenty of things to be fearful of when our scientific knowledge was more primitive. Anxiety and fear are, however, now openly expressed and more widely disseminated. The stiff upper lip has vanished. People volunteer commentary on feelings much more readily, making us more aware of anxiety in society even though this does not necessarily mean there is more to be anxious about.

---

* This can of course be a phase which reduces in intensity after rebellion from the confines of family. As Mark Twain said: 'When I was a boy of fourteen, my father was so ignorant I could hardly stand to have the old man around. But when I got to be twenty-one, I was astonished at how much the old man had learned in seven years.'

Although there is nothing new in our inability to see into the future, our confidence in our capacity to comprehend it is important to us. Anxiety varies according to our knowledge but also varies in proportion to our scepticism of the authority of knowledge. It is through greater confidence that our anxiety and fear can be controlled. Without fear, curiosity comes to the fore, which stimulates rational enquiry rather than shuts it down. So, with less fear we might be more rational.

Many of us do not want to admit to being fearful, particularly in public life. It might show lack of competence or, worse, cowardice. Instead, fear is translated into anger, and anger needs a target. Whilst naked aggression is ugly, it can often be justified by its protagonists as being for the greater good. Hence we encounter the phenomenon of virtuous aggression. Obvious targets include those who do not share our group views and in particular those who threaten the group. The stronger and more credible their arguments, the more they become a threat and a target of ostracism, discrimination, defamation and hatred.

We might naturally want to reduce fear in society and assume our leaders share that view, but with fear we are easier to govern and easier to sell to: less questioning, more obedient. Further, although there is some argument that we need a bit of fear, French writer Pascal Bruckner argues that what we crave is a focus for our fear, particularly an apocalyptic focus.[13] A catastrophe sidelines other fears, making them look manageable. Such a focus provides therapy. Over the past few years superhero movies have dominated box-office receipts. As with horror movies, for a period of ninety minutes a simplistic battle between good and evil provides focus and outlet. And during the Cold War, for example, we had a focus for our fear: all-out nuclear war – and for some, as expressed by Ronald Reagan, an 'evil empire' behind it. In our minds we could compartmentalise it and think of other things for much of the time. But now there seems to be an endless stream of things to worry about, some, it may later turn out, real and some not: fear is everywhere. Now that the threat of the Cold War has subsided (though not disappeared), climate catastrophe and other fears have taken its place. Covid-19 seemed initially a paramount threat capable of making others look relatively manageable, but unless one wants to heap blame on a specific human source (to which there has been strong aversion) it is difficult to sell as a dominant evil. In any case, the fear has abated now we have vaccines. The most lasting bogeymen are those which cannot be disproved, mitigated or otherwise deflated.

For some, there is no rest from anxiety. In our more complex interconnected modern world, we have contradictory information flying at us all the time. Are we more anxious and fearful now because today's threats (to freedom, the environment, our identities, our morals and our values) are major dangers worse than nuclear holocaust? Or has there been some change in our collective credulity? Are we simply more fearful because we are less certain about the reliability of our information?

Whether or not our anxiety is now heightened because it is at its most intense in the face of uncertain threats, the lack of pushback when fear drives mass hysteria and intolerant behaviour is a factor too. There have been a number of recent cases of students bullying staff and administrators at the most liberal university campuses in the US. At Evergreen State College in Washington in 2017, a biology professor, Bret Weinstein, objected to a proposed change to the college's annual 'day of absence'. By tradition, ethnic minority students and staff would choose to remove themselves from campus for a day to highlight their contribution to the college. In 2017, this protest was reversed and white people were asked not to attend. Weinstein argued that the exclusion was an act of oppression against those encouraged to absent themselves from campus. An intolerant reaction to his objection followed and a series of events leading to humiliation of the college president. One can understand reactions from both sides, but once morality is seen as necessitating an absolutist approach, intolerance is fostered, and with it the opposite of an environment which feels safe for all and encourages free thought and speech.

Anxiety and fear are sometimes easier to cope with when seen through simple (binary) moral perspectives – they can be categorised and this can help the anxious and fearful to move on, to stop agonising and fretting. Yet unfortunately with moral categorisation can come, for the extreme few, fanaticism, bullying and intolerance, and for others, cowardice and complicity.

THE SEARCH FOR MEANING...

Our lack of understanding creates anxiety, and to reduce it we yearn for knowledge. We create narratives to explain the world and we do this collectively. We are social animals and we benefit from the security of knowing we are not alone in our beliefs. French sociologist Émile Durkheim refers to our ability to experience certain emotions together. This happens when we transform ourselves to a higher, collective level of the sacred – and only in groups do we feel this way.[14] Religion, family and wider group myths and ideologies (which are incomplete myths) have always given us greater certainty, and the collective nature of these beliefs stabilises them and gives them permanence.

Whence comes our ability for collective views, including collective stupidity – our herd mentality. Peer pressure can make us do surprising things, such as ignoring our previous patterns of behaviour and thought and indeed our own senses. We trust the wisdom of others as a shortcut; thinking is hard work, after all. Within a group, the pressure to conform can be intense. People suspend their capacity for moral judgement. There is a significant literature of how people in crowds behave differently than when alone, and George Orwell's Winston Smith is tortured until he believes that 2 + 2 = 5. Thinking like your group can be not only the easy option amid intense peer pressure to do so but also part of your effort to support and care for the group. Heroes can risk sacrificing themselves, but it is worrying that intense care for the group is also an outstanding characteristic of suicide bombers. This psychology is being nurtured in some terrorist groups, and we could all do with a greater awareness of our own susceptibility to social forces. Whilst most of us are extremely unlikely to become suicide bombers, we should more often ask ourselves, as Michael Bond says: 'Am I doing this because it is right, or because those around me are making it *feel* right?'[15]

...AND ITS DISTORTION

Belonging to a group enables a child to make the transition from parental dependence to social life. However, should psychological development end with identification with the group, this may restrict individual, but also group, growth. This may eventually lead to catastrophic group dissolution, and for the individual be as damaging as failure to leave childhood. Failure to leave the group can lead to one of two things: decadence or fanaticism. Decadence is a rejection of all tradition, and indeed all order, its political expression being nihilism; fanaticism is a desperate effort to hold on to a belief and disregard any outside influences, and it can lead to group aggression. Just as it is part of growing up to rebel against one's parents, so it is part of intellectual and moral maturity to rebel against one's group, and there are severe problems if this does not happen.

What might someone rebel against? Beliefs can be manipulated and distorted, typically through ideology which contains a central lie (which may be a key characteristic of group beliefs or a simple conjunction of power and truth – i.e. adults or group leaders are always right). By a lie is meant not only a manufactured falsehood but also a deliberate attempt to mislead through the partial selection of information. The power of ideology often comes from its appropriation of mythical ideas, which attract, and can be sustained because they are untestable. But danger comes from its incompleteness – an ideology is a simplification which discourages thought outside its boundaries. The insistence on observing these barriers and accepting truth on authority rather than on the basis of evidence and reasoning can lead to group manipulation. Whereas one group which reveres the individual can provide a conduit to adulthood and enlightenment, another may subjugate the individual to a subservient role, denying them meaning where this is necessary to ensure absolute identification with the group. This denial of meaning to maintain group discipline can lead to hate of self and of others.

Ideologies can cause hate and other negative emotions, but their partiality can also leave them vulnerable to exposure. Every ideology has different layers of belief, and the deeper the threat from outside, the more anxiety and depression but also hope, denial, deceit and desperation in favour of the conviction. People cling desperately to their beliefs. Nevertheless, a determined and persuasive pin prick may act as a catalyst in bursting the ideological bubble, identifying the lie and freeing the individual. Then, after trauma, come enlightenment and freedom.

To prevent the lie being identified as such, defences have to be strong and targeted. Any anomaly may be a threat. It may take the form of a stranger, an unusual idea or a creative individual – all of which are categorically equivalent to a natural catastrophe. The vulnerability is greater the simpler the ideology, the more precarious a central lie or the more abstract some of the beliefs. Even the mere existence of a different set of beliefs may pose a threat – most obviously when primitive cultures first come into contact with more advanced ones. Hence the tribal need for hostility to strangers and their beliefs.

It is rationality's role to construct meaning and so avoid the trauma of challenges to belief systems and the pitfalls of decadence and fanaticism. We use rationality to construct prejudices and narratives. Our conscious selves explain to us and others why our elephant does what it does and how it is purposeful and good. This releases us from obsessive and exclusive concentration and frees up our ability to think about other things.

DEFENCES AS SIGNS OF GROUPTHINK

To keep the number of believers up, ideologies, especially vulnerable ones, require extensive defence mechanisms. Even the non-aggressive signs of such mechanisms are detectable – primarily the lack of willingness to engage in debate – although they may be quite subtle. For example, it is common, in the UK anyway, to say of someone that they have gone 'a bit mad' or 'a bit crazy', but what does that mean? It signals a desire to discount the views of the designated 'bit mad' person and may reflect the discomfort of the labeller with their views – discomfort which translates into a reluctance to engage. The catalyst could be a taboo or sensitive issue, something which seems fundamentally wrong. The labeller may not be open-minded but not want to admit it to themselves or others. They could be resistant to challenges to their prejudice or groupthink (of which they may not be aware). They are often unsure how to react, don't really want to blame the other person – not least because they are not sure what to think about their message. They don't necessarily have a view, or they may simply want to avoid thinking about it. They feel a doubt coming on, and doubt is unsettling.

OUR DIFFERENT MORALITIES

Morality gives structure to our emotions and behaviour. It helps curb ego. Some philosophers, like Mill, have been optimistic about human nature and argued that the more human energy, the more strong impulses one has, the greater the potential for good. Others see good not in our passions but in our reason and self-restraint, the better directed to the good by being constrained by family, law and morality.

Outside formal religion, there are many ideologies with central credos containing non-disprovable arguments and belief in absolute truths. Marx and Engels, realising this, wanted to avoid the charge that their ethical ideas were purely self-justifying. To achieve this, they argued that different concepts of social justice vary over time and depend on social circumstances. As Karl Popper expresses their theory: 'If a social reformer, or a revolutionary, believes that he is inspired by a hatred of "injustice", and by a love for "justice", then he is largely a victim of illusion … his moral ideas of "justice" and "injustice" are by-products of the social and historical development.' They argue that the ruling-class concept of justice always necessarily differs from that of the working class. We do not have to accept their historicist interpretation that class, or even power, determines differences in morality. However, we can perhaps agree with them that morality is a construction of human society and a function of its time and circumstances. A consequence is that the tendency to judge historical behaviour by today's morals is at best misguided; at worst it is not designed to search for truth or explanation but to fabricate propaganda.

Not only does morality change over time; not only is it inevitably somewhat arbitrary; not only can moral interpretations of other times and societies be used to buttress current ideology; but sometimes it fails us. If the moral order is under threat, the emergency button is hit, rationality is short-circuited and moral panic ensues. Fear predominates, and fear leads to anger, anger to hate. The so-called Hobbesian trap is when fear between two groups leads one of them to strike first, and this is all the more likely during a moral panic, as is the extreme persecution of heretics and those perceived as threats or potential threats. A whole society can react in an irrational and aggressive fashion. This happens when two groups misinterpret each other, when there are differences and uncertainties over where the boundaries lie between the moral and immoral and when the transgression of boundaries is seen as a threat.

So, the policing of moral boundaries is needed, but this is complicated by a lack of uniform morals within a jurisdiction. For example, liberals may take satisfaction in civil and abortion rights legislation, yet the same laws may seem to conservatives to condone what they would view as immorality. Adding fuel to the fire is that fear is the standard tool used to police such moral borders. The alternative is to minimise legislation on such issues – but then members of society must assume responsibility for policing themselves. In any event one hopes that we can be tolerant of those with other morals, but it is not easy and not always possible when people hold strong beliefs and feel threatened.

BORN TO BE RIGHTEOUS...

When I found myself in Calcutta on my year off before university, my first lesson was to understand my own hubris. My mother worked for Oxfam in Oxford, and, as I wasn't a doctor or an engineer or in possession of any useful skills, when I appeared at the Calcutta Oxfam office I was greeted with laughter when I asked what I could do to help.

As Jonathan Haidt says, 'We're born to be righteous, but we have to learn what, exactly, people like us should be righteous about.'[16] It can get us into a lot of trouble. Lionel Trilling wrote: 'Some paradox in our natures leads us, when once we have made our fellow men the objects of our enlightened interest, to go on to make them the objects of our pity, then of our wisdom, ultimately of our coercion.' For this reason, we need what he calls moral realism. It is those in certain knowledge of the truth who are truly dangerous, as Socrates knew two and a half millennia ago. This is not to belittle the good that many people do but merely to point out that intention and result are often very different, and 'doing good' is dangerous as well as difficult.

...BUT IT'S GOOD TO MAKE MONEY...

Focus on an interest can be a precursor to exploration and may help an individual discipline themselves and stabilise their understanding of their relationship with the world. We have already seen how economic interest came to be seen as capable of taming the passions. This is a moral argument, and not one which everyone agreed with in the past or agrees with now. Indeed, commercial motives have been seen as divisive since before Plato. In his *Republic*, the ruling class of guardians, mirroring the reality of the Greek tribal past as well as of contemporary Sparta, were not allowed to engage in any commercial activities, save farming. All instability in the state was considered to come from division amongst rulers, and so they had to be equal. Any trade which led to large personal wealth was seen as destabilising. The Christian church later banned usury, and there are still many today who consider making money distasteful.

So it is remarkable that money-making nevertheless managed to be elevated as the key interest to tame the other passions. One reason is that the accumulation of money is unusual in avoiding the typical dissonance between desire and fulfilment. Samuel Johnson even remarked: 'There are few ways in which a man can be more innocently employed than in getting money.' But I suspect the main reason money-making has been the passion of choice to control others is its effect on human predictability. The neutrality

24

of money, its stability as a store of value, its convertibility and its being the measure of other goods all lend it a safety in stark contrast to more fleeting and unstable passions.

...OR JUST AVOID HELL

Pursuit of one's interest may offer a carrot, but it does not provide a stick. For that the prospect of hell can provide more motivation than the absence of material comforts. As automatic induction into religion has declined, the need for group identity to protect us from the horrors of the unknown has not. Individuals need to find alternative rules to live by, which means joining some moral grouping (be it a political or activist group or a local charity or a street gang). This can also help the wider society insofar as groups encourage us to take responsibility for our actions.

Under totalitarianism or other tyrannical rule, the individual may be denied such responsibility. Totalitarianism has also occurred where the individual does not want such responsibility and passes it to a tyrant. When such a tyrant is elected and then fully cooperated with, we arrive at what Jung called, in the case of Nazism, epidemic insanity. A lesson from the violent fascism and communism of the twentieth century is that we abrogate our individual political responsibilities at our peril. To correct this, we should avoid joining groups which discourage personal responsibility, be tolerant of those who think differently and resist intolerance in others. Hannah Arendt talked of the banality of evil: evil spreads when we ignore it, when we are cowardly in the face of it and when we accept it as normal.

All too often the need for group identity has come at a cost to outsiders. The tendency to protect means hating others. The fall of organised religion has been associated by Nietzsche and others not just with the Enlightenment but with the erosion of morality and the road, via Hegel and Marx, to nihilism, totalitarianism and modern misanthropy. It has certainly led to many new mass groupthinks and beliefs which elevate the group over the individual, including credence to the nation (Hegel), one's class (Marx) and more recently one's politically correct (or politically incorrect) group identity. Even the most intolerant set of ideas can spread if labelled attractively, and they may on the surface appear unobjectionable through an appeal to common values, justice or a utopian vision.

PICK-AND-MIX MORALITY

In her book *The De-Moralization of Society*, Gertrude Himmelfarb wrote of the shift from virtues (absolute standards of behaviour) to values (which we may say we adhere to but which are more difficult to verify).[17] Joint values are our new tribal colours, and although it may sound innocuous to sign up to the values of a group, it may not be. Values are used to demarcate and then police boundaries of thought and action in the modern faiths – faiths which help us establish our self-identity and self-identification with the group. This has spilled into politics, as people with different moral systems (a moral system being a linked set of beliefs that makes us cooperate) fail to understand each other. This has led to, and is not helped by, an increase in intolerance.

Jonathan Haidt has tried to explain something which has baffled a lot of liberals like himself over the past few years: why it is that almost half (47 per cent) of the US electorate twice voted for Donald Trump? The off-the-cuff explanation that they are simply stupid will not wash. Haidt starts by describing our inner elephants, as recounted above. He then reveals (from a study by Joe Henrich, Steve Heine and Ara Norenzayan) signs of an elite bubble: nearly all psychological research is conducted on Western, educated, industrialised, rich and democratic (WEIRD) people.[18] Moreover, the dominant moral system of WEIRD people is liberal and highly focused on care for others and fairness.

Yet the set of contemporary voters in the US is broader and can be grouped in three: liberals, libertarians and conservatives. (Haidt notes the almost total absence of political conservatives in academic psychology. Maybe this is a reason for the oversight.) Each group possesses a different set of moral foundations. Haidt identifies six: care/harm; fairness/cheating; loyalty/betrayal; authority/subversion; sanctity/degradation; and liberty/oppression. Each has their associated challenges which explain their evolutionary roots, as well as their own triggers, emotions and virtues. There is a strong relationship between people labelling themselves on a scale from very liberal to very conservative and the moral foundations which are important to them. Liberals overwhelmingly focus on the care/harm and the fairness/cheating foundations; libertarians focus on liberty/oppression; conservatives, although in electoral politics often allied with libertarians, are very different – their moral systems include all six of the moral foundations in a balance. This, Haidt explains, is why conservatives understand liberals but liberals seem unable to understand conservatives.

Often, liberals do not relate to the sanctity/degradation moral foundation, but they do sacralise equality. This leads them to fight for civil and human rights and a parity of outcomes. This contrasts with conservatives and libertarians, who both tend to sacralise liberty but not equality. This leads to conflict: as conservatives do not pay as much attention to the care/harm foundation as liberals whilst liberals do not pay as much attention to liberty, the conflicts most in view are those where the means to further equality override liberty.

A symmetry is visible between on the one hand Riesman's shift from the inner-directed to other-directed, and on the other hand the shift from conservative to liberal moral systems. The inner-directed (and perhaps the conservative) value privacy more, as well as non-interference in other people's business. The inner-directed participate in politics when they have something specific at stake: a responsibility to themselves or to others, i.e. they act according to interests. Politics to them is about issues, and they neither need nor want to invade other people's privacy in the way they engage politically.

For the other-directed, what other people think of them is very important. They wish to be at the centre of political and social life, or at least to understand it. They are willing to adapt themselves to resemble others, to fit in. Many are not only naturally group-ish but capable of changing their affiliations and views rapidly – i.e. they are faddish – and may signal their group belonging by looking down on those outside the group. Yet in seeking to be like others, people lose their social freedom and individual autonomy.

Our moral defence systems make it hard to understand outsiders. When one's principles are not under threat, the result is a sense of well-being; when they are, the result is crisis. Moral reasoning is pre-experimental and a means to explain and support actions in the context of one's beliefs. If we want to reach a particular conclusion, almost whatever it is, then we will find the reasons to do so. As Haidt puts it, when confronted with a piece of information which fits with our view of the world, we ask ourselves 'Can I believe it?', but when it conflicts with our position, we instead ask 'Must I believe it?' The answer to the first question is almost always 'Yes' and to the second 'No'. In other words, moral reasoning is reminiscent of Soviet show trials, or indeed the attitude of Lewis Carroll's Queen of Hearts in *Alice's Adventures in Wonderland*: 'Sentence first – verdict afterwards.'

The key problem US Democrats face in understanding Republicans is that their focus on the care/harm and fairness/cheating moral foundations makes them blind to the other moral foundations, particularly sanctity/degradation and liberty/oppression. I further agree with Jonathan Haidt that a common blind spot of the left comes from their not properly considering the impact of their policies from the moral perspectives of others.

THE PRECAUTIONARY MOTIVE AND ITS RECKLESS APPLICATION

So, morality is in flux. Avarice in the Middle Ages was the foulest sin of all, and yet by the late eighteenth century it was seen as the means to control other passions, as well as being key to national and individual economic prosperity. More recently, we have seen a shift from religion to virtues to values. Moral systems have multiplied, values are not always shared and are sometimes not understood by others, especially by those who have moved furthest from tradition – i.e. the most liberal. Threats to moral systems are traumatic and resisted, including through hate for the other.

Into this mêlée, just as economic interests were promoted by Sir James Stewart, Adam Smith and others to aid behavioural predictability, so fear is now being used by companies, in their advertising, and more notably by politicians and governments, not least in the use of nudge techniques, which employ behavioural science to help people make 'better' decisions – but who decides what is 'better'? We are seeing an increase in mental health problems linked to fear and anxiety. It is perhaps no coincidence.

One of the prime devices to keep us frightened is the precautionary motive. Justified by care for others and acquiesced to form a sense of priority, this has replaced broader and more rational risk assessment.

WE ABHOR UNCERTAINTY...

We are surrounded by uncertainty, and this causes us stress. Sometimes we put off making important decisions because of the potential consequences and fear of making the wrong choices. We may freeze, fail to move on, avoid taking on new ideas. Yet such procrastination can also extend anxiety. If our stress becomes intolerable, we may grasp at a solution without thinking things through carefully, ignoring and failing to act on the ideas and information we need. And the less we know about how to deal with the doubt, again the more distress this causes us. Too many choices to deal with uncertainty can, ironically, give us more stress. Still, normally, the more we think we know about the ambiguous situation and can compartmentalise it, the better.

One distinction (highlighted by economists John Maynard Keynes and, separately, Frank Knight) is that between risk and uncertainty. We can define the difference as follows: both occur when we face random events, but risk is when we know the probability distribution; uncertainty is when we don't. In financial markets, this translates into being able to hedge or insure against risk, but even if there is no such ability, greater knowledge of possibilities and likelihoods helps us deal with things. As we move from generalised uncertainty towards risk, so we understand more, can compartmentalise better, worry less and maybe mitigate it. Our anxiety becomes more specific fear. We have a better chance of being able to move on and think about something else.

Also, as some uncertainties are of greater importance than others, so they can shift our attention away from others. This is the attraction of one big, apocalyptic uncertainty – it puts all others into perspective, lessening them.

To be able to narrate to ourselves and others that we are able to do something to reduce uncertainty is valuable in helping us deal with stress, even if in reality our actions have no discernible impact. Hence, to campaign with emotional energy on a global issue of moral importance can have huge attraction. We also have a psychological desire to convince ourselves that uncertainties (which we have little ability to prevent) are actually risks (which we can maybe insure ourselves against). In financial markets there is an unbalanced focus on the measurable as opposed to the non-measurable (for example, past trends in data are heavily extrapolated but major possible structural shifts often not considered). Uncertainty, defined as random events by Keynes, is often ignored and categories of risk are seen as rigid. They are projected away from (behaviourally complicated) individuals and onto financial instruments. One example is that liquidity is fetishised: investors place too much emphasis on the ability in theory to sell quickly (often when their liabilities do not require this) – but if there was a major crisis, the liquidity they assume might evaporate, liquidity being a function of others' behaviours, not simply an innate quality of the financial instrument in question.

The past also appears less risky than the future precisely because we know more about it – this is called hindsight bias. And psychologists Amos Tversky and Daniel Kahneman also demonstrated with their prospect theory that our risk appetite is anchored to our starting point – we care more about losing what we have than not gaining what we don't.[19] This is consistent with our valuing the status quo, what we know about the world now. Of course, sometimes we enjoy the thrill of risk (for example, gambling), and this is also a way some of us cope with anxiety.

...AND MISPERCEIVE RISK

We have difficulty in understanding nested (Bayesian) probability and tend to favour extremes and polarised thinking. Even judges and government ministers are regularly fooled by this. The theory is not complicated and relates to the interaction of two or more probabilities. It may be best explained through an example: if a test for a disease has a false positive rate of 5 per cent (i.e. for every 100 people without the disease who are tested, the result will erroneously show positive for five of them) and for simplicity if we assume that the test identifies all cases of the disease (i.e. its false negative rate is 0 per cent – this assumption does not significantly alter our revelation below) and the disease is present in only 1 per cent of those tested, then for every 10,000 tested, 100 will test positive because they have the disease (10,000 x 0.01 = 100) – and just a few less if the false negative is non-zero – but 495 will test positive who do not (9,900 x 0.05 = 495). Hence, 83.2 per cent (495 out of 595) of those who test positive will not have the disease. And the percentage goes up the less prevalent the disease. One worries that not everyone in the NHS who should understand this does, and similar confusion over nested probabilities has resulted in people being found guilty by judges and juries due to an inability to understand this maths.

Sometimes we do not get that far. We often have limited ability to understand simpler likelihoods, typically inflating low probability events to appear much more significant than they are. Cass Sunstein coined the term 'probability neglect' to describe an inability to factor in the denominator.[20] For example, if a rape is reported on the television, even if the risk is one in 10 million, one may not want one's daughter going out that evening – another case of fear kicking in.

When we are fearful, we expect the worst and any attempt at probabilistic thinking is excluded, our brains reinforcing this precisely to solidify our single-mindedness. As sociologist Frank Furedi expresses it, the perspective of fear 'exudes a cultural temper that rejects probabilistic risk analysis because this approach is far too open to the possibility of positive outcomes and opportunities in the future'.[21]

Even when we try hard to assess risk, we often fall into a number of traps. One is our tendency to ignore what we cannot measure. This includes information we have but which cannot be easily quantified. Risk assessment in financial markets is rife with examples of people ignoring difficult to understand but relevant information. I made a career trying to understand sovereign risk, and often this comes down to trying to see a problem from the perspective of a key decision-maker – a Finance Minister or President, perhaps – facing a limited number of choices, often in a restricted time period (which generally makes the outcome easier, not harder, to predict). Incentives, beliefs, politics, history, even anthropology may all be relevant, as well as the hard economic and financial numbers.

Risk is a human concept invented to help us cope, not an objective feature to be impartially observed. It is complicated. Yet the standard ways of representing risk in financial markets is to focus on the measurable, normally just the past volatility of a price. And because many other investors do the same – and because their doing so moves the price in accordance with their beliefs (at least for a while) – this focus adds real value for much of the time. However, it can also totally fail when a structural shift of some type occurs. Investors are often caught out by a change from past patterns, and not enough of them plan for alternative scenarios. They suffer from what is often called herd mentality, a weak form of groupthink.

Financial markets of course constitute only one environment in which risk is misperceived. But if people can get it wrong there, they can most certainly do so elsewhere.

THE DRIFT AWAY FROM COST–BENEFIT ANALYSIS

Most of the big mistakes in public investment projects (if not in policy more generally) occur in implementation.[22] It is important to gauge in detail what will happen if a strategy is adopted, including knock-on and side effects, and to continue to monitor and assess during execution. Impact can be assessed against the status quo but also against other policy choices. One can use cost–benefit analysis to do this, which, although it can be highly complex, is conceptually simply an assessment of all the costs of a policy option on one side set against the benefits on the other. To compare like with like, all the expected consequences of a policy are given a monetary value. These costs and benefits are then netted out and policy choices weighed against each other.

Such a utilitarian approach has its attractions. But what measures should be used? Different methods may lead to very different conclusions, and the choice of gauge may be determined by the chooser's outcome preference. In other words, the selection and assessment of risk measures constitute exercises of power. For many policies, a monetary value is assigned to preventing a human death, and, similarly, quality-of-life impairments are also given a price tag. There is a whole literature on how governments, insurance companies and others value human life, and of course whatever measure is used the resultant number cannot capture the true value of a person's existence. It is no more than an aid to making a difficult choice. Sometimes the lives of many can be saved tomorrow only at the cost of some today. Policy-makers can face hard decisions in the knowledge that a judgement cannot easily be ducked – refusing to make a choice, for example in a battle, or in setting economic or health policy, may also cost lives, or indeed more lives.

But how is it acceptable to value a human life or make a choice which takes even one? Depending on one's moral system, one will have a different response. By what specific chain of events and decisions a person dies is also important – indeed, it can be more important than whether they live or die. So, certain choices – for example, sacrificing the lives of innocent people through a clear positive decision to do so, even if this saves many more lives than the available alternatives – are just not acceptable (by most people) as policy options.

And the principle holds more generally. Even if lives are not at stake, if policy-makers consider too many options as unacceptable, and especially if they are concerned that how they reached certain policy decisions might be criticised in the future, this may lead to certain options being excluded outright, and so to sub-optimal decisions. If more and more policy options get closed off in this way, the choice narrows on a single objective. Wider cost–benefit analysis may not even be considered, with many strategy options discarded from the start. Groupthink can exacerbate the problem where nobody in a government department or the Cabinet raises objections or thinks outside the box. If we then add in a large dose of fear, the precautionary motive, which urges us to err on the side of caution, replaces more balanced risk assessment. Fear can also be used to justify the policy to the public. Precautionary policy focuses on one or a narrow set of objectives and designs policies to achieve them irrespective of any side effects, good or bad. In such cases, serious cost–benefit analysis is simply not used to make decisions, although a version of it may be produced to justify a decision already made.

Elected politicians are wary of any policy which can cost them votes. In today's politically correct environment, this means they are wary of any policy which challenges the extreme attention placed on care for others. Moreover, in a world of fear in which the precautionary motive has replaced more reasoned pros and cons – for example, during lockdown when people were faced with aggressive advertising implying that to break restrictions was putting lives at risk – accusation means guilt. Perception is more important than reality. Hence, the question is not simply whether a policy focuses exclusively on care for others but whether it can be spun that way. The precautionary motive has replaced balanced risk assessment. We have replaced rationality with a form of single-minded, collective stupidity, its clarion call the emergency, its certain sign the lack of balanced risk assessment or full debate of alternatives.

CODDLING

Over time, our institutions have done more and more to protect us. Whilst this is of great benefit, it has gone hand in hand with changed perceptions of what to expect. If something goes wrong, we are incentivised to look for someone to blame. There is a related tendency to rely on the state to take more and more responsibility for mitigating the risks in our lives. Is this an inevitable consequence of greater wealth and societal complexity? I do not think so. Wealth is more an enabler than a driver of this trend. It is more a moral prioritising of care for others which brushes aside other considerations (including liberty, freedom of expression and tradition), combined with hubris and a tendency to interventionism. That the dominance of care over other considerations is seen as obvious progress by some may actually be considered evidence of their groupthink. As with other examples of groupthink, one either agrees with the core belief or disagrees, with very little room in between. And, again characteristic of groupthink, there is a lack of effective (internal) opposition – the result of cowardice by those who might otherwise speak out and intolerance by those who would stop them. So, for example, to what extent should two consenting adults have the liberty to do extremely harmful things to each other – like one eat the other alive? Mill's idea of non-intervention in the liberty of the individual so long as there is no harm to others is a starting point for how far the care principle should go, but there are obvious exceptions – for the young, mentally ill etc. – and exactly where these definitions take effect is hugely controversial. In our example, should the knowledge of consensual cannibalism be considered offensive to others and so justify intervention? Could the desire to be eaten demonstrate mental illness sufficient to intervene? This is obviously an extreme example and I expect all but the most libertarian would want the state to intervene, but what about imposing a healthy diet on the dangerously obese (in hospital perhaps) or preventing retail investors investing in particular high-risk investments? My point is that choosing where to draw these lines entails moral not just technical questions.

To some extent, again mirroring Riesman's three-stage progression from tradition- to inner- to other-directed, sociologists Bradley Campbell and Jason Manning argue that there has been a progression. This is from 'honour cultures', in which men react violently to guard their reputations, to 'dignity cultures', in which people have pride whatever others think of them and are fairly thick-skinned when slighted, and finally to 'victimhood culture'. Victimhood culture has three traits distinctive from dignity culture: high sensitivity to slight, tendency to handle conflicts through complaints to third parties, and desire to appear as a victim. It features a desire to be cocooned from reality and its challenges, as well as a lack of emotional development towards self-reliance and independence. And it encourages, and is encouraged by, an accommodating bureaucracy.[23]

Greg Lukianoff and Jonathan Haidt criticise 'the coddling of the American mind' in their book of the same name. They identify three untruths: us versus them (life is a battle between good people and bad people); fragility (what doesn't kill you makes you

FOOLING OURSELVES AND OTHERS

weaker); and emotional reasoning (always trust your feelings). All three contradict ancient wisdom, are unsupported by modern psychological research on well-being and harm individuals and communities.

They argue that the us versus them mentality is a function of fear (apocalyptic and non-apocalyptic) and base tribalism. Following on from the discussion so far, we can see how the moral focus on care can, by applying to in-groups at the expense of others, ironically enhance the sense of sectarianism and lead to intolerance, animosity and harm.

We are anti-fragile. Challenge is what makes us individuals, makes us think. We need challenge in order to develop. Children in particular are anti-fragile. Paranoid parenting is bad for children. They need more free unsupervised play than they are getting. Over-protection makes them less resilient. Adults also benefit from challenge rather than constant coddling. One consequence is that we should not be so scared of giving offence; we could be doing someone a favour, making them think of something from a different angle. We also need to avoid over-coddling ourselves, and look for ideas that challenge us rather than ones which reinforce our existing views.

There is also a link with the concept of emotional intelligence mentioned earlier. The idea that one should avoid giving offence and tell people what they want to hear rather than what they need to hear is connected to the promotion of emotional intelligence in the office and elsewhere, yet may be at the cost of productive challenge. We have to make a conscious effort to take good rather than pleasing decisions, developing beneficial habits and incentives for our elephants. We should avoid many of the shortcuts and moral reasoning which lead to poor outcomes. This is very difficult, but by the end of this book I hope to have shed some light on why it is so important to make the effort, as well as on how to do so.

SUMMARY

In this chapter I have discussed various aspects of human psychology – our irrationality, our moral systems, our fear and anxiety and how we respond to uncertainty. In doing so, I have explored the pull of groupthink and its dangers. The following are key ideas covered:

- The rationalist myth has a long pedigree, and we are much less rational than we believe ourselves to be. Tribal/kin conformity has been a winning evolutionary strategy, with it being more important to look right than be right. Competence precedes and is more important than comprehension.
- But humans desire narratives to make sense of the world. Our conscious selves create such narratives and act as publicity agents to our subconscious selves. We can visualise our subconscious selves as elephants which our conscious selves sit atop but have no control over.
- The more intelligent, educated and erudite we are, the better we are at fooling ourselves and others that we are rational. Hence, elites are most likely to fall into groupthink.
- Our subconscious elephant makes decisions based on our passions. We can learn to communicate emotionally with our elephants and focus on self-interest to mould our passions. But being emotionally intelligent does not make us more rational.

- Our efforts to be rational are often trumped by powerful emotions, especially fear and anxiety.
- A single apocalyptic fear, to which we are often drawn, can be therapeutic. It can help focus our anxieties and make other problems look manageable in contrast.
- Group beliefs and moral systems can help us cope with our fears, but they also cocoon us from reality and nurture mass groupthink.
- If the moral order is under threat, rationality is short-circuited and defence mechanisms come into play.
- Following our interests often leads to more desirable and collectively logical results than attempting to impose rational solutions (which people will resist and which turn out to be irrational).
- Efforts to be righteous often involve exerting power over others and cause unnecessary conflict, pain and suffering.
- There has been a shift from virtues to values and from inner-directedness to other-directedness (from inner strength to caring more about what other people think of us). When our different moral foundations come into contact with each other, the result is often incomprehension and conflict.
- The dominance of fear and anxiety, abetted by splintered morality, has led to irrational responses to uncertainty, in particular a reckless focus on the precautionary motive in place of more balanced risk assessments.
- We have also reacted to uncertainty by withdrawing into our shells, coddling both our young and ourselves instead of seeing challenges as healthy opportunities enabling us to grow.
- Being rational is hard, as the jury in 12 Angry Men illustrated. It is often easier to fit in with the dominant groupthink, but this can lead to the worst outcomes.

CHAPTER 2

GETTING ALONG TOGETHER

'Embedded in social networks and influenced by others to whom we are tied, we necessarily lose some of our individuality. Focussing on network connections lessens the importance of individuals in understanding the behaviour of groups. In addition, networks influence many behaviours and outcomes that have moral overtones.'

NICHOLAS CHRISTAKIS AND JAMES FOWLER, *CONNECTED*

Realising that we live in societies with multiple moral systems, how do we get on? More specifically, how do we mediate between groups with various moral systems to ensure our political units – in particular nation states – perform well? We have shown that understanding between adherents of different moral systems is difficult and that some policing may be required. In the modern democratic and pluralistic state, trust is needed between the government and the governed, but we also know that the challenge and competition of new outlooks and ideas is stimulating. We do not want to stifle creativity and energy. So, the role of the state should be unobjectionable from the perspectives of different moral systems and help avoid conflict. However, it should encourage challenge and competition of ideas. It should engender public trust and stability, not try to impose its will through force and fear.

The Thirty Years War, largely driven by religious differences, devasted much of Europe, with about a third of the population of what is now Germany dying as a result. At its end, the 1648 Treaty of Westphalia cemented the principle that states should not interfere in the internal affairs of others. This amounted to allowing princes and kings to choose which religion should be officially adopted in their territories, as well as how to govern their own subjects. This non-interference enabled the peace and is still a core principle of international relations.*

Serious religious conflicts are still with us. In Northern Ireland, we still have a political divide based on a religious one. The Middle East is a hotbed of religious intolerance. Short of having a medieval prince or modern tyrant to impose common views, many societies have great difficulty in trying to please populations with a significant proportion of intolerant people. Such intolerance may come from religious groups which feel threatened, but also from other moral groupings.

Many states have long followed the US's lead in ensuring that the constitution is neutral in matters of religious faith. The model is one of official tolerance of others' creeds. But for some, this is not acceptable. There are many who believe that only their religion is true, and many who also consider that those with different beliefs pose a threat to them and their way of life. We discussed in Chapter

---

* Although it comes into conflict with the principle of the right of a people to self-determination – perhaps most destructively in living memory with the Balkan wars which followed the break-up of Yugoslavia.

1 how a perceived threat to one's group can cause an irrational response, hatred of the other and aggression. It is very difficult to persuade someone so threatened to think differently. Such intolerance and even aggression applies across the political spectrum, albeit not equally. Whilst some may regard religious intolerance as a right-wing phenomenon, from Jonathan Haidt's insight about different moral foundations, we can understand how liberals (with little identification with the sanctity/degradation moral foundation) may also think some religious views unacceptable. Although they want to care about others, including others' rights to believe in their own gods, they do not always extend this when it comes into conflict with their own strongly held views about equality. This may be considered a good or a bad thing, depending on one's point of view. My point is not to make such a value judgement but to observe that such conflict can happen. For example, many today object to abortion rights on religious grounds, arguing for the sanctity of all human life. Others refuse life-saving medical interventions for their children. Others refuse vaccination for similar reasons. Such conflicts are not new. The British banned sati (the burning alive of widows on the deaths of their husbands) in British India in 1829 (extended to all India by 1861). Such policies are violations of long-established religious customs. The problem is that sustainable political solutions will continue to be evasive until the citizens affected feel less threatened by such interventions.

Why does the call for tolerance often fail to work? It is all very well to agree to the principle that you can do what you want as long as you do not harm others, but different groups cannot agree on what constitutes such harm. Many also object to attempts to educate them to accept a different view – one person's efforts to encourage reason are another's unacceptable propaganda, particularly if that information is coming from an outside (threatening) source.

SOCIAL CAPITAL

Social capital consists of those norms and networks of human interaction which give value to society as a whole, from trust in the word of a business counterpart to law and order in the streets, to the credibility of politicians to deliver on promises. We act in ways which create such capital because we trust that others will do likewise. Our incentives and the institutions which form around us largely explain when we cooperate, when we compete and the rules of our interactions. However, one can live in a society which lacks social capital, and one can also be close to but on the outside of a rich vein of social capital, unable to benefit from it. Unfortunately, institutions can build around mistrust and fear as well as around tolerance and cooperation. Fear destroys social capital, as do policies which use fear to motivate public compliance. And as groupthink can play a positive or negative role in developing norms of thought and behaviour, so it can also affect social capital. Electorates and interest groups all too often fall into groupthinks which damage societal understanding and cooperation, leading to negative outcomes, and the more so the more closed-minded and aggressive the group is towards outsiders.

LACKING TRUST

What happens when we don't trust each other? We may not have faith in any outsiders. We may be against the vaccination of our children. But lack of trust can also be much more generalised in a society. Edward Banfield's study in Lucania in southern Italy in the 1950s, *The Moral Basis of a Backward Society*, paints a picture of a society with very low social capital.[1] He tested, using survey data, the hypothesis that local people were amoral familists, that they will 'maximize the material, short-run advantage of the nuclear family; assume that all others will do likewise'. His results were entirely consistent with the hypothesis. The Mezzogiorno had been in a state of underdevelopment for centuries, arguably at least since the Normans arrived. Banfield found a society with no tendency to change or improve. Those with secondary education or ambition simply left the region. Households would only take in an orphaned nephew if they needed domestic help. All politicians were assumed to be corrupt, and voters could be swayed by favours received from candidates but not by promises. The comparison with northern Italy is dramatic, with its long history of vibrant city states with strong civic traditions, lots of social capital and much greater wealth and dynamism.

Why should social capital develop in some societies but not in others? Having different religions and moralities may explain why we fight each other, but various theories, such as Weber's Protestant[*] work ethic, which try to explain variances in economic vigour in terms of different religions, to my mind, lack persuasiveness. Whilst supportive correlations for such theories can be found, how can one separate the impact of moral beliefs on economic actions from so many other historical factors? We know that what

---

[*] Max Weber's seminal 1905 work *The Protestant Ethic and the Spirit of Capitalism* has been widely interpreted as arguing that greater individual freedom after the Protestant Reformation led to a more dynamic capitalism than might have occurred under continued Catholicism.

psychologists call cohesion, which holds groups together, can significantly enhance effort and productivity, but it is not dependent on what people believe so much as that they all believe the same thing.* A sense of belonging is needed to volunteer and to give freely. Moral systems have evolved for the same purpose at various times and in different societies, and those which last for more than a short period have generally been consistent with economic effort and cooperation. I can see how a community with common purpose and joint identity can work hard and well together, and how such conditions existed for the early puritan settlers in New England and for European states constantly at war with each other for hundreds of years (challenge stimulates), but not why one particular, well-established religion might encourage more effort than another per se. So it may benefit us to take a closer look at how people are incentivised to react in contact with people under different conditions.

GAME THEORY

Game theory was developed to understand the incentives and outcomes of interacting parties where payoffs depend on one's own and others' behaviour. In the classic example of the prisoner's dilemma, there are two players (prisoners A and B) who have committed a crime together and are in custody. The police cannot convict either without the other confessing, but the worst punishment for either is if their partner confesses but they do not (say, B cheats on A but A cooperates with B). Given these conditions, does A confess or not? In this one-period game, the payoffs (prison sentences) can

---

* It can also cause groupthink. As Paul Collier and John Kay put it in *Greed is Dead*: 'Without pluralism, cooperation can turn into the stagnation of parochialism and errors of groupthink.'

be designed such that both are likely to confess and so both go to prison for fairly long stretches, though not quite as long as for one who cooperates with a cheat.

Things get more complicated where there are multiple players and certain pairs interact many times. In such games, building a reputation is important and affects how other players may behave when they interact with you. We can simulate, on a computer, patterns of behaviour of multiple agents working with each other. Typically, agents meet each other randomly and each has a strategy of when to cooperate and when not. They remember what happened when there are repeat exchanges with the same counterparties. Robert Axelrod developed some of the first game theory computer simulations.[2] A particularly successful strategy, which he named 'tit-for-tat', did very well in a number of them. It is initially cooperative, but if another player cheats, the player will retaliate the next time they meet, but then forgive and cooperate the time after that. This strategy is thus not easy to take advantage of. It does not pay to cheat on 'tit-for-tat' because there is retribution, but it prevents a vendetta-like feud from going on for ever. However, even though 'tit-for-tat' succeeds with a number of starting populations of different agents and strategies, there are situations in which it loses badly, not least where all other players always cheat. In such an environment, nobody does well, but the strategies which do least badly, like with our prisoners, are those who always cheat. In other words, where there is no trust, as with Banfield's Mezzogiorno, cooperation strategies are pointless.

What we have learned from game theory is that if you know you are going to have multiple future interactions with the same players, or indeed if your behaviour is more widely known about, not just by those you interact with, then you can build a reputation. And the ability to build a reputation enables you to build trust and experience more cooperative and beneficial interactions. Multiple interactions with the same players are common in contained geographical communities, but they also exist in certain markets, like the traditional Lloyd's underwriting market, where almost everyone is known to each other. In such close-knit networks, trust and social capital can be more easily built and sustained than in environments where relations are more anonymous, or where one has the option to cheat and afterwards avoid further contact with the same person. So, you may be able to build useful credibility that you will cooperate by ensuring you deal with the same counterparts often.

You may also be able to engender trust by raising the cost to yourself, should you be seen to cheat. This can be done by being consistently transparent about your actions – letting many more people than just those you interact with observe how you behave. By making public avowals that you will behave in a certain way in the future, you may impose on yourself a cost if you do not which is higher than the specific transaction payoff (in an extreme case, you may have to eat your hat!). There is the countervailing argument, of course, that you should keep your cards close to your chest to avoid being taken advantage of. Although, all other things being equal, simplicity of strategy aids credibility, your strategy may have to be more complicated than 'tit-for-tat'. But the successful approach and how transparent you are about it both ultimately depend on the rules of the game/the nature of the interaction and, importantly, who you are dealing with.

The public avowals just referred to can, of course, be part of a moral code – they can constitute values or principles not subject to alteration through reasoning on a case-by-case basis. So, having unbreakable principles can reduce your freedom to act and behave rationally, whilst at the same time increase your credibility and reputation. Such is the power but also the trade-off of having values. We know that morals can trap us in narrow modes of thought and lead to what Alvesson and Spicer call functional stupidity but also that such functional stupidity can help us in the long run.

COMMON CAUSE

Robert Putnam's 2000 book *Bowling Alone* looks at the reduction in social capital in the US in the second half of the twentieth century (i.e. before social media), as epitomised by the decline in community activities like bowling leagues. He links the reduction in social capital to a number of social problems and to the erosion of participatory democracy:

> Democracy does not require that citizens be selfless saints, but in many modest ways it does assume that most of us much of the time will resist the temptation to cheat. Social capital, the evidence increasingly suggests, strengthens our better, more expansive selves. The performance of our democratic institutions depends in measurable ways upon social capital.

He also finds possible explanations for the observed decline in social capital. His estimate is that pressures of time and money, especially the rise in two-career families, may explain 10 per cent, and suburbanisation and increased geographical decentralisation 10 per cent. The two more significant suspected causes, however, are the impact of, and the increased time spent watching, television (25 per cent), and the demographic shift away from the high levels of social capital which were engendered by the experience of living through the Second World War (which demanded and engendered high levels of trust and sacrifice, which then lessened for those population cohorts who came later). This latter explanation is partly indistinguishable from the generational shift to television-watchers, but together these two factors explain up to 50 per cent of the social capital reduction.

We need a shared culture to give meaning (interpretation and guidance) to the world. Having a national cause (like a war) can further help reinforce shared identity and culture. It is also a motivation to action. To be most effective, there needs, moreover, to be a sense of urgency and an appeal to the emergency and the fast-thinking part of the brain, as Kahneman calls it. This can either take the form of an enemy or scapegoat (an important trope throughout history), or it can be more positive and inspirational. As President John F. Kennedy put it: 'Ask not what your country can do for you – ask what you can do for your country.'

The two tried and tested means to establish a national purpose and identity – or, to put it another way, universalistic values – are through war/national service and education. We have seen how groups other than nations can also invoke identity and loyalty. National, tribal and other group loyalties share with brand loyalty a differentiating feature: in creating such loyalty, one is trying to embed an irrationality, based on an individual attachment which distinguishes one's product, group or tribe from others.

How does one model a common cause or identity? To attempt this, communitarians have moved away from a selfish model of 'economic man' towards individuals embedded in groups. They stress the importance of institutional form and social capital, and in so doing they have helped fill a gap between economics and other social sciences. Similarly, behavioural economists have formulated models of how individuals optimise objective functions adjusted for their biases and irrationalities and how incentives play out in various institutional settings. Yet by adopting such approaches something is still missing. Understanding economic decisions comes from more than adjusted optimisation and institutional form; it also comes from understanding that people often don't optimise at all (even in a bounded sense, à la Herbert Simon).* As discussed in Chapter 1, people really can be a lot more irrational than we give them credit for.

LOCAL TIES

Antipathy to the study of social capital also exists. There is an argument that social capital, which encourages us to cooperate with each other, is at variance with liberty and tolerance. Walter Bagehot talked of the tyranny of one's next-door neighbours. However, there is the 'tyranny' of having to conduct oneself in a civilised way and there is what we might call full-on political tyranny. Just as most of us would agree with the need for some parental discipline for children, or having good manners, or even (though perhaps begrudgingly) the need to get on with our neighbours, the benefits of social capital would normally seem to outweigh the disadvantages. It amounts to self-discipline, not tyranny. We can even distinguish between different types of social capital: some which bond

---

* He won the Nobel Prize in Economics for his work on bounded rationality.

and some which bridge, and which are good for different things. Putnam makes the distinction: 'Strong ties with intimate friends may ensure chicken soup when you're sick, but weak ties with distant acquaintances are more likely to produce leads for a new job.'

Ties within groups or tribes are often stronger than those across groups, as one might expect – groups are often defined by particularly strong internal bonds. A corollary one might expect, though one which is not always welcome, is that the more groups one has in a society, the more difficult it can be to establish mutual trust and society-wide social capital. Indeed, it is a conclusion of another study by Putnam that ethnic diversity can reduce both the bonding and the bridging types of social capital. Liberal efforts to not merely live with but promote diversity, whilst no doubt laudable in many ways, may lead to more social isolation in communities in response. Similarly, Haidt concludes, after listing various US liberal reforms designed to help minorities or those seen to need greater empowerment, that counterintuitively they 'may lower the overall welfare of society; and sometimes even hurt the very victims liberals were trying to help'. As with so many things, you can have too much of a good thing.

How might one build more social capital? Not in a society in which you worry your neighbours might inform on you. Not in a society of far-off, overwhelming power, or of constant Orwellian surveillance, or of societal behavioural manipulation based upon the amassing of vast personal digital information – i.e. not where China is leading and many other countries appear to be following – a society of cynicism without trust.

Building trust often starts locally. In another book, *Making Democracy Work: Civic Traditions in Modern Italy*, Robert Putnam looked at the variation in performance of regional governments, which were established in 1970 to extend democratic self-government.[3] A very clear conclusion was that the more civic traditions and social capital there were, the better the government. There was significantly more social capital in the north, and northern Italians expected better government and were prepared to act collectively, whereas southerners were cynical and alienated. However, a second conclusion was that institutional reform can change political practice. The establishment of Italian regional government benefited both north and south through gradually changing identities, values and power relationships and enabling societies to learn from their experiences. National initiatives to build social capital can be assisted through local institutions.

Unfortunately, should communities with shared identities and their rulers become liberated from geography, governance becomes more difficult. Without geographical communities there is a lack of civic traditions and social capital. By removing local constraints from our societies, we metaphorically strengthen a tide taking us backwards towards Banfield's description of southern Italy.

LEGITIMATE POLICY

There are always trade-offs in public policy. A society with more social capital will trust government and politicians more than one with less. But trust in politicians and government policies cannot be taken for granted and can be eroded if such policies are seen to act against the public interest, particularly if the public think they have been deliberately misled.

Illustrative of these trade-offs are some of the more extraordinary and seemingly nonsensical lockdown policies during the Covid-19 pandemic – most went along with them willingly, but not every-one agreed with them. What are the issues policy-makers need to bear in mind as they try to get the balance right between ensuring the public complies with lockdown (and other related health programmes) and the maintenance of both policy legitimacy and our democratic freedoms? The trap of groupthink is to focus just on compliance. The seductive means to achieve this is to invoke fear, as fear is the easiest tool to ensure compliance in the short term. In the UK, as in many other countries, an emergency was called during the Covid-19 pandemic and public statements issued asking for conformity. Fear was an element in the design of government messages to the public to ensure compliance with public health and lockdown policies. In her book *A State of Fear: How the UK Government Weaponised Fear During the Covid-19 Pandemic*,[4] Laura Dodsworth lists nine government units using psychological techniques to manipulate the British public during the period. The media further assisted the government in stoking up fear.

If policy is not seen as legitimate, if it fails to be suitably transparent, if it demonstrably fails to count the costs of lockdown, then opposition grows which threatens compliance. Worse, we risk eroding the social capital required for democratic legitimacy and trust in government policies more generally.

DEMOCRACY: USE IT OR LOSE IT

Finding a good leader is a gamble, as evidenced throughout history. We know there is a clear link between social capital and effective democracy. Unfortunately, it takes a long time to build that capital. Despite the recent progress, southern Italy largely failed to make any such headway for nearly ten centuries. Hence also the mixed success of young democracies not used to a civic culture or much trust outside the home. For those of us lucky enough to live in a society which has inherited a working democracy, we need to be ever vigilant if we are not to lose our electoral rights, and with them our freedom. Power, we should not forget, is never freely given, only ever taken. If electors take their eyes off the ball, they may have their votes taken away, or, worse for their sense of responsibility, they might find themselves following the route of 1930s Germany in actually electing someone as close to pure evil as history has to offer. Electorates do get politicians worse than they deserve (not least as power corrupts), but they do not, by and large, get better ones. The electorate has to remember always to focus, not just on who to choose but on how leaders are constrained once in office.

THE URGE TO CONTROL

During the Second World War, many public sectors expanded to command the economy in unprecedented ways. Hitler's Germany was highly competent at marshalling forces. It produced armies much more efficient and motivated than their opponents. A lot of the resistance to Germany on the Western Front was half-hearted, especially at the beginning. The French Army collapsed shockingly quickly. The British, initially not much better, were sustained by Churchill's rhetoric more than a little, and were possibly saved from an early capitulation only by Battle of Britain pilots and the English Channel. Within the British political elite, resistance to Hitler was mixed at the start of the war, with powerful establishment forces still for negotiation and appeasement. In such circumstances, a call to arms, an emergency, was in order. Churchill refused to hold discussions with the enemy. Focus enabled the British motivation required to resist Hitler, even when Britain was alone and the odds seemed desperately long.

All-out effort was required. New ministries were created to direct people and resources towards the war effort. The state expanded to coordinate the economy. Everyone got used to increased government power and control over the economy and their lives, and fear but also hope were important elements of motivation. Censorship and propaganda were seen as legitimate, not just for security reasons but to concentrate the minds of the nation on its paramount need to survive. Britain became a unified tribe, as have many other nations at war throughout history.

After the war, many were in awe of Stalin's ability to turn the Russian economy around to defeat Nazi Germany, the Eastern Front being, more than anywhere else, where the war was won. The power of the state to direct lives and economics was everywhere evident, and aside from the notable exceptions of Friedrich Hayek and John Maynard Keynes, there were very few in Europe who thought the centralised, state-controlled economy was not the way forward. Most thought small-sized (or even moderate-sized) governments had little future. Meanwhile, the regime had acquired a new habit of control over citizens and the use of official propaganda to achieve it. And it was clear that fear had played a part in making this possible.

The inhumanity, enemy status and defeat of fascism removed it from contention as a model to emulate, but Stalin's communism had continued appeal. Evidence of Stalin's crimes against humanity and the unbridled brutality of his totalitarianism was inconvenient for those sucked in to Soviet groupthink. Many foreign observers wished to be, and were, hoodwinked. Nevertheless, Western leaders, aided by their Marshall Plans, came to see the Soviet Union as the new enemy and understood that an 'iron curtain' had descended across Europe where Soviet armies halted. Was it possible that liberal democracy could survive? Socialism, if not communism, was seen by many as the more obvious route to progress than the laissez-faire, small-state model. In order for free markets and freedom to have a chance, it was widely believed that leaders and their governments had to play an active part. And against the background of the Cold War, the sense of unity in the face of an enemy was still evident.

At this point in the story, I want to refer back to the ancient Greeks. If the state was to become so much larger, there were those, following Plato, focused on how to implement policies in the national interest and to the benefit of the population. But there were also those who followed Socrates's scepticism. However wise someone might appear, they should not presume to know very much. Danger may lurk with those who put themselves forward as wise enough to make decisions for others. Whether these Socratic supporters of democracy accepted state-sector expansion or not, they insisted on power being transparent and held to account. Especially given the risk that a wise leader can easily turn tyrant, checks on power are seen as more important than the choice of leader.

There is also a problem not only of who to trust in authority but how much policy-makers and voters alike trust themselves. Both need to resist being sucked into groupthink, and specifically the belief that there is only one way to deal with a situation. There are always policy alternatives, and alternatives need constantly re-assessing and testing to ensure one is following the best course of action.

Yet politicians commit to certain policies which, even when circumstances change, they feel obliged to continue to follow. They are committed to their strategies, which have worked for them in the past and helped them gain credibility, enabling voters and colleagues to trust them. Just as in Axelrod's games, they can be unwilling to change course, because to do so may signal untrustworthiness. Bureaucratic momentum also resists plan changes and criticism. With the time pressures of high office and electoral cycles, many elected politicians have found it deeply frustrating to have to take voters with them all the time, to explain complex details and gain legitimacy for every policy.

The press holds them to account on behalf of voters. So, how appealing it is to try to co-opt parts of the press to help with one's agenda rather than be constantly probing it. The desire to persuade, to include critics and potential critics into one's groupthink, arises at this point. During the Second World War, the need for propaganda was clearer than in peacetime, so the unsophisticated direction of what the media could report, and how, was a lot easier. In peacetime the desire for such control continued: if only the press were less difficult for the sake of it and would understand the essential need for certain policies. If they are reasonable and enlightened people, they surely must see the good sense of what is being attempted?

An effective check on central power can only occur with an electorate which cannot easily be fooled and a media which is not captured by the government agenda. Both these conditions are constantly under threat. To sustain democracy, vigilance is required at all times.

But how does a country acquire an electorate which cannot be fooled? A strong democracy rests on citizen participation in the democratic process. There has to be some trust between leaders and people, and this requires social capital. Without it, there is no constructive political engagement, just passivity and protest. Putnam's work on the impact of the introduction of local government to the Mezzogiorno shows that progress can be made, even where lack of trust has been ingrained for generations. But social capital and trust only grows as the result of lots of successful interactions with other members of one's community. All such trust needs to be learned and earned.

Electorates also have to learn to distinguish between good and bad policies and people, and that means making mistakes and learning from them. Unfortunately, there appears to be no shortcut to this. Electorates do not learn by observing the mistakes of others, only by making the errors themselves. And that means electing candidates and parties, finding out the hard way that they are no good, and trying the same again and again until a better result is reached.

Our politicians also have to work hard at supporting democracy. A shortcut for them, if they sense they are losing the public's confidence, is to benefit from, or call, an emergency – play the fear card. A month after the 9/11 attacks, President Bush polled over 90 per cent approval – the highest level on record for any President. Michael Bond, in his book *The Power of Others*, reports on a study by Solomon, Greenberg and Pyszczynski which polled (Democrat-leaning) students six months before the subsequent presidential election. Half were primed to think about their emotions facing death, and the other half, the control group, asked to think about being in pain. All were subsequently asked which candidate they were more likely to vote for. 'The outcome was pretty astonishing. Those in the control group favoured Kerry over Bush by four to one, while those primed to contemplate dying favoured Bush over Kerry by almost three to one.' Fear works. This can go to a leader's head. We know that our elites are more capable of convincing themselves and others that they are in control of their inner elephants, that they are more prone to hubris and groupthink. Elite superiority complexes can lead to our leaders avoiding optimal, let alone full, policy transparency and accountability. An elite bubble can drift into legitimacy deficit and technocratic administration.

TECHNOCRATIC DRIFT

James Burnham, in his 1941 book *The Managerial Revolution*, predicted the replacement of capitalism not by socialism but by technocrats – administrators in business and government.[5] This was seen by some as a credible alternative to socialism after the Second World War, but such subtleties were sidetracked by the Cold War and the domestic battles between socialism and more laissez-faire ideologies. Over time, however, there has been a technocratic drift and, more recently, a resultant political reaction to perceived lack of legitimacy.

The technocrats have gradually become more powerful. Independent agencies (IAs) – parts of administrations which act without direct government control or much parliamentary oversight – are growing. They are often enabled by politicians who do not want the political liability which goes with responsibility for various functions. Moreover, whilst it may be a gamble for a politician to hide behind the decisions of advisers they are responsible for, that hasn't stopped many attempts to do exactly that. And the more distanced they are organisationally, the better the odds of getting away with it.

Separation of powers, as suggested by Montesquieu, can aid accountability; creation of IAs not liable, or only distantly responsible, to anyone often does not. The intention is to give balance and credibility. Many value competence over legitimacy and somehow think you cannot have both. Particularly where undue political interference and the electoral cycle may interfere with judicious policy, IAs may be able to extend the timeframe of policies beyond that of an electoral cycle. However, the argument that politicians cannot be trusted, and so power should be taken away from them, is dangerous. In a democracy, the fact that issues are complex and technical does not alter the need for proper oversight. If you are with a toddler in an armoury, and if you feel competent in supervising the toddler's handling of a slingshot but not a loaded pistol, that does not justify deliberately leaving the room the moment the child picks up the gun. Yet this is what our leaders appear to be doing when delegating so much power to IAs. And yes, people not subject to checks and balances, especially the intelligent ones, do often behave like toddlers much more than those constantly in the public eye and held to account. It is no more than human to revert to our toddler state of emotional impulses whenever we can get away with it.

Whereas credibility can be enhanced by a transparent rules-based system, this is not always the case. Natural monopoly regulation is a case in point. A natural monopoly can exist when economies of scale lead to a country or region having only one provider of a good – such as with certain infrastructure networks. The two standard ways for a regulator to set the prices a monopolist can charge are a rigid rules system (say a cost-plus model, which sets a fixed profit margin above reported average cost) or one which leaves more discretion to the regulator. Both systems have flaws. The rules-based system can be gamed, for example, by artificially inflating reported costs. Regulators with more discretion, even if incorruptible, can be captured over time through a barrage of unbalanced and partial information being provided by the well-resourced entity being regulated.

The problem is, as our societies have become richer and more complex, more and more government functions have been acquired. The laissez-faire view of a minimal state has to contend with the reality, as Adam Smith and many others have pointed out, that the private sector, left to its own, has strong incentives to collude and reduce competition. The substantial expansion of state capacities in nineteenth-century Britain was in large part to regulate and create the infrastructure to enable competition. New technology is often creating new economies of scale and new potential monopolies, and so also new demands on the state to ensure that innovation, growth and consumer protection are promoted via market competition. There are some public goods (such as national defence) which require not just regulation but provision by the state. So even if one wants a minimal state, there are still plenty of functions for government. Many of them create complex incentive problems, on which there is a substantial literature. And because we live in a complex, uncertain world, more and more discretion is being handed to IAs, where before there may have been simpler and more easily observable rules-based systems.

Paul Tucker, after a distinguished career at the Bank of England, has written a thorough and thoughtful tome, *Unelected Power*, about IAs.[6] In it he lays out the case for when and how authority should be delegated. IAs include not merely regulatory institutions, which try to oversee and regulate particular activities in the economy and society, but ones which have powers to take new initiatives and create new policies and means to deal with future unforeseen problems. An independent central bank today does not merely enact a simple set of pre-agreed rules; it has discretion on how to reach pre-agreed objectives. They have unelected power which can impact millions of lives.

There are now hundreds of IAs in the UK – more than parliamentarians can effectively keep an eye on. Although government, parliamentary or congressional oversight may take up substantial time and resources, it can lack real challenge. Ideas and conclusions are often presented without alternatives. This is worrying and brings us right back to Socrates versus Plato again. However wise those staffing an IA may be, if they are not being effectively and rigorously challenged or kept in check, there is a risk of them making decisions without taking their political masters or the public with them, and that way lies potential tyranny, albeit of a specific type.

When IA executives communicate directly to the media and public in more than a completely factual way, they can also compete with government in providing an interpretation of events. They can spin too. They become active in political issues and benefit from the status of being experts without the direct need to be accountable. They have the ability to justify their actions, bypass government and reduce the options available to politicians as they make crucial choices, but they cannot be replaced by the public when they get things wrong in the same way. They do not have the same responsibility.

A further problem is that of transparency. Some issues are secret, most obviously those concerning security and national defence. Representative oversight is made difficult and certain details may have very limited circulation. The discretion of what to withhold may effectively lie predominantly with the executive, not those overseeing, including information supporting alternative courses of action. Partly in realisation of this problem, public sector actions requiring secrecy are typically not delegated to IAs. Even so, defence procurement is a good example of how lack of competition and inadequate oversight within the public sector can lead to high levels of waste and cost inflation.

An independent central bank is a particularly important IA, with more discretion given to it than to most regulatory agencies. And transparency is currently lauded as a great benefit in central bank monetary policy decision-making. As Paul Tucker puts it: 'The revolution in economic ideas that promoted transparency as an instrument of policy efficiency had the invaluable side effect of helping to align central bank practice with the values of democracy.' If by the values of democracy he means paying lip-service to transparency, then all well and good. However, there is a big difference between optimal and maximum transparency, and this can be especially marked when objectives conflict. By saying one is being transparent, and being so somewhat, market confidence can be maintained. However, as I write central banks are meeting massive fiscal expansion through almost identical amounts of government bond purchases, equivalent in economic terms to little more than printing money, whilst at the same time trying to keep a lid on inflation expectations. I say more about this in Chapter 4.

For leaders (and citizens) trying to keep national institutions honest and open-minded and thus effective and acting in the national interest, it is important to identify and mitigate harmful groupthink within public organisations. Central banks may be secretive, but some state bureaucracies are far more inward-looking, wedded to hidebound ways of doing things, wasteful and ineffective. Hierarchical organisations are particularly vulnerable to groupthink. Internal dissent is generally discouraged. As the influential pre-WWII American writer and Democrat politician Upton Sinclair put it: 'It is difficult to get a man to understand something, when his salary depends on his not understanding it.' In a culture where technical expertise is promoted and respected, decisions can be taken by a small clique of people who can successfully disarm potential internal and external critics. Facing such a bureaucracy, politicians can be persuaded or cowed into submission, not wanting to confront a concerted front of experts.

What I have been describing is a shift (each step of which may be justified, but not the overall effect) towards power without responsibility, and with it the growth of a bureaucracy increasingly difficult to control. This has helped feed the replacement of balanced risk assessment with the precautionary principle. For balanced risk assessment, one needs a person or body, with all the relevant facts, able and willing to take the best decision. But what we now have is thousands of choices being made every day by people pursuing limited objectives without full consideration of side effects or alternatives. One can sympathise with those responsible for important decisions in the absence of the full picture, and indeed with their reliance on the precautionary principle. However, what is needed is organisational change to ensure that for a particular decision there is someone capable of doing better than using the fall-back precautionary principle, and moreover who does not have a skewed incentive structure. We would also like a political leadership capable of appropriate delegation which allows efficient and sound decisions to be made, but not at the cost of lack of accountability. In other words, decisions do not all have to be centralised, indeed many decisions are best decentralised, but it does require a degree of independent challenge (important for identifying and mitigating groupthink), and reporting and transparency for leaders and voters to verify that delegated decision-makers are acting in the public interest. Yet also required is that decisions are not second guessed or amended by those higher up the hierarchy with less command of relevant detail. Unfortunately, our government structures have evolved in a sometimes dysfunctional way, and the use of the precautionary motive is increasingly common, not least as an insurance should things go wrong. And there is insufficient central governance able to check whether delegated decisions are being well made, only a political leadership separated from the detail and so manipulable by technocrats and lobbyists.

SUMMARY

In this chapter we have explored trust and social capital, which are important for democratic engagement and effective government. We have noted a drift towards technocratic policy-making, which may reduce accountability, lead to stilted policies designed without proper challenge or consideration of alternatives and create a legitimacy deficit which is damaging to democracy.

- If we are going to get along together, we have to fear each other less. The state needs to be neutral on some moral issues and encourage trust and cooperation. The state should not be engendering more fear, which it often appears to be doing.
- Game theory has taught us that optimal cooperation strategies depend on the network and the behaviour of other participants. Computer modelling has illustrated the value of building a reputation which engenders trust and so cooperation (but also inflexibility).
- Social capital is important for political engagement. Without constructive and open social capital, we risk voters disengaging from their electoral responsibilities.
- The choice of political leader is a gamble and less important than holding power to account. Democracy, if not exercised, can be lost, with the road to tyranny taking its place.
- The government has a strong urge to control but has to earn trust from citizens, which means less use of fear to cajole cooperation. Use of fear to aid policy compliance can work for a while but can also destroy social capital and so damage future cooperation and political engagement.
- Social capital and political engagement are also damaged by the erosion of geography and by a lack of national purpose and universalistic values.
- As the state has become more complex, we have seen a drift to technocratic solutions and lack of accountability.

- The result is that policy ideas are not sufficiently challenged. There is a lack of balance in decision formation and over-attention to the precautionary motive.
- When there is no one looking at the big picture, nor asking contrary questions, nor holding power to account, we risk the building of elite bubbles and large-scale groupthink.

As we shall see in the next chapter and later in the book, if this were not bad enough, we also face another threat from new forms of communication technology: the revolution of social media which is both liberating and stupefying, empowering and dangerous. It has unleashed new economic and personal potential, but at the same time led to myopia, irrationality, intolerance and victimisation. This has also combined with excessive focus on rights without concomitant responsibilities, together with multiple identities and victimhood culture. To cope with this, we need more defences: more social capital, more trust, more tolerance.

CHAPTER 3

SOCIAL MEDIA

'The French Revolution ended up with the Committee of General Security, which had a law passed. It said you could take a piece of paper saying something like "Citoyen du Roque is an enemy of the Revolution", put it in the central square on a post, and that person would be arrested. It's basically the same as tweeting it; it's exactly the same idea. It's a denunciation, a shaming without evidence, an assertion.'

STEPHEN FRY, 2018, *POLITICAL CORRECTNESS GONE MAD?*[1]

TECHNOLOGY: THE GREAT DISRUPTOR

Since prehistoric times, the development of technology has been irreversible. New technologies can be highly disruptive, and there are many precedents of communication technology changing the way we think and behave. Socrates was against the written word, as he thought it wrecked memory. Gutenberg's invention of the printing press enabled on the one hand the Vatican to print indulgences and on the other hand access to the Bible in one's own language. The buying of indulgences was widely seen as corrupt. Martin Luther understood that the new technology created popular access to the word of God and so made laymen theologians. This access helped unleash the Protestant revolution, and with it decades of war in the seventeenth century – war which affected all members of society in an unprecedented way. Later, the telegram shrank distances and enabled a fascination for 'news', events far away, often of interest only because of their newness. We have already heard how Robert Putnam ascribed 25 per cent of the reduction in social capital to television in post-war America.

The telephone, telegraph, television, personal computer, email and internet have all had an impact on our culture, changing the way we interact and learn, often in highly disruptive ways. More even than transformations in transportation technology, change in communication technology has been ideologically laden. It has not only introduced new words but altered the meaning of existing ones. And one should not have rose-tinted glasses – it is no respecter of culture. It can tear up all before it. It is unstoppable and cannot be slowed down as long as people believe in the inevitability of progress.

Advances in communication technology in the past, as with innovations in transport, have had the attraction of massively increasing access to information. This can be initially disruptive, as it leads to people experiencing new ideas and communicating regularly with people over greater distances, often with very different perspectives. This has enabled greater individual freedom and power and may also cause conflict with leaders and elites, in some cases fomenting major political changes. In general, we can observe winners and losers, but ultimately a sense of overall gain, especially for people not previously empowered or fully realising their potential.

New communication technology has, however, typically been accused of dumbing down. In catering for the demands of the now wider, often less well-educated group, content becomes more popular and, initially at least, often simpler in its messages. But this can change as education and mass consumer tastes develop, which in the past they have done, as seen by the gradual increase in the range and sophistication of written material following the invention of the printing press, and also the broadening range of radio and then television content. And as this happens new media can still cater to the tastes of elites, just not exclusively.

The internet and social media have been the most recent disruptive forms of communication technology. They have expanded our networks and increased our access to information, with clearly beneficial, but also contentious, effects. For example, deep reading, denoting the ability to read a book thoughtfully and deliberately so as to comprehend meaning thoroughly, is become rarer. Just as Socrates lamented the dying art of memorising long epics due to the written word, so today we can lament that reading without being distracted has become more difficult for many people who have developed short attention spans and got into the habit of scrolling social media. Skimming and being easily distracted are becoming more common, and there is even some neurological evidence for changes occurring in the brains of heavy social media users.

NEW COMMUNICATION PATTERNS

We used to communicate more slowly and make political and other important decisions slowly. The ancient Persian custom (according to Herodotus) was to take decisions twice: when sober and when drunk. Anxieties were expressed about the introduction of the telephone: its interruptions, deleterious effect on physical social visits and, compared to communication via letters, the lack of time it gives users to reflect. Riesman observed mass media contributing to our political confusion, invading our privacy 'with its noise and claims'. He says: 'This invasion destroys the older, easy transitions from individual to local, local to national, and national to international interests and plunges the individual directly into the complexities of world politics, without any clear-cut notion of where his interests lie.'[2]

Robert Putnam's observation about television eroding social capital is also instructive. The option of being entertained and gaining information from the comfort of one's own home meant certain types of socialising went out of fashion. He considered that this loss had an impact on local connections and trust, and with it democratic engagement. So, in the past there has been a pattern of concern that new technology reduces our time to reflect and our ability to sustain democracy. Such past concerns may seem overblown and do not apply to all new modes of communication – email can allow more time for reflection than the phone. People are also quite capable of making quick decisions. However, from what we now know about thinking fast and slow, is there a limit on how much faster we can speed up our thinking and how many distractions we can cope with in quick succession before falling into bad habits of letting our emotional responses dominate? As we, with the advent of social media, start to react in seconds, constantly, maybe the habit of reflection really does atrophy a bit.

One is a passive recipient of information from the television and largely also from browsing the internet. Email is a two-way communication, but it is limited by users not being able to see each other and take in the subtle behavioural signals we give off. Many of us will know from experience that some emotionally ambiguous messages are best not communicated via email. We mentioned that there is more information going into the eye than coming back – sight is a confirmation, more than a discovery, activity. Likewise, much of every communication is confirmatory. It is easy to read negative messages into an email when defensive and looking for things to object to. In this respect, video conferencing is better but still not as good as meeting in person. Emails can also be copied to others by mistake, and this can cause all sorts of embarrassments and difficulties. But how much worse is social media in this respect, when we have no idea who is reading what we have said?

Traditionally, we have been used to talking mostly in a binary way, one person with another. Sometimes we also listen in an audience to a speaker, who is in transmit mode, with rules or a moderator deciding who can speak when. Should some of the audience decide to transmit at the same time, we can easily end up with cacophonies, shouting matches, chaos. The need to be heard above the noise can cause participants to talk louder, to over-simplify and to express views in more extreme forms so as to stand out and be noticed – they play to the gallery. Unruly meetings, when tempers run high, can inflame, prompt emotional responses and even descend into violence.

The great thing about email and social media is that it helps group communication by enabling us to receive all the things being said, without having to shout. And one's physical safety is typically not at risk. It also saves a lot of travel time. However, social media, or more specifically the way it has developed since 2009, has changed how we communicate. All one's friends, and their friends, and their friends' friends and so on, can see and comment on your behaviour, appearance, embarrassing mistakes and any aspect of your personal online history. They can do this with you but also behind your back. In large groups they can, in effect, do so anonymously and without the normal constraints of even a large debating room.

Email has been with us for a while and not caused major problems, but something worrying has been happening more recently with social media. Facebook only became open to all in 2006, and the iPhone came in 2007. However, 2009 is the key date. This was when Facebook added the 'like' button and Twitter the 'retweet' button – and social media became highly addictive. These features transformed a window into, as Zuboff puts it, 'a blizzard of mirrors'.[3]

The 'like' and 'retweet' buttons massively expanded the ability of people to pass instant judgement, and the ease of doing so has encouraged instant emotional, as opposed to more thoughtful, reactions. This is causing serious damage to some of the generation brought up since social media took off – specifically those born since 1996, called Generation Z, or Gen-Z. As Greg Lukianoff and Jonathan Haidt explain in *The Coddling of the American Mind*, Gen-Z girls have been affected worse than boys. Boys and girls bully as much as each other, but boys are more physical. Girls' bullying is relational. Girls are more affected by constant social comparison, and they suffer more from the fears of missing out and being left out. Girls also talk more about emotions, and whilst sharing feelings with others can help alleviate problems, this sharing can also provide networks for negative ideas and feelings to spread. Whereas the threat of physical violence has reduced by socialising online instead of in person, the possibilities for emotional bullying have expanded.

Not only have smartphones and social media led to sedentary life-styles but also to a significant increase in anxiety and depression and related suicide attempts, especially for Gen-Z girls.

This is not to say that there are not health benefits coming from increased connectivity. In his book *The Four: The Hidden DNA of Amazon, Apple, Facebook and Google*, Scott Galloway suggests decreasing deaths from violence is one amongst many positives. However, there is a strong link between increased Gen-Z mental health problems and high use of mobile phones and other electron-ic devices.*

Although violent death has decreased, so has tolerance. Indeed, violence is now seen as acceptable by a surprising number of this generation. Referring to recent changes in US university campus life, Lukianoff and Haidt summarise that in one late 2017 survey, 20 per cent of students thought violence by other students was ac-ceptable to prevent someone speaking on campus, and in a second survey about the same time, it was 30 per cent. I find this quite shocking, and the opposite of civilised progress. John Milton, the seventeenth-century poet and, as author of *Areopagitica*, defender of free speech, might well be turning in his grave.

It would appear that the 'like' and 'retweet' buttons have greatly increased our mutual animosity and the speed at which outrage can spread. It is now common to react at a speed which does not allow for reflection.

Lack of reflection matters. There have been numerous experi-ments which illustrate people's susceptibility to irrationality in the

---

* Lukianoff and Haidt convincingly make the case that these links between on the one hand Gen-Z girls' mobile phone and social media use and on the other hand anxiety, depression and suicide attempts are causal, not just correlations.

face of peer pressure. For example, and as related by Michael Bond in *The Power of Others*, Solomon Asch's line experiment involved two cards which were shown to volunteers. On the first was a single line, and on the second three lines, one the same length as on the first card, one significantly longer and one significantly shorter. Volunteers were asked to identify the line matching that on the first card. Simple enough, at least for the first four rounds. But in twelve of the remaining sixteen rounds, associates called out the wrong line. The purpose was to see if the volunteers could be persuaded to stop trusting their senses. Only a quarter of volunteers answered correctly every time. Such is the power of suggestion.

However, I believe it also offers a clue as how we will eventually learn to cope better with social media. If you realise that you are in an experiment and that such experiments have been conducted in the past (Asch's tests were conducted over seventy years ago), and you suspect that your susceptibility to influence might be being investigated, then you might trust your senses a little more. Likewise, eventually people may learn to be more discerning of algorithm-generated suggestions, and people using social media may learn to consider consequences a little more carefully before joining in with the herd. It takes time, though. As Tocqueville put it: 'The taste for material enjoyments ... develops more rapidly than the enlightenments and habits of liberty.' We must develop these habits.

Being occasionally misled by experimenters is one thing, but we are now being constantly bombarded by emotional messages. Psychologist Patrick Fagan calls for a discussion about this trend: 'Smartphones, social media, and the internet more broadly tend to produce a shallower style of thinking – that is, more emotional, more impulsive, and more stereotyped.' This bombardment, he says, 'likely makes us more susceptible to mass hysteria than ever'. It should be no surprise that there are cases of psychogenic contagion in which the anxiety of others makes us sick. One student thinking they can smell a gas leak can convince others that they have gas-induced symptoms and cause a school to evacuate when there is no leak.*

By making decisions faster, we give our rational selves little chance. As discussed in Chapter 1, we are not even vaguely rational. We seek information to bolster our existing views and find network connections that help us reduce, not increase, challenges to our existing prejudices.

NEW NETWORKS

Jonathan Haidt describes the coming of the 'like' and 'retweet' buttons as akin to God deciding to change the gravitational constant. More than the way we communicate has changed; our networks have too. And from our discussion about game theory in Chapter 2, we can see how this may be important for how people behave.

Networks can be of many different types and lead to different patterns of connection and contagion. We can visualise the simplest as a single line, with the person at each end having a connection to only one person, and everyone in between having a connection to two others. Alternatively, a network may branch, as a tree, with each person knowing several others but these others not knowing each other. Such a network is said to have low transitivity, as opposed to a network where everyone's friends know each

---

* As related by Christakis, N. and J. Fowler (2009) in the case of Warren County High School in McMinnville, Tennessee, in 1998.

other, which is said to have high transitivity. We can also say that the more one is connected to others who have relatively high transitivity, the more central one is to the network. And we know that the more central one is, the more prosocial (likely to trust/cooperate but also transmit and adopt new ideas without questioning). Some networks have a clear centre (some place God there), and some have several clear nodes, with many more connections than others. Such nodes can enhance contagion but also be the focus of attacks. The most stable networks often have a number of super-connected nodes rather than a single one. Just as a power grid can experience cascade failure if a central node power station goes down, so in social networks a change from a key communicator can have huge impact.* So, to summarise, we can think of four parameters of one's social network and place in it: its size, its density (how transitive it is), how central you are in it, and whether there are some super-connected centres or nodes (individuals or small, tight-knit groups).

We have impressive but limited capacity to form connections with others. Humans, like apes, are social animals, only much more so. We can live in larger groups than apes, because we have developed the ability to maintain a greater number of trusting relationships. Indeed, one explanation of why humans developed language is that it enabled us to build such relationships. Unlike the apes' alternative of grooming each other to build trust, talking can be done with more than one other person at a time and can occur

---

* As a hypothetical example, what would happen if, say, Greta Thunberg decided she was wrong about CO_2, that she had been worrying needlessly. What would happen if she started to blame global elites for causing her, and her whole generation, unnecessary mental anguish? Although many influential communicators repeat and reinforce the same messages, which is needed to attract followers, if and when they do present genuinely new and challenging ideas these can have a major impact.

whilst performing other tasks. However, there is a limit to the number of people with which humans can maintain stable relationships, and it is, more or less, 150 – known as Dunbar's number after anthropologist Robin Dunbar. A community beyond this size has trouble maintaining collective group discipline without formal enforcement mechanisms, as it is easier to cheat and get away with it. This has been observed in many contexts and throughout history. An army is a particularly clear example of an organisation which asks for extreme individual risk-taking for the good of the group. Effectiveness is dependent on soldiers caring for the welfare of each other, requiring strong bonds of friendship. It is noticeable that effective army company size (150 or a little larger) has not changed from Roman times to the present. Likewise, Malcom Gladwell and others have observed decreasing effectiveness of workforces beyond 150 employees.[4]

What this means is that, as we add new contacts to our networks using social media, which can jump geography, we also inevitably cut off others. As we become more attached to like-minded groups, many of which reduce the range of new and challenging ideas we may come across, we reduce traditional, family and local ties. Significantly, these more local ties have to a greater extent not been chosen by us. Hence, the ideas we encounter may be more random than in our social media groups. This may not always hold, but before social media, as one moved geographically one would be likely to encounter new ideas, and, moreover, in a fashion we could understand and learn to cope with. Understanding where ideas come from has always been important in how we weigh them: their veracity and importance. With social media, much of that context is lost.

Within our network are reference groups, and they have two functions: firstly, we use them to compare ourselves against, and secondly, they influence us. Your influence or the degree to which you are influenced is going to be determined by your own sources of ideas and susceptibility to the ideas of others. But it will also be affected by the precise structure of the network you are in, the sources of influence and the susceptibility to influence of many others in the network. You are not likely to know any of this (though the likelihood is rising that Big Tech observing you does). We have discovered a few things, though. One is that if one wants to immunise a population, it makes sense to try to prioritise those who are most connected, most central. One way to do this is to survey random people and ask them who their acquaintances are, and then start immunising their acquaintances rather than those surveyed. According to Nicholas Christakis and James Fowler in their book *Connected*, such a choice 'informed by network science could be seven hundred times more effective and efficient'.[5] This reflects the importance just mentioned of random encounters and local geography. Such a surprisingly large difference indicates the huge impact non-random, as opposed to random, influences can have on our networks.

Christakis and Fowler have investigated and reviewed the properties of social networks. Our ability to map real behaviour in social networks is increasing due to greater online presence, not least with the advent of large-scale gaming involving millions of people's avatars. One conclusion is that there are often three degrees of influence: one's contacts, their contacts and their contacts' contacts. After this, in most networks, other influences predominate, from advertising to news items to more random thoughts and events. Another finding is that, when it comes to problem-solving, teams often work together most effectively when there is a mixture of people who already know each other together with some who do not. This is better than if either nearly everyone already knows each other or almost nobody does. When we know people with different levels of familiarity, a mixture of strong and weak ties is best. In a medical setting, the Zollman effect describes much the same phenomenon: well-connected researchers tend towards a consensus quickly, but sparsely connected networks are more likely to form a correct consensus. In making decisions quickly, some challenges and alternative thinking are missed. In other words, the closely networked are prone to groupthink: they can reach a conclusion quickly which ends up being wrong.

Networks also evolve with the adoption of new media, and the way they have evolved with social media in particular has had a huge impact on the mix of our encounters and received views, impacting in turn our group loyalties and tolerances for outsiders. In the last chapter we looked at game theory and at multi-period games where agents interacted many times with each other. Suppose, however, that one had a choice how much and whether to interact or not. Those who communicate rarely if at all can be seen as on the periphery of a network, which might be a preferable strategy should the alternative be being constantly taken advantage of. Those who interact a lot are the most prosocial. So, in trying to emulate social networks, we might think of several types of agents. There are those who are trusting and cooperative, those who cheat more often, those who punish the cheaters (as 'tit-for-tat' does) and those who retire to the periphery of the network.

Another observation is that social media has been linked to

increased loneliness, with those at the periphery cutting themselves off, but often not before infecting the few they know with a sense of loneliness too. So whilst overall social media has massively increased connectivity, it has led to exclusion for others, and with it related mental health and other problems.

Avoiding social media is not an option any more for many children who want to socialise; everybody else in their network is using it. There is quite literally nobody in the street to play with as an alternative. But it is a network in which fear and a strong desire to conform can dominate. This constrains thoughts and identities, creating more uniformity of views. You never know who is watching, and there is intense peer pressure to conform, leading to anxiety.

NEW GROUPTHINK

How do our networks, communication patterns and information flows affect our understanding of meaning? Learning occurs when we come into contact with novelty, which is why social media, with its less random or private interactions, is becoming a major problem. New perspectives may not be sought, and existing thoughts reinforced rather than challenged by a network of like-minded contacts and associated outside information sources. This is especially true when one can be ostracised or cancelled for stepping over acceptable thought boundaries. Randomness in our experiences and information has also been reduced and we (and the algorithms trying to guide us) have become more efficient in surrounding ourselves with contacts who think the way we do and information sources supportive of our groupthinks. Yet we lose something important in the process. Not only is randomness vital in our thinking, enabling new connections and ideas to form, but lack of enlightenment is linked to inability to think outside a given narrative. This requires a self-awareness which cannot flow from the narrative's internal logic. Just as Godel's theory helps us understand the limits of computers to become self-aware,[*] so no matter how much we look only to the internal logic of a current narrative (however confident this may make us of its veracity), we cannot verify its truth. The collective can be seductive, but to critique it we have to get outside.

Furthermore, growing up in an environment with more anxiety, with not only constant distractions but also reminders of things to worry about, doesn't help. Fear trumps all other emotions and stops us being curious. For those constantly feeling anxious, something of a bunker mentality may even develop. Conformity, lack of novelty, leads to slow cognitive development and inability to develop one's own concepts and test them. Much evil is caused by unthinking group conformity.

To have enemies and use social media is dangerous. One can be accused and condemned without evidence or objectivity or much chance of response or defence. In general, there are only two ways of surviving a social media attack, and neither involve an appeal to truth. The first is heavy use of PR, and the second is being in the right group to start with, as people forgive those in their group

---

[*] Godel's second incompleteness theorem shows how certain formal logical systems cannot demonstrate their own consistency. The consequences are neatly explained by the mathematician and Nobel Laureate Roger Penrose in *Shadows of the Mind*. The basic idea is that we can demonstrate that we can draw a conclusion about computers which it is impossible for a computer, as we understand the laws of physics, to draw. Penrose claims that this in turn affirms that we know neither how to build a self-aware computer nor how our own minds work. Penrose believes a possible explanation may lie with some aspect of quantum theory which we do not yet understand.

much more readily than those outside. It comes back to a point made in Chapter 1: if it bolsters our groupthink, we ask ourselves if we can believe something (yes, we can), and if it doesn't, we ask ourselves if we have to (no, we don't). In an environment where anybody can be subject to attack, and there are always excuses to think badly of them, this behaviour feeds the growth of groupthink and hardens group boundaries.

Intelligence is the selective destruction of information, but when this is done thoughtlessly (driven by fear, not careful consideration), collective intelligence is lowered. When this is done systematically, based on group adherence not objectivity, it is lowered even further. In short, new networks and ways of thinking are creating more collective stupidity, more groupthink.

Furthermore, where there is groupthink, having more people involved in the decision makes things worse, not better. It can increase the efforts and resources in squashing challenges, reinforce our views and increase the likelihood of stubborn persistence along the wrong course. Where there is independent thought, crowds are often better estimators than individuals (for example, taking a crowd's average estimate on the weight of an object is often very accurate) but not when there is groupthink. The bigger the lie, the greater the need for intolerance to sustain it, but the bigger the group, the more achievable this is. The largest bubbles are the most ruthless – heresies and heretics are most completely excluded. The collective can be both all-powerful and fundamentally wrong.

Individuals still crave understanding and rebel in order to achieve enlightenment. But those of us who rebel (often the young) are typically now doing so inside the bubble in repeated patterns which do not lead to enlightenment. The way in which children and young adults rebel is increasingly a form of compliance to various groupthinks – for example, extremist views on climate change and political correctness. It may seem counterintuitive, but activism can give the impression of rebellion, meet a desire for challenging authority, enhance one's sense of ability to change the world and thus one's empowerment, all whilst being completely supportive of the dominant groupthink. We even teach them how in school and university. Such activism, which attacks straw men – superficial representations of opposing thought – is distinguished by acceptance of authorised truths rather than by scepticism of dominant theories and independent assessment of opposing views, experiments and data. And again fear, and especially the need for catastrophe to focus our fear, keeps us grounded within the orthodox narratives. The effect of such activism dressed up as rebellion can also further discipline those who may be wavering. Young people are often the most effective mind guards and the most intolerant of others. For extremists, violence, the threat of violence, and even self-harm are considered legitimate ways to enforce their views on others.

Furthermore, Big Tech employs tens of thousands to censor content. Whole networks are on occasion simply deleted. Censoring decisions are determined by the views of the handful of owners of Big Tech and the majority views of those they pander to. Outliers and dissent are systematically excised from the public sphere.

The amount of effort made to stop dissent or debate may be itself a sign of weakness. Unless it is rejected entirely, when a narrative constantly fails to explain the world satisfactorily groupthink members are driven away from rationality and evidence. If views are contrary to empirical observation then evidence is rejected, and if necessary reason and science. Instead come dumbed-down acceptance of trite memes and explanations. Thoughts are repeated, reinforced but not elaborated. We don't create new ones. Insanity, as Einstein supposedly said, is doing the same thing over and over expecting different results. The alternative is to stop trying to explain the world, to acquiesce, to comply, to self-censor one's rebellious thought, to seek escapism as therapy. We will do almost anything to keep in the safety of our group, to protect our prejudices.

PUBLIC VERSUS PRIVATE

Plato's totalitarian dream, and that of many tyrants since, has been to eradicate all that is private or individual. Privacy has been practically limited, and so all the more valued, in many societies in the past. Public life, in the sense of being known to and communicating with more people than one can know personally, has until recently been limited to leaders, artists and others famous for their deeds or social position.

It may require some nerve to have a public persona, especially if in so doing one is likely to create and encounter enemies. Politicians need a thick skin. Andy Warhol said in 1968 that in the future everyone would be world-famous for fifteen minutes. That future has now arrived, and many embrace it willingly. We now have celebrities who are well known simply for being well known (and who are instantly forgettable as a result). Although some of us want no public attention or fame, most of us appreciate some as a form of recognition. It gives us a sense of self-worth. However, one can have too much of a good thing. Many, like one-time richest person in America Howard Hughes, prefer to be reclusive. Few of us want to be under constant surveillance, and the strain of being constantly hounded by the media has left a catalogue of unhappiness.

Most people, however, have no experience of mass public attention or the trauma it can bring when they start using social media. Its tyranny is made possible through users not understanding or coping with it being public not private. It can come as quite a shock. Years can go by before a tweet is dragged up from your past to publicly shame you. The term 'offence archaeologist' has been coined to describe those who do the digging.

Psychologist Gregg Henriques highlights a crucial distinction between private and public domains of justification. Filters between the two are important, as one needs to nurture both a stable self-view and a stable (but different) presentation of self to the outside world. The filter from private to public (called the Rogerian filter) determines what we share with others.[6] Confusion about who we are talking to on social media, especially thinking a conversation is more private than it turns out to be, is how many people miscalculate, with disastrous effects.

Many social media users are children who are trying to form their own identities. The erosion of traditional moralities and geographical and family group identities puts additional pressure on children to form their identities early and on their own. With their peers all online, there is also not much choice but to make one's way in finding identity online too. Moreover, that online environment is overseen by companies which are harvesting personal data and moulding behaviour in line with commercial interests.

Such commercial interests want predictability in people – in their buying habits and in their thoughts. Yet reaching decisions is often and necessarily chaotic. The more creative and innovative our ideas (the more out of the box they are), the more apparently chaotic the route in reaching them. To maintain our creativity, to be free in our thought, we need individual and small-group privacy to experiment with ideas we then discard, including the outrageous – not least so we understand why they are outrageous.

To have our private ideas kept as a record confuses the private/public distinction and inhibits the process of self-definition, especially in a world of political correctness and taboos. For those spending a good proportion of their days online, forming identity and ideas is thus constrained. One has no space to work things out on one's own – all one's workings are on display, indelible for all time. Also, feeding the needs of others at the expense of private time leaves less time for self-construction. The task is often not done well and a lifelong instability between one's inner and outer self may result. Many adult personality disorders may emanate from this.[7]

The fear of even thinking one's ideas might become public creates self-censorship. A consequence is groupthink. As Henriques says: 'Human consciousness functions, first and foremost, as a social reason-giving system, one that seeks a personally and publicly socially justifiable path to legitimize action. If we understand this … groupthink, along with many other social psychological processes, becomes readily understandable.' Our reasoning is a derivative of circumstance, and designed to justify action. As a consequence, altering our motives can easily alter our reasoning, even to Orwellian limits.

NEWSPEAK

'The purpose of Newspeak was not only to provide a medium of expression for the world-view and mental habits proper to the devotees of Ingsoc, but to make all other modes of thought impossible. It was intended that when Newspeak had been adopted once and for

all and Oldspeak forgotten, a heretical thought – that is, a thought
diverging from the principles of Ingsoc – should be literally unthink-
able, at least as far as thought is dependent on words.'

GEORGE ORWELL, *1984*

George Orwell's Newspeak is, within certain groupthinks, gaining footholds. The same words mean different things to different
people. When you talk in public, you now have many publics to
consider. What you say can be critiqued by any group, with a wide
range of agendas and intolerances, now or in the future. Someone
may easily take offence when none is intended, and so nearly all
high-profile communication which goes beyond platitudes is dangerous for the speaker. There are those who wilfully misinterpret.
Saying things which cannot be reasonably misinterpreted does not
mean they will not be. This makes it nearly impossible to sustain
principles in public. In effect this robs us, even politicians who are
experts at it, of the ability to communicate effectively to different,
or indeed any, groups. The result, too often, is trite statements, am-
biguity, not challenge or leadership. Language starts to fail.

   With groupthink, central ideas are never properly challenged or
justified. Taboo subjects are widely held, often lacking any effective
challenge for many years. This is despite them sometimes being
highly vulnerable to even cursory examination. Consequences are
not understood as standard skewed memes have always been assumed. They are not thought through.

   And who decides what is and what is not taboo? In a world dominated by the fear of being cancelled, the list of what is taboo grows
ever longer. Its domain is constantly expanding. One sign of its cancerous growth is the reduction of acceptable joke topics. I was told

in my youth that fascism could never happen in Britain because Hitler would simply be laughed at. Maybe that counterfactual was never valid, but one worries that it may be less so now. We joke less but sneer more. Some of us learn to hate instead of laugh. In George Orwell's *1984*, there is a daily collective 'Two Minutes Hate' session. Everyone is encouraged to express their hate whilst footage is shown of the state bogeyman, Emmanuel Goldstein. This daily therapy releases frustrations, making people more complacent.

SURVEILLANCE SOCIETY

In 2012, a man stormed into a Target store with a fistful of coupons for baby products, demanding to know why the company was sending them to his teenage daughter. He accused them of encouraging her to get pregnant. What he did not know, but the company's algorithms did, was that she already was, and that was without her having bought any pregnancy products from them... yet.

There is a strong case for public policy to protect privacy. Yet identifying individuals from anonymised data is often ridiculously easy: three pieces of publicly available information – date of birth, postcode and sex – are often enough. Also, individuals can be found by their physical location, obtainable from their mobile phone. Tech companies have now also established the right to use facial recognition to identify anyone in the street without their consent. The EU's GDPR (General Data Protection Regulation) may form a basis for constraining the surveillance business model, but its main impact so far appears to have been to restrict competition. However, without surveillance the business model of many currently dominant mass-use technology solutions which are free or almost free at point of delivery, fails completely. The battle is all going the other way at present. A public sector nudge unit (i.e. a government policy design/communications unit which tries to mould our motivations and so choices towards options considered best) could focus on protecting our privacy and individuality, but too often a government's preference, like that of commercial interests, is to mould more conformity and uniformity into our behaviour, not less.

Huxley's *Brave New World* seems to be coming into focus all too quickly. In it, he describes a world of hedonistic simpletons whose behaviour and whole lives are programmed from birth to death. The next step is to dumb us all down further. In Plato's *Republic*, education was necessary for an elite to be able to govern, but it was considered highly dangerous and so only for the old – those well set in their ways and not likely to think differently or challenge the political order.

Probably the most influential American psychologist fifty years ago, B. F. Skinner was both admired and reviled. He was famous for his ambitions to mould human behaviour and his support for the argument that knowledge releases us from the illusion of freedom. This extreme determinism has been found of limited use, until now at least, by the impossibility of central understanding, let alone coordination, of millions of individuals and their decisions. As a result, Friedrich Hayek, for one, prominently argued against ambitious central planning. The failure of Soviet economics supports his analysis.

Fifty years ago, following in the footsteps of Plato, Skinner wrote about the possible use of technology to gradually squeeze more and more of our lives from the private to the public sphere. The influence of his vision was largely subdued after the horrors of twentieth-century war, fascism and communism, but it has been resuscitated by the internet of things, the surveillance of our every action, the increased amount of our lives digitally observable.

Four companies dominate Western digital lives: Google, Facebook, Amazon and Apple. The dominance of these companies is not only monopolistic but international, powerful enough to negotiate with governments and internationally tax evasive. Their business models are based on what has been coined 'surveillance capitalism', an essential part of which is to collect massive quantities of data on users which are then used to sell products. In *The Age of Surveillance Capitalism*, Shoshana Zuboff has compared this collection of data to the Spanish conquistadors' taking of Latin America. The right to collect and own, and sell on, the personal behavioural data of others is asserted without paying for it, indeed without explicit consent. The technologies which extract this personal information are hidden. They fit into the background and steal the information unnoticed. This theft is necessary, as when asked for consent most people say no. In a 2015 survey, 91 per cent said they did not think surreptitious collection of personal data was a fair trade-off for lower prices. But without this surveillance, the business model cannot work, which is why it seems no stone has been left unturned to protect it, be it via lobbying legislators, taking legal action, predatory business practices, careful branding, academic funding or perhaps even helping political friends win elections and giving them lucrative jobs in their retirement.

Zuboff refers to the collection of personal behavioural data as rendition: 'If rendition is interrupted, surveillance capitalism cannot stand, for the whole enterprise rests on this original sin.'

Where there is reluctance to part with personal information, three strategies are employed. The first of these is to point to significant cost savings. The second is to present the behavioural monitoring as somehow fun or diverting. The third is to promote the sense of inevitability – your data will be collected sooner or later, so you might as well not struggle. As the Borg in *Star Trek* say: 'Resistance is futile.'

If a user is presented with a product for free, that is a sign they are not the customer. When you use a service from a company like Facebook or Google but do not pay for it, you are not the customer. The customer is the company who is paying for the information and analysis provided from surveillance of your behaviour. Data, having been extracted, is analysed to find patterns which can aid future sales. Products and communication to users can be personalised and, in order to elicit more sales, experiments can be carried out, automated and in secret and often continuously, to understand user behaviour patterns better.

But the interaction with users is not simply one of observance and analysis; it is also designed to make the users more uniform in their habits and so more predictable. More predictable users translate into more valuable data for third parties and more reliability that marketing and advertising spend will lead to sales. Highly sophisticated algorithms are now active in not just exploiting but shaping behaviour for commercial motives. Smart devices are here to spy on you, conduct experiments and nudge and mould your behaviour in the best interest of the corporations' customers. This means, in a profoundly sinister way, that our privacy is being eroded and our behaviour programmed. This shaping of actions is not in individuals' or society's best interests. It caters to our selfishness and emotional responses, encourages profligacy and addiction, not self-restraint, prudence, reflection or toleration.

These companies are simply getting away with it. Although there are many addictive design features on the internet and social media, the most dangerous are those which prompt rapid response and sharing across a social network. Given this, why, for example, are the 'like' and 'retweet' buttons still available to teenagers when we suspect they are major contributory factors to excessive, addictive social media behaviour, as well as anxiety, depression and suicide? No one is taking the necessary responsibility. Companies are motivated to turn a blind eye to negative consequences: more time on social media means more profits. Politicians have been largely spineless.

Also, and inevitably, changed behaviour alters self- and group identities. It affects the structures of our networks, and not in a random way. We have seen the enormous impact changed networks can have, with the spread of ideas hundreds of times more effective. Not only our behaviour but our morals are being eroded and, in effect, shaped by algorithms for others' commercial gain. Big Tech branding today has the potential to go far beyond what was possible in the past. Groupthink can be produced, emotions channelled, hedonistic reward given, independent thought discouraged, certain values and worldviews encouraged, others censored.

There is also money in predicting and changing voting patterns, with prediction seamlessly leading to manipulation. Where the line is between the acceptable and unacceptable is hard to draw. Cambridge Analytica's analysis of voter information used the same techniques in the political arena as are widespread in the commercial. Foreign interference in elections is unacceptable, but the intelligent use of social media by, for example, Obama's team to win the Democratic primary against Hillary Clinton, acceptable.

There is also little competition in this space. Monopoly power comes from the huge economies of scale in the use of the personal data being extracted. Once monopoly power is established, prices can move up with little to stop them. That may or may not happen, and we do not yet know whether more jobs will be destroyed or created by the new digital economy. But we do know firstly that consumers believe they are benefiting from cheaper and more convenient services and secondly that monopoly profits are huge.

We also know that social capital has reduced significantly since our digital age took hold. As far as Big Tech is concerned, social trust is becoming increasingly redundant. The objective is to reduce uncertainty in our behaviour, which has the side effect of us not having to trust others so much. Indeed, such trust might lead to unpredictable behaviour. It might lead us to have novel ideas, a clear danger, as Plato knew, to the natural and fixed order of things. We are not asked to take as many chances as our ancestors, so we neither conduct nor need risk analysis. All that is needed is for us to respond to behavioural cues. The precautionary motive is the best and only risk-related response our Pavlovian selves need to be programmed with.

BIG TECH AND THE NEWS

Google and Facebook are not only selling goods. They have now entered the news and politics business, shaping how we see the world. They can provide users with news for free because it attracts traffic, because they extract personal behavioural information in the process, and because they can use customised newsfeeds to mould us. Indeed, it is but a short step beyond measurement and prediction to algorithm-driven continuous experiments being performed on us, moulding our thoughts and behaviour to be more predictable (and so easier to exploit commercially).

More traditional media is thus facing tough competition, especially for the attention of young readers. One advantage of reading a newspaper is precisely that it is not customised for you personally, and thus gives you a sense of relative importance of the news, at least from the editor's perspective. This is not to say that it is balanced, as the purpose of a newspaper editor is to sell newspapers. Consistent with our observations so far, fear sells, and has done so since before newspapers existed. Disasters and other negative news and scandals sell. Royals, sports and fashion also sell. Good news is less interesting. Foreign news will always lose out in the battle for column inches against similar domestic news. Nevertheless, adjusting for all these biases, the layout and relative profile given to different stories does convey information about how the world is changing.

A newspaper separates truth from falsehood. It can be a tutor in tolerance for those who want to hear novel views, though in practice often within limits; it can provoke indignation for others. In other words, existing views cannot only be challenged but can be reinforced, opinions rehearsed for re-use. But such reinforcement, for which there is strong demand, is now available from many sources without the same challenge. Newspaper reading is shrinking as a result. Potential readers have a massive choice of news feeds. Anyone interested in regular information on a highly specific topic may find a more reassuringly consistent, less provocative source somewhere on the internet. Editors are trying to survive in an environment in which people are becoming more intolerant of others' views, an environment in which balance and impartiality are less attractive to the reader. Why read a newspaper? For some it is mere habit, and for others a source of entertainment. These reasons are selling fewer and fewer newspapers. The business model is being squeezed. Add to that dwindling resources and dumbed-down competition, and the trend is to lower standards. Investigative journalism, for example, is difficult to protect from vested interests and particularly expensive.

Google and Facebook have business models more indifferent to high standards of journalism. They are not dependent on truthful reporting or impartiality. They appear to have little interest in diverse views – indeed the opposite. This is simply a logical extension of their desire to understand and control human behaviour. The pity is that many people can no longer notice the difference between their product and that of mainstream media – increasingly because there isn't any.

They are eroding the demand for traditional journalism, but are they responsible for their content or not? They seem to want it both ways. On the one hand they claim they merely provide a platform for others and are not responsible for content. On the other hand, they employ tens of thousands of employees to monitor and censor that content. The entire purpose of such censorship is to exclude certain types of communication and certain communicators. The basis of this is largely defined by political correctness, by group-think, and is not limited or controlled by anyone outside these private companies.

They can even exclude the President of the United States. President Donald Trump was permanently banned from using Twitter in January 2021 after he voiced support for protesters storming the US Capitol. Did the US President cross a line in challenging the constitution, threatening the balance of power necessary to preserve democratic freedoms? But then again, by what right, and who at Twitter, should be able to stop the US President communicating with his public?

Short of banning or censoring, traffic can also be sidelined away from undesirable places and views. To aid those responsible for this process, machine learning fairness (MLF) has been introduced. The purpose of MLF is to take judgement-making out of human hands in the selection of getting from place to place on the internet. MLF learns from patterns, but that just means it learns from collective human judgement rather than that of an individual. In doing so it helps to cement, not to challenge, groupthink.

Since the Covid-19 pandemic, we have seen several cases of censorship in action. Several prominent scientists, and also Richard Dearlove, previously head of the UK's MI6, directed attention to the possibility that the virus was man-made. Dearlove was ostracised, criticised heavily on social media for pointing out the uncertainty, which for those believing the official sponsored groupthink on the issue at the time translates as believing in a ridiculous 'conspiracy'. However, a year later, in June 2021, this alternative explanation was accepted as more than a highly unlikely possibility. Yet the evidence had not changed, except insofar as there was an erosion of credibility in the alternative explanations of the virus jumping species – the longer the inter-species link remains unproved, the lower the probability of it as the explanation.

Another example is the shunning of Oxford University epidemiologist Sunetra Gupta, who in March 2021 presented the case that compelling children to wear facemasks, and telling them they pose a risk of life to others, inflicted deep psychological damage. This was posted on YouTube but was erased by the company three weeks later. A spokesman said: 'We removed this video because it included content that contradicts the consensus of local and global health authorities regarding the efficacy of masks to prevent the spread of Covid-19.' The term 'thought police' comes to mind. I am not saying Gupta's argument is valid or not valid, but I do think it wrong to close down debate on the side effects of a major government policy, and entirely inappropriate that executives at the commercial company YouTube should be making such judgements about what version of the truth is acceptable. Not only do they not have a monopoly on truth, but I have illustrated that companies in their industry do have an incentive to promote uniformity of views and thus predictability of behaviour as this can lead to more profits for them and their clients.

FAKE CULTURE AND FAKE NEWS

Intolerance to new ideas has been spreading. Reaching many US university campuses around 2013 was the idea that students, rather than being challenged with different views, should not be subjected to ideas perceived by them as offensive. This is entirely contrary to the purpose of a university, which is to educate and learn through encounter with new ideas. Lukianoff and Haidt report on a 2017 survey, in which 58 per cent of college students agreed it 'important to be part of a campus community where I am not exposed to intolerant and offensive ideas'.[8] A new moral culture of safety-ism is spreading, in which the precautionary motive has let rip and in which safety has become a sacred creed. It has led to safe spaces, trigger warnings, the concept of microaggressions, bias response teams, the idea that speech is violence and call-out culture. Unfortunately, some have become obsessed with there being a single lens (or set of lenses) through which to view the behaviour and ideas of others, be it race, gender, climate, or some other all-encompassing view. These characteristically build on the Marxist idea that understanding power relationships between groups is more important than respecting people as individuals. Anti-intellectualism, cynicism, bigotry and chaos follow close behind.

Into this environment of reluctance to be open-minded to the views of those who do not share one's particular lens has come fake news, by which I mean false information and news known to be false by those ensuring its widespread distribution. This definition is not straightforward, however, as people can believe the most outrageous and non-credible things. They can distribute information which they do actually believe to be true which to most people is clearly false, and which others would call fake news. This is perhaps in part an unfortunate consequence of widespread abandonment of the concept that there is a single objective reality out there for us to study and try to understand. Whereas we can entertain many possible truths, a breakthrough during the Enlightenment was the modern scientific method, which we come to in more detail in Chapter 5. Its role is to seek not immutable truth but only testable hypotheses which have not been disproved to date. Scepticism is essential to scientific advancement in this sense, and efforts to close off public debate in the name of public safety or because the truth is already known is poison to it. In a world in which fewer and fewer care for such a view of science or scientific progress, or who even think there is a single objective truth, fake news can be thought of as an important tool in furthering paramount objectives. It is the harvest of the hubris and patronisation of elite egotists – be they Big Tech owners or public sector technocrats who think they know best. For others who have cynically given up on trusting anyone to be objective, it is viewed as mere propaganda and entertainment. For some, it may be interesting and sophisticated – more so than traditional news, with its emphasis on objective truth. Fake news easily crowds out truth, as it is designed to spread well across social media. But it can also spread across traditional media desperate to compete, particularly when a fake news item has real-world consequence which can be construed as real news. Fake news can be a deliberate effort to confuse, close down debate and prevent understanding of the truth. There is, for example, evidence that Russia tried to manipulate the US presidential election. Yet some people are just nihilistic. Some people crave war for its own sake. Some like smashing things up. Some simply love social media for the amount of hurt they can cause – their egos unconstrained.

CONSEQUENCES

Both H. G. Wells and Aldous Huxley thought that we were in a race between education and disaster. Big Tech's strategy of surreptitiously extracting behavioural data, and then experimenting on and manipulating people, is fundamentally antidemocratic. Evil is so often banal, and the banal is often evil. The ease with which various totalitarian regimes acquired power in the twentieth century was in part because they solved existing problems. The ridiculousness of the distorted egos that drove them was no bar.

Technology generates opportunities to expand our networks and gives us access to much more information, but it also activates the fear of change. We typically adjust too slowly, with fear trumping any stimulus to new thinking. Hence, whilst our new-found communication abilities create exciting capacities to roam in larger spaces than before, without courage and self-discipline (not yet learned), we lack the ability to escape groupthink and, in consequence, decadence and fanaticism, as discussed in Chapter 1.

With new technology comes new responsibilities but also real empowerment: a new Great Enfranchisement, as I shall call it. The question is whether we shall reach a positive and stable relationship with our new technology without first suffering a form of dystopia. The race is on.

SUMMARY

- New communication technology has often been highly disruptive, changing the way we communicate, our networks and our morals.
- Social media, especially since 2009, has led to instant reactions, less reflection, more intolerance. Children have had little choice but to socialise online. There has been, in girls in particular, an increase in anxiety, depression and suicide attempts.
- As we increase social network connections, so others reduce in importance. Our interactions have become less local and less random. Reduced randomness can have a very large impact on a network, and our networks have become more prone to groupthink.
- Groupthink has not only increased but becomes more, not less, robust with size, as defence mechanisms kick in. The bigger the lie, the greater the need for intolerance in order to sustain

it, and the bigger the group, the more achievable this is. Fear, and especially the need for catastrophe to focus our fear, keeps us grounded within the orthodox narratives. Highly connected individuals can have a major influence on many others and tend to promote uniformity of views.

- Loneliness is one consequence for some people who cease engaging with others in their network, though not before inducing loneliness in others.

- The way in which children and young adults rebel is increasingly a form of compliance to various groupthinks, for example extreme alarmism on climate change and political correctness. Contrary evidence is rejected.

- There is a crucial distinction between private and public domains of justification, and this has become confused. The lack of individual and small-group space to test non-consensus ideas has narrowed, and this seems to have damaged cognitive development.

- Nearly all high-profile communication which goes beyond platitudes is dangerous for the speaker. This makes it nearly impossible to sustain principles in public.

- Groupthink prevents consequences being thought through, from private decisions to government policies.

- We have explained the business model of surveillance capitalism. The right to collect, own and sell on the personal behavioural data of users is asserted by Big Tech companies, without paying for it and indeed without explicit consent.

- Highly sophisticated algorithms are now active in not just exploiting but shaping behaviour for commercial motives.

- Social capital is at best redundant for surveillance capitalism and may be inconsistent with the business goal of moulding predictable consumer behaviour.

- Big Tech is now also dominant in determining the content of our news sector.
- Public sector nudge units and other government policies could focus on protecting our privacy and individuality, but too often a government's preference, like that of commercial interests, is to mould more conformity and uniformity into our behaviour, not less.

CHAPTER 4

FROM ONE CRISIS TO THE NEXT

'I used to think that if there was reincarnation, I wanted to come
back as the President or the Pope, or as a .400 baseball hitter.
But now I would like to come back as the bond market.
You can intimidate everybody.'

JAMES CARVILLE, POLITICAL ADVISER TO BILL CLINTON

We have heard in Chapter 1 how the erudite, intelligent and educated are the most prone to groupthink. We now illustrate
this in finance and economics, populated with high achievers, yet
capable for all that of immense collective folly.

Arguably the most important thing to happen for most people
on the planet since the Second World War has been the end of the
Cold War. The foreign policy of developed countries has largely
stopped propping up regimes for ideological reasons and this has
allowed the preferences of domestic economic actors (consumers
and producers) to determine prices. Most people now live in societies in which prices reflect these choices, and in which institutions
are evolving in response, including norms of behaviour. With this
competition of ideas there is plenty of challenge. There has been a

deliverance from a particularly unpleasant form of political group-think, namely Soviet communism. Yet there are nevertheless persistent irrationalities.

My interest in groupthink originated from my experience in finance and economics, where herd mentality appears even though there is plenty of competition of ideas. It is manifest despite financial markets being the epitome of private competition, with many buyers and sellers focused on maximising returns and, to ensure competition, extensive regulation of both firms and individuals. Maybe it is because it can be such a complex environment with a lot at stake, but there often seems to be a lack of thinking outside the box. Being in the crowd can be beneficial for much of the time, and this is bolstered by incentive patterns. Much chatter and commentary is repetitive and predictable.

Compared with the complex and often highly politicised world of policy-making, the clarity of purpose in financial markets can be refreshing. In her book *The Nature of Economies*, Jane Jacobs contrasts the public and private sectors through a Platonic dialogue.[1] One of the key differences she highlights is between the zero-sum thinking common in politics compared with the positive-sum thinking typical in commerce and trade. The benefits of openness and cooperation are much clearer and more abundant in the private than the public sector. Government is territorially competitive, control-obsessed and bureaucratic. It tends to restrict innovation with its dead hand (see Matt Ridley's *How Innovation Works*),[2] even with the best of intentions.

Echoing Socrates's support for democracy, and contrary to Plato's preference for political stasis, recent history provides plenty of evidence that liberation, democracy, free markets and societal progress can be highly compatible, not least much of the history of the growth and prosperity of Western democracies over the past couple of centuries. And some form of what might be called capitalism has been with us ever since trade began. It evolves, sometimes in unpredictable ways, the result of millions of decisions.* Where there is competition in goods and services and also competition of ideas, innovation can flourish and hence progress.

However, the optimal mix of state and markets is not simple. Just as an overweening state can be harmful, so dogmatic laissez-faire and a minimum role for the state can be too. Lack of government and free markets are not the same thing as competitive markets, not least as private actors have incentives to collude. Financial markets provide some excellent examples of why regulation is essential not just for competition but to avoid financial crisis. This chapter will focus on some recent events to illustrate how many people (often millions of them) can get things seriously wrong. But first, to set the scene, some remarks are in order both about how financial and goods markets differ and about the role of incentives.

FINANCIAL INSTABILITY

The standard economic link between price and demand does not apply to financial markets – more specifically, when the price of a good goes up, demand normally falls, and vice versa. There are luxury goods, where demand can go up as goods become more expensive, but making them more exclusive arguably changes their

---

* I find the deterministic thinking of Marx and Engels unconvincing. The capitalism Marx described and criticised was gone even before he finished writing his magnum opus, *Das Kapital*. Before the ink was dry, capitalism had evolved – not least with the Factory Acts – beyond the ruthless extremes of exploitation he described so well. The contradictions he identified as inevitably leading to a great crisis are no more. Capitalism has a long track record of evolving before catastrophe strikes.

nature. A less ambiguous exception is the Giffen good, where the increase in the good's price has a major impact on the pattern of consumption due to its impact on purchasing power. This is very rare, the classic example being the potato in Ireland in the 1840s. The rise in the price of potatoes (due to potato blight-induced scarcity) caused an increase in demand because it was still the cheapest food. As potato prices rose, their necessary purchase significantly squeezed the amount of household money left for purchasing anything else, so much so that other foods were no longer affordable.

Such seemingly perverse demand behaviour, whilst very rare for goods and services, is common for financial assets. When a financial asset price rises, demand often goes up – at least for a while. The fear of missing out and sheer greed, exaggerated by incentive distortions, often results in bubble chasing. On the flip side, panic and fear can lead to mass selling. Investors repeatedly run through a sequence of fear, emotional focus on capital preservation and liquidity (ability to sell quickly), as well as flight to those instruments perceived as low-risk or so called 'risk-free'.* This may be done without analysis of the herding it involves and may lead to increased exposure to assets which may later move suddenly from highly liquid to illiquid and lose substantial value. Liquidity in particular, though also other financial market characteristics, is seen as reliably pertaining to particular financial instruments. However, it is more fundamentally a function of the behaviour of other market participants, which can change dramatically.

What is safe? Where is it best to invest? Answers are complex

---

* There is no such thing as an asset without any risk at all. Government bonds are often thought of as 'risk-free' even though they can default and their value can be eroded through devaluation and inflation. Assuming that some assets are risk-free is part of a conceptual framework in which risk is considered additive – a gross simplification.

and ever changing, because they involve the actions and beliefs of others. Popular ideas may work for a while simply because they are popular. Memes, with self-reinforcing characteristics, often emanate from analysts and thought leaders, who are as prone to fashions as other mortals. Ideas can be true for a while then suddenly untrue – items of common knowledge, of groupthink. Use of such advice and other shortcuts in thinking are both inevitable and dangerous, yet the perils are often poorly perceived. Why else did so few do simple accounting due diligence on Bernie Madoff? The conservative is often conflated with the prudent. Yet they can be opposites.

Inherent capacity for positive feedback is behind systemic crises. In part this is due to lack of clarity of what fair value for a financial asset is – a matter of opinion which may change quite substantially. Goods and services are consumed or otherwise put to productive use soon after purchase in a way that financial assets are not. Without what we might call near-term contact with reality, the expected future values of financial assets become much more important for estimates of current value – i.e. the extension of the timeframe adds significant value uncertainty. If the price of an asset is seen to rise, does that mean others know something you do not? With uncertainty over any true fair value, the price momentum often becomes a guide. And, moreover, it may be profitable to follow financial market changes for a while, simply because others are also doing so. This is the dynamics of booms and crashes. Financial markets are inherently unstable.

Another important consequence of uncertain fair value is the statistical behaviour of financial markets. Inappropriate models sustain misunderstanding and contribute to collective irrationality.

It is convenient to assume that normal distributions describe financial market prices, yet when there is any momentum or trend-following investing they may not.* Magnify this so that it looks like herd mentality, add in lots of leverage (borrowing using the asset as collateral) and shared incorrect views of the world which may be exploded simultaneously, and one has the makings of a market crash. Investors often have similar crisis reactions, possibly due to having similar liabilities. In such conditions, the normal distribution can become a serious misrepresentation of market behaviour.

Coping with uncertainty does not mean just ignoring it. Uncertain extreme events may be rare, but they can lead to large permanent losses. Whilst market participants can observe and learn from past patterns and each other, just looking backwards and expecting history's patterns to repeat is never going to deal with all new eventualities. New situations constantly occur. Also, investors often conflate uncertainty with fear, which as we have seen is normal for humans. The common reaction to both is minimal thought and avoidance of financial exposure, but they should be dealt with and dealt with differently. The limits of uncertainty should be as clearly defined as possible, and scenarios thought through carefully. Fear should be recognised as a function of human psychology and mechanisms put in place to minimise its effect on investment decisions.

In attempting to model reality better, one can try to alter the

---

* The normal distribution is a symmetric bell-shaped curve with probability or frequency on the Y-axis plotted against the value of the variable being described on the X-axis. In our case, the X-axis shows the price of a particular asset. The curve is plottable using just two parameters – the mean (average) and standard deviation (a measure along the X-axis of the spread of the curve such that two thirds of observations lie within one standard deviation from the mean). Whereas with a normal distribution the mean and standard deviation are known, in financial markets they are often not.

shape of the normal curve, skewing and flattening it to include the possibilities of extreme sell-offs, but when facing uncertainty as opposed to risk, this amounts to guesswork. One cannot calculate the probability of encountering a 'black swan' before having encountered a few, and certainly not when one is ignorant of its existence.* As discussed in Chapter 1, we define uncertainty as where we do not know the probability distribution – there might not even be one – as opposed to risk, where we do know it. Past extreme events (black-necked swans, perhaps?) may have little bearing on the future, so just incorporating them into one's distribution is still a poor guide. One needs to indulge instead in some scenario planning to think of the consequences of events which are possible but have not happened before.

Believing past patterns will always repeat can give a false sense of security. As the joke goes, one farmer was boasting to another that he had been increasing the profitability of his donkey by feeding it less and less every day. It had worked so well that he was going to try giving it less water, but unfortunately the donkey died. The common oversight in finding patterns in past data and extrapolating is that it can blind one to looming structural shifts (donkeys dying of starvation). Not that this prevents there being plenty of equivalents to our farmer in financial markets. Many investors are encouraged by being correct most of the time. Hyman Minsky, building on the insight of Keynes, pointed out that stability in financial markets breeds complacency, confidence and greed and so leads to excess and instability. When investors get it wrong, they

---

* A 'black swan' is an unexpected (extreme) event, as when black swans were discovered having previously being thought, by Europeans, not to exist. The metaphor was popularised by Nassim Nicholas Taleb in his book of the same name.

can do so spectacularly, and all at the same time. In this way, credit cycles build and collapse.

More useful for understanding financial market stability than the normal distribution, or even than searching for potential financial crisis triggers, is awareness of the existence or not of critical states. Critical states often pertain to serially uncorrelated events without average value but which display power laws, in which the probability of an event is proportional to the inverse of a power function of its magnitude. Critical states occur often in nature, for example with Californian earthquakes, which have no clear average value and are unpredictable using past data. Illustrative of critical states is a well-known physics experiment (simulated on a computer), in which identical particles of sand with certain viscosity are dropped from the same point each period.[3] A cone of particles builds up on the surface below until there are millions of them. Parts of the cone can be said to be in a critical state where the steepness of the surface is sufficient for avalanches to be likely. The adding of the next particle may cause an unpredictable number of other particles to move – none, ten or maybe 10 million. Significantly, not only are different particles indistinguishable (and so give no clue as to their impact) but the action of a particle is independent from that of its predecessor. Hence, extrapolating from past data is practically useless as a predictive tool. Insofar as financial markets display this pattern, momentum investing would be inadequate for foreseeing crises.

So, the relevant question to ask is not what might cause a crisis but are we in a critical state. Specifically, financial markets can be said to be in a critical state when there is complex, dangerous connectivity and when panic selling can cause others to panic sell (reinforcing positive feedbacks). A systemic crisis can ensue when there is a lot of leverage and when many investors, all at the same time, come to believe their previous assessments of risk were dramatically wrong. An event may have a ripple effect of limited extent or one that collapses huge global institutions. When markets are vulnerable in this way, it can feel like being in an earthquake zone. Or it would but for the possibility that the state can, unlike with earthquakes, intervene to bail out financial institutions and so break the spread of selling.* One should pretend neither that markets are always efficient nor that there is no role for state intervention in financial markets.

INCENTIVES

In a market prone to booms and busts, where behaviour is collectively stupid, the intelligent thing may be to do the stupid thing first. Collective irrationality (groupthink) can be fully consistent with individual rationality.

To put this another way, people face different risks and different incentives. Risk varies with liabilities, timeframes, decision-making capacity, relative speed of action, ability to alter events to reduce risk and behavioural constraints. Even if investors are rational, many investment decisions are not made by the owners of capital but by agents acting for them. As the owners of capital (whom we will call principals) may not be able to observe perfectly the actions of their agents, and any incentive contract may be imperfect, this may also affect incentives. Moreover, such principal–agent relationships may have several links in the chain.

---

* The possibility of this may create moral hazard, such as excess risk-taking in the expectation of future bail-out.

For example, consider a public pension fund, which is a good example as pension funds and other similar institutional investors have come to be significant holders, percentage-wise, of listed financial assets globally. The ultimate owners, or principals, are members of the public entitled to pension benefits from the pension plan. They are the principals to the board of the pension fund (their agents) or possibly to the politicians who oversee (and in turn are the principals to) the board of the pension fund. The board itself acts as principal to the pension fund staff, as well as, possibly, to outside consultants. The staff of the fund may also act as principals to outside consultants, and acting with their advice may set asset allocations and delegate the management of specific mandates to external asset management companies, who become the final agents in the chain. Quite complex.

With each step in the chain, incentives are altered. For the various agents in the chain, performance much better than that of the peer group (other pension funds) is rarely rewarded well; performance in line with the peer group is seldom penalised (even if it means dramatic losses); but bad performance when peers have done well may lead to the sack or other serious repercussions.

Hence, incentives are skewed towards the herd – groupthink and herd behaviour are rewarded; initiative often dangerous. Narratives, which humans crave, become dominant in explaining and justifying market behaviour. They satisfy our elephant-sitting selves – our desire to convince ourselves that we understand what is going on. It matters less what one's view of the world is but that one understands what everyone else's view is. Unfortunately, these are sometimes wrong. When they change, they can do so dramatically fast as everyone realises the flimsy rationales behind them. It was just in their interest, they thought, to go along with the consensus. As in the fairy tale, sometimes the emperor wears no clothes.

If that were not complicated enough, and by way of illustration of how distortions in financial markets affect all of us, politicians also have relationships with their electors, some of whom (sticking with our example) are pension fund participants. This can lead to conflicting objectives, such as when it is in the interests of taxpayers to reduce the real value of the national debt. This is because this aim may be reached via various pieces of legislation and regulation effectively forcing pension funds to invest in low-yielding government bonds – a common practice as part of a policy of financial repression.* With complex principal–agent chains, there are often incentives and opportunities to hide information and mislead principals. All of this provides rich nourishment for the growth of groupthink.

THE 2008 CRISIS AND WHY IT MAY HAPPEN AGAIN

John Maynard Keynes understood the radical role of uncertainty in financial markets and the knock-on impact this can have on goods and services and the wider economy. Yet his insights were inconveniently contradictory to the prevailing orthodoxy in economics.

---

* Financial repression is any policy which captures domestic savings to fund the government, and at an interest rate lower than would otherwise be possible. There are different ways to use pension fund assets to fund the government. They can be converted into a new currency or be locked up and so devalued. Pension funds can also be prevented from investing more than a small portion overseas. However, such methods are fairly obvious, and obviously objectionable. More subtly, pension funds can be mandated by their regulator, ostensibly to reduce risk, to invest a certain minimum proportion of their assets in high-quality investments as defined by a rating agency of the government's choice. This effectively gives pension funds no choice but to hold domestic sovereign debt – i.e. fund the government. This is quite a common form of financial repression.

He was busy with the war effort and died before he could correct the misinterpretation of his ideas, meaning the central role of uncertainty was largely written out of the standard view of Keynesian economics. The preference for equilibrium models prevailed over his insight that markets, especially financial markets, are inherently unstable.

The expansion of financial markets was boosted in the 1970s by the commoditisation of financial products, made possible by new developments in finance theory and widespread adoption of computers. The increased scale led to the need, in order to stay competitive, for the traditional merchant and investment banks to increase massively their capital bases. This could not be done within the constraints of the capital resources of the families which until then had owned and controlled them. So, they went public – i.e. issued new shares in the stock market. It is no coincidence that the banks with the best reputations did this last (Lehman Brothers and Goldman Sachs). Owners and managers were no longer one and the same, which led to a shortened incentive timeframe (the earlier families, like the Barings and Rothschilds, acted to preserve the business for future generations of their families). Even if they had wanted to, the new scale and complexity of investment banking meant senior management could not observe all important transactions – hence the new possibility of rogue traders.

Another major change was the growth of pension funds, as mentioned, dominated by professional managers, which came to replace individuals as the main owners of listed companies. Listed companies in turn represented an increasing proportion of companies in the economy. In this way, businesses became more and more dependent on the stock market, shrinking time horizons but also increasing management sensitivity to fashions in thinking about how they should behave.

In their book *The Puritan Gift*, brothers Kenneth and William Hopper describe the post-Second World War success of the great American company. A company would have two people at the top, both having spent decades in the firm, with maybe seven years' difference in age. One would start as president, then CEO and president, then CEO and chairman (when one's senior colleague retires as chairman and a new president is appointed) and then chairman (handing the baton of CEO to the new president). This model ensured that firm-specific expertise was retained, and it countered myopic incentives. However, the model started to go into decline in the 1970s, as executive bonuses and short-termism took hold to please stock-market analysts and investors. Companies came to be judged only on what external analysts could easily observe. Company-specific expertise was valued less, and this shift was magnified as Taylorism (scientific management) came into fashion.[4] In these ways financial markets played an increasing role in the economy. The institutionalisation of savings aided investment and expansion but also made the economy more vulnerable to knock-on impacts from problems in the financial sector.

We have had bank crises almost as long as banks have existed, and big systemic crises since central banks started to print fiat (i.e. not commodity-backed) money. An early example was the crisis in France in 1720, engineered by John Law. To assist the French government, which initially rejected his plans but later turned to him in desperation, he created a central bank (Banque Royal) and issued paper on the back of expectations of financial gains from its investment in the Mississippi Company. It all ended in tears when the Mississippi Company was found to be worthless. Financial crises have been occurring ever since. Following John Law's mistakes and proof that even central banks can blow up, the ability to exchange notes into gold and silver remained the mark of the most credible currencies.

Moving forward a couple of centuries, at the Bretton Woods conference at the end of the Second World War, the International Monetary Fund (IMF) and the International Bank for Reconstruction and Development (the World Bank) were created, as too (conscious of pre-war inflation) was a system of fixed exchange rates between major currencies. The US dollar was central to this system. It remained pegged to, and convertible to, gold, whilst other currencies were pegged to the dollar. However, this system came under increasing stress in the 1960s. In 1971, the promise to convert notes into gold on request was ditched by the US (the 'Nixon shock'). This was an inevitable result of global monetary imbalances. The United Sates liabilities to foreign dollar holders had been growing faster than its ability to meet them through the 1960s, and efforts by the main central banks to intervene to keep the dollar stable against the price of gold became less and less tenable. Nixon's decision has been largely seen as his to make, but although he chose the timing, he did not have much choice. He could either, as he did, suspend convertibility to gold and keep the stock of gold in the US, or meet mounting conversion requests until he had none left and then suspend convertibility.

The importance of this action was that it freed countries, who were able to sell government bonds in their own currency, from the discipline of fixed exchange rates and the (indirect) peg to gold. Pretty soon inflation was rife, and then stagflation (inflation and unemployment), leading eventually again to a strong reaction – the rejection of budgetary indiscipline in the UK and US in the early 1980s. However, memories are short, and more recently new imbalances have been allowed to build again.

Enter the emerging economies as key players. In 1971, Nixon had to come off gold because US creditors (mainly European central banks) started to lose faith in its currency, the dollar. After the Asian financial crisis of 1997/98, Asian central banks lost faith in the ability of the IMF to provide crisis liquidity for them, and so they instead built up their own reserves to insure themselves against external shocks, as did a number of oil producers. In doing this, they became the new dominant global creditors, and specifically major holders of US Treasuries. By investing so much in Treasuries, they not only boosted the dollar but also pushed down US borrowing costs significantly. This created an artificial measure of risk in US financial markets and fuelled financial asset price excesses into bubble territory.

The other thing which happened was a failure to control US house-price inflation. Without the same welfare state provisions as in Western Europe, upward social mobility was long important in keeping the US electorate happy. As described in Raghuram Rajan's book *Fault Lines*, President Clinton worked out that it was not necessary to raise incomes to keep voters happy; it was enough to raise their consumption, and that could be done by allowing a housing bubble to raise people's estimations of their wealth.[5] So, a regulatory blind eye looked away from what happened next.

As an example of the commodification of financial markets already mentioned, mortgage originators were incentivised to sell on mortgages as fast as they could generate them. By not retaining any exposure to these loans on their books, their assessments of household affordability became little more than cursory. Their incentives were no longer aligned with minimising default but with pushing out as many loans as possible: the sub-prime mortgage market boomed. These mortgage loans were aggregated by the Wall Street banks and sold on in highly leveraged special purpose vehicles called collateralised debt obligations (CDOs). These CDOs were companies with mortgages as underlying assets. To finance the purchase of the mortgages, they issued various tranches of debt to investors. The least senior of these tranches would take all first losses from any future mortgage defaults but offered investors the highest return if there were no defaults. The next senior tranche would take the next losses if there still were any after all the investment value of the lowest tranche holders had been wiped out, but the return was less and so on. These various tranches were sold to different types of investors, with the most senior ones attracting top ratings from the rating agencies.

These rating agencies were paid handsomely to value the CDO debt tranches on behalf of the investment banks who created them. They made elementary mistakes in their assessments of default risk. Elementary, but with the same pattern, as already mentioned, as for many other risk-related errors made in financial markets – they simply looked at the easily measurable past and extrapolated. They looked at historical default rates. They ignored the possibilities of major structural shifts ahead in the mortgage market – shifts which were increasingly obvious given the very clear and catastrophic fall in the quality of mortgage origination decisions. They assumed, quite without adequate foundation, that previous housing market conditions would continue – conditions without the new level of aggressive house lending and before the national pattern of pushing loans to all and sundry. They erroneously supposed that geographical diversity would naturally pool risks. When events proved them wrong, carnage followed. As we shall see with other examples in this book, when modellers are incentivised to reach certain results, they reach them.

The US mortgage market was, however, merely the trigger. The success of low and stable inflation and economic cycles – what central bankers had come to call 'The Great Moderation' – had created over-confidence. It seemed as if crises could always be mopped up easily afterwards if necessary, and the increased size of financial markets, both absolutely and as a proportion of the whole economy, was seen as inevitable and a sign of the triumph of free unfettered markets.

Although finance theory was a new area of study, it had come to dominate thinking in financial markets. My previous book, *Emerging Markets in an Upside Down World: Challenging Perceptions in Asset Allocation and Investment*, is a critique of finance theory, and I would refer the reader to it for more detail, but I do want to mention the importance of the efficient market hypothesis, which amounts to a belief that all available information is instantly represented in market prices, and hence the market price always represents the best available assessment of value. This theory has strong and weak forms, but indiscriminate belief in it prevented appropriate regulatory action to stem excess. Its ethos can perhaps be summed up by a joke. Two economists are walking along a street and they see a $20 note on the ground. The less experienced of the two starts to reach down to pick it up, but the other stops him and tells him it must be a mirage, because if it were real somebody else would have picked it up already.

The faith in the efficiency of markets received a serious dent from what happened in 2008, but it was not sufficient to create enough political capital for much more than bank recapitalisation. Indeed, even that has been nugatory in some jurisdictions. Leverage in financial systems has reached new highs outside the banking sector; global imbalances have not been addressed; and some of the intervention powers in the US have been removed due to legislators' concerns about moral hazard. The three warning signs of financial crisis I detailed in my first book were: a) a homogenous investor base; b) a misconception of risk which may shortly change; and c) a lot of leverage (borrowing) somewhere which could affect behaviour in a crisis. None of these measures look much improved at time of writing in 2022 compared to the position just before the 2008 crisis. If anything, fear has become more conflated with uncertainty, and global views more homogenous, more unrealistic and more vulnerable to explosion. Although the 2008 crisis killed belief in efficient markets, it may take the next crisis to create the political will to reduce systemic risks more permanently. We often choose not to learn from trauma. Misunderstandings about causes of and solutions to global financial crises, with at least some of the characteristics of groupthink, remain in place for now.

FOOLING OURSELVES ABOUT QUANTITATIVE EASING

When the 2008 crisis started to get serious, Ben Bernanke, the head of the US central bank (the Federal Reserve or Fed for short), was well aware of the risk of depression. The contagion was so powerful in the financial sector that the largest banks were at risk of collapse. Lehman Brothers did fail, and other financial institutions, some much larger, were facing similar risk. Without financial support, and fast, the whole banking sector was headed for meltdown. And that would likely cause enough uncertainty to tip the economy into another great depression, as in the 1930s. Massive intervention was called for and arranged. But once the initial stabilisation was achieved, the banks still needed help to recapitalise themselves. No one wanted these institutions to end up in public ownership.

A large part of the policy response was quantitative easing (QE). QE involved the central bank buying vast quantities of government debt but also swapping illiquid bank assets for cash. Even design choices in the first QE programmes were taken to further help banks, engineering a steeper yield curve than many expected (banks can make money from a steep yield curve). This bolstered bank balance sheets enough that they could then issue new paper into the market – i.e. capitalise themselves with fresh private money.

Many did not realise that what was going on was, primarily, a massive bank bail-out by another name. If financial markets, journalists and the general public knew that was the main purpose of QE, they might ask why. And if so, they might then realise the scale of the threat of depression which the Fed was trying to prevent and the chance that it wouldn't work. That knowledge in turn might have caused enough uncertainty to create the very depression which every effort was being made to avoid. Hence an alternative narrative, with at least the merit of partial truth, was publicised – that the QE programme was intended to stimulate the economy.

If that had indeed been the main motive, banks would have been encouraged, and observed, to increase their lending to companies. But they did not. Was that evidence after the event of a design flaw of QE? No – the Fed money was used to pay off bank debts, as intended, not to lend to the wider economy.

QE has become so large that central banks can smooth market volatility. Large-scale front-running is no longer the profitable strategy it was for very large bond fund managers. The belief in the efficiency of the market to match supply and demand in setting interest rates was already skewed by the global monetary imbalances from the large build-up of emerging market central bank reserves. But with massive QE, it bore even less relationship to private sector conditions, including, as long-term as well as short-term interest rates were distorted, the likelihood of future inflation.

With banks capitalised better in the US, UK and parts of the EU (though only parts), policy-makers could relax a little. They moved from a phase of intense panic down to merely furious brain-racking. As the time horizon of policy-making extended, the question of how to cope with now much larger national debt started to occupy minds.

There are various ways to reduce national debt. The most obvious is through a combination of fiscal consolidation and growth, both of which may release sufficient tax revenues (net of government expenditure) to not just pay interest but reduce the stock of debt. This means lower government expenditure than might otherwise have occurred, and this strategy can take some considerable time. For example, after the Napoleonic Wars, the UK's national debt stood at around 240 per cent of GDP, its servicing eating up 70 per cent of government revenues. It took most of the rest of the century to get it down to what, pre-2008, we would consider normal levels.

But tight government spending is difficult politically. It may also simply not be enough if there is an aggregate demand deficiency – i.e. if reduced government expenditure or higher tax rates result in lower growth and so lower tax revenues. Tight fiscal policy may simply shrink the economy, and with it tax income to service and reduce the debt. The alternative may be some combination of default and devaluation, unless a foreign government or the IMF wants to bail you out anyway – as, for example, the EU decided to bail out Greece after 2008.

However, in the twentieth century, two new ways to reduce government debt were found. The first is financial repression, which we have mentioned and defined already, as a means to generate negative real interest rates (i.e. nominal interest rates below inflation). This enables the value of debt to gradually erode over time. This was highly successful in reducing Second World War debts in both Europe and the US.

Secondly, with the suspension of the US peg to gold in 1971, countries could choose to inflate debt away. Like financial repression, inflation also reduces the real value of the stock of debt. However, as happened after 1971, it all happens more quickly and much less subtly, with political promises broken, expectations dashed and much general economic and social disruption.

So, post-2008 policy-makers had these two new tools to consider. The preference was to use financial repression. QE (the central bank buying massive quantities of debt from the government) became an important tool in keeping interest rates rock-bottom.

Indeed, in several countries, QE managed to push long-term yields into negative territory. On top of this, all that was needed (to keep real interest rates negative) was to have modest inflation.

But why would investors willingly buy government debt with a negative yield? For some, they had no effective choice, as their regulators forced them to buy government paper. For this, the rhetoric of government bonds being super-low-risk needed to be maintained. After the debacle of the rating agencies' grossly mistaken evaluation of US mortgage risks (for which they were paid handsomely), they had the temerity, given the ballooning of sovereign debt in the developed world, to consider downgrading some EU countries. This would have made it more difficult for those countries to argue that domestic sovereign debt was the safest of investments. The EU at one point indignantly reacted by threatening to set up a new (presumably more compliant) credit rating agency instead.

Other investors, who did have the choice, were simply fooled...

TRANSPARENTLY MISLEADING

There is a difference, for a central bank policy-maker, between optimal and maximum transparency. When one is trying to encourage investors who have the choice to buy sovereign debt, it may be wise not to point out that it is your intention to generate a negative real yield. A negative yield hurts savers, of course, which policy-makers are normally concerned about. But this may have to be weighed against the greater need to reduce the stock of debt without having to make hard fiscal policy choices (an example of the so-called independent central bank being co-opted by wider government objectives). Also, insofar as much of the sovereign debt is owned by foreigners (including emerging market central banks) about whom there is no such concern, the balance of argument in favour of obfuscation becomes more pronounced.

Central banks are now clearly in the business of observing and trying to use mass psychology to build credibility and tame inflationary expectations. The Fed, for example, created an index of common inflation expectations to collate sentiment in 2020. As magicians can attest, a lot can be achieved by distraction. A central banker may distract with his right hand whilst with his left he allows inflation modestly higher than interest rates. Every eight weeks or so, market expectation may become somewhat settled about future inflation and interest rates, which means it is time to make a statement. Typically, this will be in cryptic language, open to different interpretations worthy of many column inches of analysis (in English: vague and distracting). To be most effective, it must raise doubts about market expectations which were becoming well established before the statement. It must create some dust to obscure vision. Then, after a further eight weeks or so, as the air clears and a consensus once again starts to form, the process is repeated: more dust must be stirred up again before the previous lot settles.*

---

* My favourite Peter Sellers film is *Being There*. He plays a simple-minded gardener who has worked for decades in the roof garden of a Manhattan town house. He is naïve about the world and never leaves the property until evicted after the death of his employer. Not being familiar with road traffic (he has not been out for a very long time), he is knocked over and rendered unconscious in the street. The worried wealthy woman whose car hit him can find no identification on his unconscious body, but she notices his expensive tailoring (given to him by his employer). She is naturally extremely concerned she might be sued. So, she looks after him. She thinks his minimalist, largely incomprehensible statements extremely wise. He is treated with great deference and ends up advising the President and the nation on economic policy. In advising on national economic policy, his Delphic quotes include: 'As long as the roots are not severed, all is well' and 'There will be growth in the spring.' What better model for a modern central banker?

People are taken in, especially when they are embarrassed by their partial comprehension of complex topics. Although financial repression was successful post-war, that was when there were widespread restrictions on the international movement of capital and international transactions were controlled by a few Western central banks, whose dealing rooms talked to each other every day. It may well be that the subtle extraction of value from savers will not be so easy to maintain now.

How might QE end? One of the problems, should inflation expectations pick up markedly, is that central banks' inflation-fighting credibility may be questioned. If there are substantial increases in interest rates before central bank balance sheets are pared of government debt (i.e. before QE is reversed), then the value of said balance sheets could fast plummet into negative territory. Instead of providing dividend income from its investments to its owner (the government), the central bank might need government funding for a massive deficit. A more attractive option may be not to raise interest rates in the first place and let inflation rip. This would also suit the government as, if and when subtle financial repression fails, a period of higher (double-digit) inflation may well be the next-best plan for eroding the national debt.

This is not, as no doubt the reader expects, the current official version of what should happen (at time of writing). Rather, the ideal way to exit QE is simply to gradually reduce the stock of government debt on the central bank balance sheet before substantial rises in interest rates. But this route is not credible in any short period, and especially not in a crisis. It would mean less financing for government – in other words major fiscal austerity.

One way to ignore this inconvenient truth is to invent a new economic theory and hope it might be true. Hey presto! It is called modern monetary theory (MMT). I am indebted to Liam Halligan for pointing out that the same initials, appropriately enough, stand for magic money tree, which is a good proxy for its core hetero-doxy that bond issuance is somehow not the means for financing government but only a tool of monetary policy. One does not have to be an economist to be sceptical of a theory which appears to imply that the government can issue as much debt as it wishes, or alternatively that government expenditure is merely the derivative of central bank bond buying, not the other way round.

The problem with this irresponsible theory is that at some point private market participants may see through what is happening: the government (broadly defined to include the central bank) is printing money and then spending it, without any demand for the debt from the private sector (the debt stays on the central bank bal-ance sheet).* This means that the government can avoid any hard budget constraint. So, why raise any taxes at all? Indeed, why not spend ever more?

As debt levels grow higher, the credibility of the government's willingness to honour the debt reduces.† And crucially, the level at which the government can borrow is still dependent on its continued ability to raise a significant portion of new funds from uncoerced private buyers. Without this, the fiction that interest

---

* An exchange of letters between the Treasury and Bank of England (BoE) in 2009 assures that the government will not alter its issuance strategy as a result of BoE bond transactions executed for monetary purposes. However, there is no credible argument that the BoE has not found monetary 'reasons' to use QE to absorb huge amounts of new debt issued by the Treasury. In practice this is what has been happening.

† Honour it in real terms, that is (after inflation), bearing in mind that rich countries able to issue debt in their own currencies default by other means – namely through inflation and devaluation.

rates are market-set explodes. This would be a disaster for private sector expectations, confidence, uncertainty, investment and innovation. The danger may be nearer than perceived. The emperor's clothes may be hard to discern given all the dust floating about and nobody looking in the right direction. But should such an awful truth become apparent, it may be instantly accepted by all. Policymakers can exploit market groupthink, and even manipulate it, but excess is ill-advised. Should government expand fiscally without limit, at some point private markets may make a sudden reassessment, because when expectations change they will likely do so in a reinforcing way very fast. They may want no more government bonds at all.

MMT, reminiscent of our farmer's views on donkey productivity, is premised on being able to fool private sector investors indefinitely. It has worked for a bit in the past, and so the pattern is extrapolated, the theory apparently vindicated. A likely structural shift in expectations and investor behaviour is simply ignored. This groupthink around MMT and monetary policy more generally has left the UK and several other countries saddled with huge national debts and associated risks of major inflation and economic disruption. Of course, some of the fiscal expansion was due to Covid-19 and the extraordinary economic policies of lockdown.

COVID AND LOCKDOWN

The appropriate behaviour of ministers during a crisis is to take advice based on data and clear analysis in the best overall interests of the country, and to be prepared to change course as data comes in. However, skewed incentives,[*] myopia, reluctance to change course and lack of willingness to take responsibility have been as common as ever. None of this has been helped by massive uncertainty, especially before effective vaccines were developed, and society-wide fear.

In several countries, preparations for an epidemic were either not adequate or largely ignored when panic set in. Procedures and policies may have been bypassed due to their inappropriateness to meet the specific challenge, but bizarre choices seem to have been made through jettisoning wholesale, rather than adapting, existing plans. In the UK there was extensive planning for a major influenza epidemic in 2011. All twenty-two recommendations of the UK Influenza Preparedness Strategy 2011 were adopted by government. The current official line is that some of the measures recommended were not appropriate for Covid-19, but the existence of plans from 2011 is undeniable. Only time and access to government papers will establish the degree to which the existing strategy really was adopted, albeit with amendments, or whether it was basically ignored in favour of more wholesale reinvention of the wheel in a very short time under huge political pressure. It would seem that a number of basic mistakes were made which should not have happened with a half-sensible strategy in place. Why, for example, were there so many UK hospital-contracted cases of Covid-19? Why were new hospitals built and then never used to isolate the infected from

---

[*] Incentives, as we saw with our earlier pension fund example, can be distorted by principal–agent relationships. It is not merely that responsibility for hard decisions may be inappropriately avoided but that they can be delegated to experts, advisers and others who not only lack the necessary perspective and full information but may respond to personal and professional incentives, including unconsciously, which lead to poor decisions.

non-Covid-19 patients? If it was due to lack of staff, as subsequently claimed, this should have been determinable before the hospitals were built. Why were so many patients with Covid-19 discharged into nursing homes full of vulnerable people? Perhaps groupthink was at the fore, combined with and fed by panic, with inadequate reason being applied to the problem at the very top of government. However, it may be that, faced with the inadequacy of existing plans, there was nobody willing to defend them – a case of blame avoidance. The alternative of rethinking everything from scratch in panic mode is the perfect environment for groupthink.

Dominic Cummings, former senior aide to Prime Minister Boris Johnson, had this to say during his seven hours of testimony to a joint parliamentary inquiry on lessons which can be learned from the handling of the Covid pandemic:[6]

> The problem is that in this field of behavioural science, there are a lot of charlatans. Anybody who has been involved with the political world knows that the whole field is riddled with duff studies and memes that people believe are true but are not true. There is no doubt whatsoever that this was a critical part of the false groupthink.

Then, in arguing for an earlier lockdown:

> You read about these things in history books. It was literally a classic historical example of groupthink in action. The process was closed, and that is what happens in closed groupthink bubbles: everyone just reinforced themselves. The more that people from the outside attacked, the more people internally said, 'Well,

they don't understand, and they haven't got access to all this information' and whatnot. It was this classic groupthink bubble.

Bearing in mind that all policies have negative side effects, the strategy of isolating everyone in lockdown so uniformly and for so long may well be judged as unnecessarily costly in hindsight, in terms of both economics and social impact, but also, quite shockingly, in non-Covid-related preventable excess deaths. At the time these decisions were made, there was no vaccine, and so they were seen as justified, but as the vaccines were rolled out and immunity built, and as it became clear that younger people were less vulnerable, the justification became less clear. The original rationale in the UK for lockdown was to prevent the health service from being overwhelmed. This was achieved long before the lockdown was lifted. I suspect that in fact the political priority was to avoid blame for bad decisions. This translated into a fear of stop–start decisions on lockdown (which is not to say that this perception was altogether avoided). Although the government said lockdown duration would be driven by data not dates, it was understood by all that this did not (until right at the end when Johnson did end lockdown earlier than some were recommending) include ending lockdown earlier than targeted, only the possibility of extending it. This indicates the costs of lockdown were not sufficiently important in decision-making – an indication of the precautionary motive being used recklessly in place of more balanced and rational cost–benefit analysis.

It may be that thorough cost–benefit analysis was used to look at the possibility of raising lockdown at various points. If so, this was not made publicly available, and was not used as public justification for any policy. What the public was fed was a series of scary scenarios about new strains, which kept citizens in a constant state of fear. The UK government approach seems consistent with giving priority to the precautionary motive in decision-making. Indeed, the public is now conditioned to expect this. Yet precaution is not, and should not be seen as, justified at any price. This is most obvious in terms of non-Covid-19 health risks. It may well turn out that more people in the UK die of the policy responses to Covid-19 than from Covid-19. As the National Health Service was transformed into a National Covid Service, surgeries and cancer treatments stopped, diagnoses were not made and preventable illnesses went untreated. Many people stopped consulting doctors, as they feared contact and were made to feel that their complaint was less important than the national emergency. This has caused massive health problems for preventative medicine and especially cancer, where early diagnosis and treatment is crucial for reducing deaths. Schools have been disrupted, businesses bankrupted, lives put on hold. To understand but discount these factors amounts to abhorrent cynicism. To not take them into account at all could be construed as myopic at the very least, if not downright stupid and uncaring. The precautionary motive should be a tool to help achieve benefit for the nation, not an end in itself. However, group-think has all too effectively elevated the precautionary motive to be an unquestioned goal in itself, to the extent that even mild criticism of its paramount position, as is the pattern for central tenets of groupthink, is seen by some as morally wrong.

EXPERT BIAS AND RECKLESS PRECAUTION

The precautionary principle replaces proper consideration of various policy options and their full costs and benefits. It helps politicians who prefer narrow certainties to the uncertain whole. In so doing it is reckless with people's lives and well-being.

It is the very nature of an expert to focus on a specific set of related questions. Experts bring with them standard assumptions and ways of analysis which, in dealing with a problem outside their previous experience, may turn out to be justified or may not. Experts also suffer from groupthink. The wider consequences of certain policy options may be totally ignored by experts as lying outside their field of expertise. It is not their responsibility. Their judgement might even, they may think, be clouded by attempting to consider them. Yet such consequences (and the incentives of expert advisers) should be considered by decision-makers. Decisions may be assisted through listening to advisers with different areas of expertise, but how to weigh experts with different views, and how to assess unknown and unknowable factors, is up to the decision-makers with whom ultimate policy responsibility lies, and them alone. It is their obligation to make the effort to equip themselves to make such choices.

The problem is that survival in politics is often the consequence of avoiding heavy criticism, and in a world obsessed with just one risk, any policy that is perceived as inadequate in dealing with that single threat is a vulnerability, however justified or rational. It becomes, in that context, convenient to insure oneself against errors by making much of one's following of expert advice. Indeed, to promote experts' personal media profiles and advice may indicate the very opposite of confidence in the recommendations themselves. As a PR exercise this might make sense, but as a way to actually make decisions it is clearly an abrogation of responsibility. Unfortunately, in a mass hysteria it is easy to get carried away, as we have seen many times. From the Bay of Pigs to weapons of mass destruction in Iraq, groupthink easily prevails when the stakes are high, uncertainty abounds and time is short.

It is also arrogant to believe that electorates are so simple-minded as not to notice. Politicians often mistake indifference for stupidity, but people are occasionally roused. Treating the public like idiots, as if only one priority matters, has its limits. Hiding behind experts when things go wrong fools very few as to where responsibility lies and can simply be seen as a combination of cowardice and evasiveness, even mendacity. Efforts to scare are deeply resented, as are efforts to mislead. Behavioural manipulation, once revealed, can destroy trust and social capital. Attacks on individual privacy and autonomy can lead to pushback. People stop cooperating with a state they no longer trust to be truthful and competent.

LOCKDOWN ECONOMICS

It is in this context that one can start to ask, at this very early stage at time of writing, how appropriate was the economic policy response to Covid-19? The UK furlough scheme was well received and prevented many businesses from going bust and employees being made redundant.* Lockdown has forced change in working practices and speeded up some structural changes towards greater productivity. The scale of the daily commute will not revive for the simple reason that many people could have been working much more from home before lockdown – improving productivity in the process. Wasted time travelling to and from meetings has been

---

* However, it has been partial, in particular excluding many sole traders and self-employed people, and has prevented allocative efficiency in the economy through the normal process of the death and birth of firms.

saved, much of it permanently. Retail and home-delivery trends have accelerated.

The fiscal costs, however, I am less optimistic about. When Covid struck we had just experienced a decade of monetary expansion following the 2008 crisis. Banks had been recapitalised in the US, the UK and much of the EU, but major fiscal consolidation had not occurred, leaving historically high debt–GDP ratios. Quantitative easing had pushed trillions of dollars' worth of government bonds into negative yields, and central banks were even discussing negative short-term interest rates. Productivity seemed to be stuck at low levels, making eventual growth out of the indebtedness problem seemingly more difficult.

With expansionary fiscal policies since Covid-19 being paid for by extra borrowing, debt levels have risen even more. The massive cost of furlough and other increases in public expenditure has been matched by almost identical further expansion of QE. This gives the lie to independence of the central banks and to the idea that QE is a policy to control inflation. It also, as discussed, exposes as nonsense modern monetary theory's assumption that bond buying is an inflation management tool rather than primarily a means to finance government.

The increase in debt may be bearable whilst interest rates remain low, and this was still the case when the first draft of this book was written in early 2022, with expectations of low inflation stretching over the next couple of decades. However, my predictions at the time of the first draft about higher inflation (which readers will have to take my word for) are now, in late 2022, becoming fact, and interest rates are belatedly catching up with that reality. Inflation has not been helped by Russia's invasion of Ukraine and an ineffective (to say the least) energy policy which has dramatically failed to provide affordable energy to domestic consumers and businesses. Whilst, at the time of writing, there are still some who believe inflation can be controlled in a few months and that much higher interest rates will not be needed to control inflation, this view is increasingly coming under pressure. Given the historic amount of money printing, there is a heightened risk that our move to higher inflation is not temporary and will go well into double digits. Even if the war ends soon and cheap gas flows with abundance back into Western Europe, the consequences of the build-up in debt since 2008 and through lockdown are not going to evaporate. The groupthink that we live in a world of permanent low inflation and that central banks can keep on buying more and more government debt without inflationary implications is down if not out. Moreover, a crisis in one Western country is highly likely to trip expectations in others. In 2008, our banks were in a critical state, highly vulnerable to external events tipping them into systemic crisis. Now (a) the non-bank leverage is higher than ever and (b) low-inflation expectations are in a critical state, with the potential for a rapid shift in government policy from financial repression to 1970s-style inflation. The groupthink that we still live in a low inflationary world, albeit with a blip caused by Putin, is useful for controlling inflationary expectations – hence not being discouraged by our leaders, even those who now understand that the future is to be different.

Another area of competing groupthinks is the future viability of the Eurozone, indeed of the political arrangements which constitute the EU. The single currency is not sustainable without a considerable increase in cross-border fiscal transfers, which is unlikely to garner political legitimacy any time soon. Yet to discuss a possible breakdown of the euro and the political fallout thereof is heresy to many.

Many investors may consider that they will have time to adjust their portfolios and exit, but they may not. They will not only have to move faster than policy but faster than market expectations. Moreover, they will also have to face the possibility that new capital controls will emerge, though they might be called something less threatening: an extension to macro-prudential regulations, possibly. If one asks UK pension fund managers from the 1970s why they invested in a UK stock market which lost real value, the standard reply is that they had little choice: the only other alternative investment they were allowed to make was in UK government bonds, which were an even worse prospect. The lesson is that if domestic institutional investors face a government hungry for funds, there are only two outcomes: such funds can be provided willingly or unwillingly. They may simply not be allowed to invest abroad and only be allowed to invest a certain amount outside domestic government bonds.*

As the crisis develops, and it is looking that way as we head into a European winter energy crisis and wider tensions in the bond markets over inflation, the race will be on to be a (relatively) safe haven. Much money may flow back to much safer parts of the world – the emerging markets – but prejudice being what it is, much will also remain in the richer, highly indebted, countries.

---

* My policy advice to the UK government at time of writing is to prepare for the worst, but discreetly. It is to be hoped that capital controls will not be necessary, not least as it would be likely to scare off foreign inward investors, including foreign central banks, so best not to mention it until absolutely necessary.

To attract that money, a finance ministry will have to try to make a credible case that a major fiscal contraction is likely as soon as the immediate crisis is over. The country to slash expenditure plans fastest and furthest is the one which may be more able to continue to finance its government with investment coming in from abroad, in the process also pushing up its exchange rate and so also squeezing inflation.* However, for that to happen the relevant government would not only need to have ditched the groupthink of permanent low inflation; in order to push through new very painful fiscal measures, it would need to have garnered enough political support from others of the same mind.

CRYPTOCURRENCY DELUSION

Major differences of views on how the world works constantly vie with each other. In choosing one further example, I have tried to pick an issue which is fairly binary in outcome and likely to come to crisis soon.†

Belief in private cryptocurrencies as a replacement global money constitutes, I believe, a groupthink – one likely to reach crisis sometime in the next few years. There has been much excitement over bitcoin and other cryptocurrencies. However, I consider it wrong to think of these private digital units as currencies. Currencies perform three tasks: unit of account, preservation of value and means of exchange. Aside from the vast energy required to mine

---

* The anecdote of reference here is the story of two friends in the remote forests of North America who see a bear. One of them puts his running shoes on. The other says to him: 'Why bother putting running shoes on? A bear can run much faster than a man.' The first replies: 'Yes, but I don't have to run faster than the bear; I just have to out-run you.'

† Hence, I leave Brexit for another day. The prejudice against emerging markets, which I call Core/Periphery disease, I covered extensively in my first book.

bitcoin (that of a small country), it is not even vaguely stable in its valuation and so is pretty useless either as a unit of account or as a store of value. That is not to say people do not see it as an investment, but investments can go down in value as well as up. To be a store of value, holders should be sufficiently confident in its ability to retain value that they need not look at it for long periods of time. Bank accounts and houses can be stores of value. Ponzi schemes are not. Its exchange use is nevertheless real, especially if one wishes to evade government regulations. Cryptocurrencies are the exchange media of choice for criminals.

Cryptocurrencies are also attractive for libertarians and anarchists who want to bypass the state's monopoly on money creation. Unfortunately, many have deluded themselves on this front. Just as the state has the monopoly in the legitimate use of force in a country, so the central bank has the monopoly in the legitimate issue of base currency. They also have means to control non-base money, even if not entirely effective.* As ex-Bank of England Governor Mark Carney puts it: 'It is simply untenable in democracies that the core of the monetary system could be based on forms of electronic private money...'†

So why have central banks been so lax in light of this threat? Since the take-off of the craze for private digital currencies, global central banks have been in the post-2008 world of super-loose monetary policy. Monetary policy tightening is more reliable in

---

* Central banks do this through the setting of interest rates available to banks and through setting their minimum reserve ratios (the percentage of bank reserves which have to be kept on deposit at the central bank), which in turn limits how much money banks can create through lending.

† The US especially may have more to lose than most from a global competitor to the US dollar – its reserve currency status. This 'exorbitant privilege', as then French Finance Minister Giscard d'Éstaing coined it, is a form of self-perpetuating myth and thus vulnerable.

its impact than is loosening. Raising the cost of money (interest rates) leads to reduced economic activity; loosening (cutting interest rates and also QE) may stimulate economic activity, but, then again, it may not. It can be like pushing (as opposed to pulling) on a string. If cutting interest rates simply and always stimulated the economy, depressions wouldn't happen, but they do. It is easier to generate fear and uncertainty than restore confidence. In a world full of central bankers terrified of depression after 2008, they have been very relaxed about new private money proxies which might stimulate economic activity.

However, as we shift from a low inflation to a high inflation world, the benevolent attitude of central banks to private cryptocurrencies is changing. There are plenty of historical precedents of currencies being made illegal, punishable by whatever is necessary to dissuade further use – including various historical laws banning private ownership of gold, efforts to ban alternatives to tobacco (the main currency at the time) in Virginia, and a California law (repealed in 2014) making it illegal to introduce any currency into circulation except the US dollar. It may simply be made illegal to hold any cryptocurrency except one explicitly sanctioned and regulated by the central bank – and not just in China.

There is an important exception. Central bank digital currencies (CBDCs) are increasingly seen as a policy option. The benefits of a central bank issuing a digital currency are several. In particular, it would enable greater control of banks and banking sector leverage and help the central bank regain more control over monetary policy. After stepping down as Governor of the Bank of England, Lord King wrote his book *The End Of Alchemy*, in which he argues for extending QE further as part of a policy to move from fractional reserve banking towards narrow banks over a long transition period.[7] This would replace much of the banking system with accounts directly with the central bank, disintermediating banks and so reducing their capacity to cause systemic crises – i.e. taking the system out of its critical state. There are problems with a full transition, not least that banks are still needed to make credit assessments and lending decisions. For this we need them to be in business. So, a two-tier system may well emerge whereby the central bank takes deposits itself, using its new CBDC, but also continues to allow some leverage in the banks, so they can still make money from lending out more than the level of their deposits. A CBDC could boost central banks' ailing abilities to enact monetary policy and could also trace criminal sources of funds. A caveat is that such additional power in the hands of the central bank does raise questions about accountability. It could be another reason why central banks, who have with QE already acquired quasi-fiscal not just monetary power, should either face much more scrutiny or even lose their independence from government.

The actual course of whether private cryptocurrencies will be banned or simply fall out of use, what official digital currencies might replace them, and the degree to which the public is comfortable with such changes, will all be prevented, mitigated or made possible by changing attitudes to what is and what is not legitimate money. People have accepted all sorts of money as a means of exchange in history, but there has to be joint belief that it can be used in exchange in the future and hold its value. And that can change. Where such belief is based on false assumptions, it is a form of groupthink.

SUMMARY

My explanation of how the global economy has recently evolved is necessarily complex, which is a reason why it is generally so poorly understood, even in financial markets. A common lack of the big picture has nurtured groupthink. In giving an interpretation of recent global financial events, I hope I have shown that mass irrationality and groupthink are not confined to society and politics but are more ubiquitous. The consequences in financial markets are poor decisions and a series of crises. Emotions and the psychological factors reviewed in Chapter 1 remain important, but so too are incentives, which differ enormously from person to person. Economics and finance have their fads and collective blind spots, just as in other walks of life. Collective behaviour can be stupid, even as individuals behave more rationally. Those most confident in their views, as we saw in Chapter 1, are also those most likely to be most exposed and to lose most when the tables turn. The more intelligent, erudite and educated are the most prone to groupthink – hence mighty investment banks full of very bright individuals are prone to making enormous errors. That is the nature of groupthink.

- Financial markets are prone to instability and crisis. In part this is because fair value is more difficult to assess than for goods and services, in part it is due to conceptual simplification of risk and in part to incentives.
- Uncertainty and fear are conflated and often not managed well by investors. Overly simplistic models are used in finance to assess and manage risk, uncertainties are often ignored and fear often trumps rationality.

- Past patterns are extrapolated at the cost of insufficient attention being paid to structural changes and different scenarios.
- Different theories of the world can become entrenched. Some adherents retain open-mindedness and can quickly change their views. For others, however, belief in the exact same worldview is more determinedly held, constituting a weak form of groupthink. Only near or actual crisis is capable of changing adherence.
- There has been groupthink in economics. Keynes's insight into the role of uncertainty in economics and the inherent instability of financial markets was inconsistent with dominant views and largely ignored for decades. Finance theory is largely not fit for purpose.
- The causes of, and policy reactions to, the financial crisis of 2008 mean that another crisis is very possible. Large structural problems remain in financial sectors. Whilst we have not made the same mistakes in monetary policy as in the early 1930s, monetary policy has borne the brunt of adjustment. Governments have no more than tinkered with structural and fiscal policy.
- Quantitative easing was initially expanded to save banks and avoid depression. It subsequently became a tool of financial repression – keeping interest rates low whilst allowing slightly higher inflation to erode the real value of national debt. It's magnitude now amounts to a dangerous experiment in money printing which will probably not end well.
- It is too early to assess the epidemic's wider economic impact. Covid-19 has, however, made the debt overhang problem worse.
- The widespread fear of the disease, encouraged rather than reduced by government nudge techniques, may have also caused a reduction in social capital and trust in the government.

- Belief that private cryptocurrencies are a credible alternative to money is a delusion – one which may shortly face hard reality.

For investors, as for everyone else, it is becoming increasingly difficult to keep an open mind, determining the real from the hype. In our new media world, an important part of the financial professional's job will be looking for signs of groupthink and therefore sudden future reversals: a lack of real debate, certainty around a consensus, passionate pleas for urgency and aggressive denigration of dissenting views.

People can change their views remarkably quickly. The real world can impinge particularly fast and hard in finance. However, most people are still polite to each other and try hard to listen and be rational. In this respect, finance retains more resistance to groupthink than politics and also academia, to which we turn next.

CHAPTER 5

SCIENCE AND ANTI-SCIENCE

'A new scientific truth does not triumph by convincing its opponents and making them see the light, but rather because its opponents eventually die, and a new generation grows up that is familiar with it.'

MAX PLANCK

'Science is the belief in the ignorance of experts. When someone says, "Science teaches such and such," he is using the word incorrectly. Science doesn't teach anything; experience teaches it. If they say to you, "Science has shown such and such," you might ask, "How does science show it? How did the scientists find out? How? What? Where?" It should not be "science has shown" but "this experiment, this effect, has shown". And you have as much right as anyone else, upon hearing about the experiments – but be patient and listen to all the evidence – to judge whether a sensible conclusion has been arrived at.'

RICHARD FEYNMAN

There are many different ways of looking at things, many competing ideas claiming to be the truth. When I worked for the Inter-American Development Bank in the early 1990s, I was told a story, probably apocryphal, about the Nicaraguan dictator General Anastasio Somoza. He loved horses and had a farm with beautiful stables, though he would work in a caravan on the farm. Prospective Cabinet ministers would have to drive out of town to his farm and enter the caravan for their interview. Somoza would then ask the key question: suppose you are walking along a beach and see a turtle up a tree – what is the first question that comes into your head? Most people would reply: how did it get there? If so, that was the end of the interview. That was not the right answer – not the one indicative of the necessary political acuity for inclusion in Somoza's Cabinet. The correct answer is not even: who put it there? The correct response is: what was the motive of the son of a bitch who put it there?

The same evidence can mean different things to different people, and we normally mix in our own ideas of purpose in our under-standing of events. Different meanings need not be contradictory but reflect different narratives. We choose our own interpretations out of many possible ones. For example, the meaning of a specific drinking cup can be that of a work of art to one person, a useful object for drinking out of to another, a reminder of a loved one to a third. These particular meanings do not contradict each other. But we also select evidence to support our beliefs, and these beliefs can often be more clearly contradictory. We might have noticed that the cup has been broken, and we might believe this was an accident or that the breakage was deliberate, and we might have different theories of who did it and why. We learned from Jonathan Haidt in Chapter 1 how we adopt or reject different interpretations of reality (i.e. different evidence). If new evidence is consistent with our view, we ask: can I believe it? The answer is always yes. And if the evidence is contrary to our view we ask: do I have to believe it? The answer is always no. That is what we are up against if we are truly inquisitive and wish to learn new things about the world. The thesis of Justin Smith's book *Irrationality* is that 'irrationality is as potentially harmful as it is humanly ineradicable, and that efforts to eradicate it are themselves supremely irrational'.[1] Moreover, not only are we irrational but we keep forgetting we are.

With this psychology, analysing the world scientifically has not come easily to human beings, and as we shall see a relapse is all too easy. Scientific advance can occur during periods of moral conflict and war, as was the case during the Reformation, when modern science made major advances. Moral conflict can undermine knowledge's authority, in turn leading to societal fear: our fear of uncertainty is not the result of a lack of knowledge but a failure of its authority.

As one moral system's authority is questioned, a new approach may be accepted (as in a religious conversion). However, more independent reasoning may also be the consequence. Kant defined enlightenment as occurring when people overcome the fear of reasoning for themselves, and the ideals of the Enlightenment spread as religious authority became questioned. A concern today is that as fear becomes more prevalent we may be losing some of our ability to question authority.

SCIENCE

There are different interpretations of what science is, so what follows is to some extent a partial view. Some definitions, particularly ancient ones, have little bearing on what I am going to describe. Others have slipped from the ideal, often losing credibility for the sake of expediency.

Aristotle, following Plato, believed we can visualise essences and by intuition find correct definitions. This may help us explore ideas, but it cannot be a route to truth. Likewise, in normal discourse we may build ideas, one based upon the next, but in doing so we constantly make implicit assertions and guesses consistent with our moral system, worldview, groupthink. Words are ambiguous, and our directed meaning in using them helps mould ideas and facts to our purpose. Word meanings can not only be ill-defined but change meaning during the steps of discourse and so enable our thoughts to be channelled, consciously or unconsciously, as convenient – often as our inner elephant desires.

In modern science (as opposed to this Aristotelian 'essentialist' thinking), knowledge, whilst requiring clarity of meaning, is not built on definitions. Scientific definitions are instead said to be 'nominalist'. They are but a convenience of language, a shorthand. Popper puts it thus: 'The scientific view of the definition "a puppy is a young dog" would be that it is an answer to the question "*What shall we call* a young dog?" rather than an answer to the question "*What* is a puppy?"' Scientists can be said to read definitions backward, from right to left – from thinking of a young dog to a puppy (which is definitional and thus incontrovertible), rather than from a puppy to a young dog (which is one of many interpretations of what a puppy is). He goes further, saying that every discipline 'as long as it used the Aristotelian method of definition, has remained arrested in a state of empty verbiage and barren scholasticism'.

There are no end of disputes when we all play at being Lewis Carroll's Humpty Dumpty.*

Science is still in a constant competition with such Aristotelian essentialist thinking. Socrates famously argued that, in contrast with the 'Sophists' who were confident in their superior knowledge, the wise man knows that he knows nothing. He is full of doubts and questions – a sceptic. This idea underpins the modern Popperian (after Karl Popper) conception of science.[2] This may be roughly summarised as the idea that we cannot prove anything, but we can disprove hypotheses, a hypothesis being a testable proposition capable of being disproved. Although all thought is based on some assumptions which we have to take for granted, if there is no conceivable evidence which could disprove a hypothesis, then it does not qualify as scientific knowledge but as some form of non-scientific assertion. If not disproved, a hypothesis might be used as if true, and so science progresses with a set of ideas which are not absolute, which are capable of being challenged and which change over time. We gain progress but can never be certain of the truth.

Plato and his followers thought Socrates's view of wisdom must be due to his lack of scientific success in his day, but this displays, as Popper says, 'the pre-Socratic magical attitude towards science, and towards the scientist, whom they consider as a somewhat glorified shaman, as wise, learned, initiated'. The rationalist myth was a trap for Plato, who thought reason our most noble attribute, making us like the gods.

---

* From Lewis Carroll's *Through the Looking Glass*: "'When *I* use a word,' Humpty Dumpty said, in a rather scornful tone, "it means just what I choose it to mean – neither more nor less." "The question is," said Alice, "whether you *can* make words mean so many different things." "The question is," said Humpty Dumpty, "which is to be master – that's all.'"

At science's core is a separation of facts from the motivational presumption we attach to them, creating an objective rather than subjective meaning. It was thousands of years before humans realised the importance of this necessary separation and acted on it. Before science, there was moral thinking; moral thinking is pre-scientific.

Whether scientific or not, though, knowledge changes. It is not fixed but a process of accumulation (and forgetting/reprioritising). To know certain truth is to stop looking. The history of ideas can help us understand how our current ideas and morals evolved (including scientific knowledge) and how transitory they can be. It can help direct our scepticism and inquisitiveness. Cicero went as far as to say: 'To remain ignorant of things that happened before you were born is to remain a child.' To learn from history in this way, though, we have to recognise that history is constantly reinterpreted to justify current political narratives and identities – a fog we have to penetrate and clear. Moreover, if the study of history is to provide new insight (as opposed to being used as evidence in support of our own contemporary moral system), we must, with an open mind, attempt to understand its meaning from the perspectives of those who lived at the time. History is a series of mysteries and puzzles to be solved. The facts of history are not restricted by the imagination of an author or a current-day propagandist but provide case studies of human behaviour under different moral systems, and so, by showing different perspectives on human fallibility, may offer us insight into our own prejudices.

This assumes we are inquisitive. But we have a choice: either accept a set of ideas as truth and not look any further, or search for new ideas and progress, most notably through using science. As

Popper explains: 'We can say that in our search for truth, we have replaced scientific certainty by scientific progress.' And the way it progresses is not gradual, as Aristotle thought, but via convulsions impelled by radical ideas. Popper continues:

> This view of scientific method means that in science there is no *'knowledge'*, in the sense in which Plato and Aristotle understood the word, in the sense which implies finality; in science, we never have sufficient reason for the belief that we have attained the truth. What we usually call 'scientific knowledge', is, as a rule, not knowledge in this sense, but rather information regarding the various competing hypotheses and the way in which they have stood up to various tests; it is, using the language of Plato and Aristotle, information concerning the latest, and the best tested, scientific *'opinion'*.[3]

This contrasts with common modern interpretations of science as a body of unquestionable authoritative truth. We cannot prove scientific ideas, only disprove various hypotheses. Scepticism is the basis of science, and so of progress too.

We can check that all our reasoning is correct, all our definitions nominalist, much easier than we can identify our prejudices. What the scientific community collectively knows is thus largely bounded by the limits of our experimentation – but also by the assumptions used by scientists. We can question our assumptions, but there are always more assumptions behind them, however far back we go. Pascal assumed his senses were to be relied on, but we know them to be unreliable. We know, moreover, from Godel's incompleteness theorem, that any system with propositions which are internally consistent and logical, including any moral system which ascribes to certain truth, must necessarily be based on assumptions outside that system.*

A fact, capable of multiple interpretations, unlike a scientific (nominalist) definition, is also not straightforward. It does not stand in isolation. Scientists cannot work without a conceptual scheme. A fact is an empirically verifiable statement which scientists try to make sense from. To do this, they formulate hypotheses consistent with various facts and not contradicted by others. These hypotheses can be refuted, not proved, and if they are not testable they do not constitute scientific knowledge.

This is clearly exemplified by the natural scientist doing controlled experiments which can be repeated by others at a later date with the same results. Some branches of science, however, are limited by the practicality and ethics of conducting experiments. In such areas (including clinical and social science), data from cases are observed and hypotheses tested against the data available – and not 'cooked' by pre-selection of only those cases which are supportive. This is a crucial point, for any such pre-selection motivated to achieve a positive result (sometimes subconsciously) breaks the separation of facts from motive. By hiding some of the evidence in a systematic way, proper science is no longer being conducted, as we shall see later in the chapter in medical science. Insofar as one defines a lie as the intention to mislead, lies are being created (the sin of omission). As Einstein said: 'The right to search for truth implies also a duty; one must not conceal any part of what one has recognised to be true.'

Much of what passes for science fails to meet these standards.

---

* See footnote at page 85, Chapter 3.

Only presenting supportive evidence in statistical and other areas where this makes a big difference to conclusions is lamentably common, and not even perceived as a source of bias by many. Activism and wishful thinking are categorically not science. Group belief that such practices do constitute science (because science is believed to be whatever scientists do) is a form of groupthink, especially should there be other signs such as strenuous efforts to stifle criticism. Theories and models which have unrealistic assumptions and no testable results (common in my own discipline of economics, and numerous types of modelling), whilst possibly of heuristic value, can also misdirect us away from scientific progress.

Thomas Kuhn's *Theory of Scientific Revolutions* describes how science occurs in paradigms. Hypotheses are made assuming that past results and their underlying assumptions are valid. As more and more experiments yield more results and facts, these are tested and understood within the paradigm. Newton said that if he had seen further, it was by standing on the shoulders of giants. And so, the paradigm builds, result building on result.

However, verifiable experimental results may arise which are contradictory to other experimental results already established as true within the paradigm. If this happens, it requires that previous experimental results, which form part of the assumptions for more recent experiments, be checked. If these are valid, then their assumptions and the experimental results they were based on need verifying and so on, until either an error is found or one reaches the foundational assumptions of the paradigm – assumptions which have previously been taken to be self-evident. In this way, our prejudices, which are only identified after they have been removed, can be revised. In practice, this often happens only when we have run out of alternatives. In contrast to earlier philosophical approaches, objectivity in modern science is not a function of the far-sighted and independent views of individual scientists but a collective consequence of the scientific method.

However, finding contradictions will not, by itself, demolish a paradigm. Just because a Newton finds himself not on the shoulders of giants but on a funnel of the *Titanic* does not mean either that sinking occurs immediately or that all the people on board can, or will choose to, abandon ship. Scientists spend whole careers within certain paradigms and are understandably loath to part from them. Thus, they ask Haidt's question of the new thinking – do I have to believe this? It is natural to think there *must* be an error in some experiment or reasoning, an error that it is somebody's else's problem to locate and resolve. For a new paradigm to replace the old, as for example relativity and quantum mechanics replacing Newtonian physics, the new should explain everything that the old did, plus experimental results contradictory to the old paradigm. Even then, it takes years for a paradigm shift to occur, as Kuhn tells us and as referred to in Max Planck's quote at the beginning of the chapter: 'A new scientific truth does not triumph by convincing its opponents and making them see the light, but rather because its opponents eventually die, and a new generation grows up that is familiar with it.' Though many consider scientists as authoritative by virtue of their being scientists, they are as human as the rest of us, just as irrational, and they may have a particular set of vested interests.

To progress, we need work within paradigms to occur, but also for the paradigms to be tested fundamentally now and then, especially if more and more contradictory experimental results amass. As scientific knowledge has grown and become necessarily specialist, this task remains vital to progress, requiring at least a few independent minds. And it requires that these independently minded paradigm critics not only exist but be heard. We educate our students for this purpose. As Allan Bloom says in his *The Closing of the American Mind*: 'Most students will be content with what our present considers relevant; others will have a spirit of enthusiasm that subsides ... a small number will spend their lives in an effort to be autonomous. It is for these last, especially, that liberal education exists.' He goes on to say: 'Without their presence (and, one should add, without their being respectable), no society – no matter how rich or comfortable, no matter how technically adept or full of tender sentiments – can be called civilized.' This is because without the occasional paradigm shift, progress eventually stops and the dogmatism necessary to stop it becomes tyrannical.[4]

Yet challenging scientific paradigms can be lonely, intimidating and career destroying. Groupthink lives in the academy, not least due to a greater than average number of its inhabitants being erudite and intelligent and so prone to groupthink. It is also a result of the funding environment. Moreover, academia is a relatively closed environment, with multiple repeat transactions between the same participants. We know from game theory that this can discourage rogue behaviour. As mentioned in Chapter 3, the Zollman effect describes the observation that well-connected groups of researchers tend to come to consensus quickly, whilst sparser networks are more likely to settle on a true consensus. There can be strong incentives to keep heretical views to oneself. Indeed, the sin of omission, driven by fear, is rife when it comes to certain issues – some of the alternatives to the orthodox green views on CO_2 emissions and the importance of rapid adoption of renewable energy sources, for example.

An interesting example of how scientific consensus spreads is that of smallpox variolation in the early eighteenth century. Similar to vaccination, variolation involves exposing pus (in this case smallpox pus) to a scratch on the arm. Lady Mary Wortley Montagu observed the practice of smallpox variolation whilst in Turkey and on her return to England tried to convince physicians to use it. Her efforts failed, but she managed to persuade Princess Caroline to adopt the technique, and once this became known the practice spread. This spread had little to do with either evidence or belief but was largely a social phenomenon. In encountering the choice of whether to change allegiance, one weighs beliefs against the desire to conform.

An entire population can appear to reach a consensus on an issue, but that does not mean it is a true consensus, and sometimes it isn't. 'The science' is a phrase often used to denote a fixed set of incontrovertible knowledge, which as outlined above may have very little to do with actual science. For example, the idea that the science is established on the causes of climate change is often used to stop further debate. Yet there is substantial uncertainty about this hugely complex area of study, and a very large gap between the often hedged and tentative conclusions of the panels of scientists on the Intergovernmental Panel on Climate Change (IPCC) and the more politically directed conclusions drawn from these studies, let alone the alarmist presentation of them in the media and by activist groups. 'The science' can be convoked, in an appeal to authority, not reason, to spread or defend a bad idea as easily as a good one. If the authority of 'the science' is being used to shut down debate and stop any further enquiry, then one should perhaps be suspicious.

To echo my earlier President Somoza vignette, when faced with something which flies in the face of reason but which everyone else appears to go along with, don't only ask how a turtle got up the palm tree (or indeed how 'the science', however nonsensical, became accepted), but what the motive was. Since long before Jonathan Swift started to make fun of them in *Gulliver's Travels*, there have been a lot of vested interests in academia, a lot of careers and reputations to protect, and there are now a lot of studies funded by corporate and government bodies with particular agendas. There are many groupthink members wanting affirmation, which they are happy to fund, from the academic community to aid credibility and help defend against nonbelievers.

SCIENCE UNDER ATTACK

Science, as we have seen, separates facts from motivational presumption. It is hard just to describe, stay impartial and present all the important data and findings, not just that which supports your hypothesis or view. Yet that is what science requires – and where it often fails. The struggle between rationalism and irrationalism (in the Middle Ages, scholasticism and mysticism) has a long pedigree since at least Roman times. Rational argument will not sway those without a rational attitude; groupthink has deep roots in our psychology and is not new.

THE ANGRY LEFT
Loretta Breuning has studied the neurochemistry of science bias. She says:

> Rousseau asserted that nature is good, and 'our society' is the
> cause of that which is bad. A social scientist who finds evidence

to support this presumption can expect rewards. The result is an accumulation of evidence that:

1. Animals are good (they cooperate and nurture each other)
2. Children are good (they grow to perfection automatically, unless miseducated by society)
3. Preindustrial people are/were good (in harmony with nature and each other)

A reader may think these assertions are indisputable facts because the effortless flow of electricity through well-developed pathways gives us a sense of truth.

Breuning's findings are interesting rather than the last word on the topic, but her identification of Rousseau as a major source of current thinking about man's place in the environment, as well as his apparent misanthropy, is a common one.[5]

The urge to rebel against authority is a common human trait, as discussed in Chapter 1. It feeds the anarchic revolt against society which is as old as our civilisation itself. As new beliefs substitute for religion, so new authorities have been created to feed this revolt.

Hegel was an advocate of scientific intuition and Aristotelian thinking. He embraced contradictions and proposed a theory of history with a dialectic process of thesis and antithesis, which contradict each other and from which is formed a synthesis. This synthesis then develops into a new thesis, with, in turn, its own contradictory antithesis etc. In this way, contradictions do not disprove theories but adjust them. His practical conclusion, in a period of political upheaval, was support for the status quo.

This, after the wreckage of Napoleonic misrule in Prussia, was the restored government of Frederick William III. Hegel has been accused of inventing irrational ideas to forestall political change and win himself favour with Frederick William. Schopenhauer (quoted in Popper) said: 'Hegel, installed from above, by the powers that be, as the certified Great Philosopher, was a flat-headed, insipid, nauseating, illiterate charlatan, who reached the pinnacle of audacity in scribbling together and dishing up the craziest mystifying nonsense,' adding that the widespread acclaim of his nonsense 'enabled him to achieve the intellectual corruption of a whole generation'. Modern science sees contradictions as impermissible and avoidable; Hegel sees them as desirable and necessary for scientific progress. His approach is, however, destructive of knowledge accumulation via the scientific method as I have described it and indeed of all progress. His is nothing short of an attempt to stop reason.

He has, unfortunately, had many followers. Kant tried to stop the scribblers but failed to stem the tide. Hegel's most influential philosophical descendant was Karl Marx, who with Engels described very movingly the plight of the industrial working poor and inspired socialism in its various forms. Yet, despite the monumentality of his efforts, his so-called scientific analysis of history and critique of what he coined capitalism were deeply flawed. His ideas helped justify totalitarian communism and statist policy solutions to almost any problem.

Various milder versions of democratic socialism were more successful in Western Europe, and they have achieved many laudable results. However, the desire for rebellion, including against reason, has remained a core motive for many. By the mid-twentieth century, George Orwell observed that many socialists didn't really like the poor; they just hated the rich. As social ills have lessened, the revolutionary urge has not gone away, merely found different people to hate. Rolling the clock forward to the present, lower economic class has all but evaporated from the postmodernist list of criteria used to determine society's deserving victims. The honorary working class are indeed the very opposite of poor, comprising middle-class intellectuals. As Roger Scruton says of the 1960s: 'This was the age of "intellectual production", in which the identity of the intellectual as honorary member of the working class was established – precisely when the real working class was disappearing from history and could be guaranteed survival only in this theatrical form.'[6]

POSTMODERNISM

Society has been analysed through a series of lenses obsessed with power relationships, labelled deconstructionism, poststructuralism, postmodernism or simply Marxism. The fashions and some of the terminology changes, but the distance from testable refutable hypotheses, and the modern scientific method as being the key process of knowledge accumulation in society, remains. I focus here on postmodernism, but the arguments apply to its close cousins, and there is no space (or appetite) here to review the subtle differences. My point is simply that there has been a lot of academic activity meandering away from the reasonable if not from reason itself, which has now destructively leaked into society at large and is feeding anxiety, confusion and groupthink.

From Marxism to postmodernism, there have been many iterative steps and branches, but one constancy has been that everything is about power. Leftists of various hues see structures of domination everywhere, where others see just instruments of civil order. The idea is that by unmasking behaviour as a function of power relations, we come to understand them better. Yet we invariably learn nothing from such revelations. The truth is either more complex or already transparent. Power relations are only universally dominant in tyrannies, and liberal democracies are not tyrannies. Indeed, being tolerant and reasonable and giving voice to people means rejecting power as the explanation for everything. Instead of classifying people and identifying victims, many problems can be solved by enabling and trusting people's ability to work things out for themselves – which is at the core of liberal democracy. To be enlightened is to reason for oneself, to escape from the idea that one is defined by one's group identity. This transcends power relationships between classes of people.

Postmodernism is a post-Second World War philosophical approach, distinguished from previous left-wing philosophies by its reaction against perceived failures of liberalism and of the nation state (specifically in France and Germany). Following disillusion with Marxism and its numerous deficiencies, postmodernism is an aggressive pessimism and gut reaction against authority. It owes a lot to Marxism's destructive fantasies and hatred of the status quo and shares its intolerance to anything not in perfect agreement with its own ideals. If postmodernism is the rebellious adolescent son of Marxism, its other parent is nihilism. Nihilism, the alter ego of totalitarianism, is a response to experience without certain meaning and denies its adherents the ability to find meaning. French social theorists of the 1960s (Foucault, Derrida, Lyotard) were particularly important in postmodernism's development (creating what is known simply as 'Theory') and also the Frankfurt school (Horkheimer, Adorno, Marcuse and others). Horkheimer and Adorno attacked the Enlightenment as part of a hysterical critique of bourgeois society, with its perceived herding of people into the capitalist model of exchange and justice and its replacement of mystery, authority and self-discovery with reason, entrepreneurship and technology.

As with a normal virus, postmodernism has evolved. It has done so in a seemingly arbitrary way – the consequence of the struggle of ideas to survive in a cut-throat but ever-changing environment, where survival defines truth and not vice-versa. Postmodernism in its initial strain was almost incomprehensible to the uninitiated. Incomprehensibility, following Hegel and many other philosophers, is a protection from criticism and a proven survival technique. It never made it out of academia. Although its first iteration was disruptive in an indiscriminate fashion, its second iteration, building on New Left political activism coming out of the Frankfurt school, was into dismantling hierarchies and reordering power relationships. Its third iteration, now infecting the whole of society, can be described in very general terms as a dogmatic insistence on political correctness in its various, often contradictory, forms.

Postmodernism shares with other elements of the left no knowledge of the socialist future, only that it is necessary and desirable. Its energy is negative, directed against established behaviour and ideas, suspicious of reason and of a broad swathe of establishment views, considering them determined by ideology and power relations. It is cynical of all progress to date. There are various versions, a minefield of thoughts, largely nonsense and contradictory. But it has been described as having four pillars: the social construction of identity; the idea that morality is socially constructed; the deconstruction of art and culture; and the notion that borders between all peoples are social constructions, to be crossed and eroded. According to Steinar Kvale, central themes include 'doubting that any human truth provides an objective representation of reality, focusing on language and the way societies use it to create their own local realities, and denying the universal'.[7] This follows Orwell's observation (and Antonio Gramsci's) that every revolution targets language as a priority and gives maximum authority in determining truth to the new high priests. It is also, following Aristotle, essentialist not nominalist.

People do see reality differently. As an attempt to understand the human mind, this at least has some merit, but postmodernism, though it may attempt to dress itself in acceptable clothes, is not designed simply for passive knowledge discovery but to classify the world according to its own dogmatic vision and then to change it. Perhaps most clearly at variance with science, postmodernism denies the boundary between subjective experience and objective reality. We are all entitled not merely to our own view but to our own truth. There is thus no objective reality. This completely contradicts the most basic premise of modern science and is fundamentally anti-science; not a philosophical move sideways but a move backwards. Moreover, instead of understanding that science is a process based on scepticism and capable of constant revision, postmodernism considers liberal reasoning and science as meta-narratives which they wish to replace. They wish to destroy all ideology and certainty yet have no mechanisms of, or ability to learn from, self-criticism. The irony is that their own absolute methodological truth has hardened into a dogma, a meta-narrative, to use their own terminology. This dogma is theoretically incapable of change as a result of outside challenge. Yet it does adapt, mauled by those inside it with the strongest voices, the biggest bullies, the most outrageous.

The hard left has often insisted on total discipline to tenets set by a small intellectual elite. For example, Althusser insisted on the sacredness of Marx's *Capital*. Likewise, it can only be admitted that you understand postmodernism if you first believe it. In short, postmodernists abound in universal cynicism but consider their own methods above any criticism. And as the centre left does not criticise the extreme left, whether through ideological loyalty, lack of perception or cowardice, the lunacy simply grows more and more extreme.

Plato's use of the word 'justice' in his *Republic* was a reversal of its everyday meaning, and so it is today for those following his totalitarian desires. In its more virulent later forms, postmodernism has now jumped via activists to the general population in the form of campaigns for 'Social Justice' (with a capital S and capital J). And in keeping with Orwell's Ministries of Truth, Peace, Plenty and Love, so the reader will not be surprised that postmodernist 'Social Justice', whilst eminently cynical, is neither particularly social nor particularly just. Advocates of the concept dogmatically believe society is structured with obscure identity-based systems of power and privilege. These construct knowledge through controlling language. They also aim to describe the world critically in order to change it – i.e. their aim is the very opposite of science, which seeks to separate facts from motives. It is from here only a short step to deciding what knowledge to share with others. And by trying to mislead through the sin of omission, this amounts to the manufacture of lies. As to what lies, though, this can be arbitrary.

Postmodernists may not believe in an objective reality, and it is difficult to identify what they do believe in with much confidence.

Science, which provides explanations for social phenomena not requiring social constructs to explain everything important, is deemed factually and morally wrong. The lunacy is sometimes stranger than fiction – indeed laughable. A senior university manager I know told me about a disciplinary event for one of their academic staff. The staff member failed to appear at the pre-arranged disciplinary meeting, which happened to be on a Wednesday. When later confronted and asked why they did not make the appointment, the reason given included the words: 'Well, Wednesday is just a social construct,' to which the reply was: 'And so is my paying you.'

History is also considered fair game. Aside from it being used to classify one's ancestors, and so determine whether today one is victim or oppressor, it is largely forgotten or rewritten. Postmodernist history is simply a litany of injustice. One consequence is that, with history simpler to understand, it also appears more certain. This contrasts with a future which looks ever more uncertain. The contrast helps to feed our fears, keep us in place. This helps to solidify the groupthink: by giving certainty to the past, the explanatory power of postmodernism is promoted; by fostering fear of the future, the case is made for action not thought, discipline not debate, aggression to outsiders not compromise or tolerance.

As further evidence that postmodernism is a form of groupthink rather than something we might describe as contributing to intellectual progress, and just as Orwell predicted in 1984, postmodernists restrict thought and criticism by monitoring and restricting words and eligible arguments. Social Theory (again with a capital S and capital T) can only be criticised according to its own language, on its own terms. Disagreement is not tolerated. To disagree simply shows lack of comprehension and thus ineligibility to pass judgement.

So, how is truth established? Pluckrose and Lindsay summarise the current fad:

> It is impossible for humans to obtain reliable knowledge by employing evidence and reason, but, it is now claimed, reliable knowledge can be obtained by listening to the 'lived experience' of members of marginalized groups – or what is really more accurate, to marginalized people's interpretations of their own lived experience, after these have been properly colored by theory.[8]

Because people have different 'lived experiences', any attempt to find objective reality is full of complexity and contradiction. In practice, those selected as being authentic are selected for their agreement with the prejudices of whoever is declaring them as authentic. What we have is a groupthink in which it is morally wrong to question the dogma.

Postmodernism can be seen as a virus, a cause of mental health problems, a painful addiction. For the uninitiated it can appear not merely counterproductive but quite mad. The postmodern agenda has spilled out of academia and is now crowding out public discourse and eroding social capital and mutual trust. The most common expressions of it relate to race and gender issues. Although in its legal setting and other applications Critical Race Theory has been of constructive use for several decades, some radical adherents to its newest versions assume that racism is everywhere – the relevant research question being not whether it is present but in what form. By trying to force everyone to think about racial categories all the time, it is perpetuating, not alleviating, intolerance and feelings of aggrievement and separation. It is 180 degrees away from Martin Luther King's dream: 'I have a dream that my four little children will one day live in a nation where they will not be judged by the color of their skin but by the content of their character.'

Unsurprisingly perhaps, unconscious bias training does not appear to work. Telling someone who is white and who does not consider themselves to be (and is not) racist, not only that they are racist but that there is nothing that they can do about it is prone to make people more angry and more fearful and less, not more, tolerant. It is reminiscent of the twelfth-century test by water – if the suspect is accepted by a body of blessed holy water and drowns, he is innocent, but if he floats, guilty.

Whilst there is plenty of criticism of postmodernist ideas from outside, it is often responded to with a sneer, derision of the individual making the criticism, rather than honest debate or reasoned argument. The totalitarian viewpoint does not allow compromise. One is either innocent or guilty, resentful or the cause of resentment.

Conflicts between different postmodernists do abound and often take the form of vigorous and unpleasant personal attacks. Tolerance appears to play very little role in discussion. One might think that outright contradictions would cause pause for thought and reassessment, but far from it. The legacy of Hegel's embrace of contradictions, of which there are many, and the abandonment of the scientific method and objective reality have seen to that.

Proponents of decolonisation have argued against the way science and reason are taught; diversity of thought, according to

Michael Harriot, is just a euphemism for white supremacy; and Robin DiAngelo has explained 'how white people who see people as individuals rather than by their skin colour are in fact "dangerous".⁹ Also important to some is not just what is said but who says it. There is a lot of jumping to conclusions in the culture wars on both sides, but it seems to me we are getting further away from mutual tolerance.

The lack of tolerance combined with an obsession with language can easily cause a breakdown in communication. As Pluckrose and Lindsay say: 'In practice, deconstructive approaches to language … look very much like nitpicking at words in order to deliberately miss the point.' Words are also a battlefield chosen by those who want to impose group discipline. I witnessed this when chairing a video meeting during lockdown at which great offence was taken at the use of the word 'chairman'. Although the man who used the term, and who clearly intended no offence, immediately apologised to the woman who claimed to be offended, this was not enough. Several minutes of lecturing on why it was so important followed before we moved on with the agenda. By this time the emotion of the woman was such that she simply hung up. Tolerance of other people's views and use of language was not enough for her. She wanted others to completely comply with her ideological agenda. Hers was a moral argument. The belief that definitions and choice of words matter so much stems from the idea of Chomsky and others that words help define the structure of our thoughts. A desire to control our thoughts is behind the desire to control our language, like Orwell's Newspeak. It is also a sign of groupthink in action: by creating an unreasonable fuss, the woman was marking the boundaries she expected others to comply with, and by getting angry she was indicating the sort of negative cost others might expect in future if the transgression occurred again. Not only did she consider it appropriate to feel aggrieved and offended when no offence was meant; she also felt it right that she should dictate the use of words by others. For others not to accept her definition of a word was, in her mind, to victimise her, when from another perspective one might think she was the bully.

This links right back to the earlier point about Aristotelian essentialism in which words and their precise (if changeable) meanings are the building blocks of academic endeavour. The contrast is with science, which, as we have seen, denotes no great importance to definitions. Whereas scientists, who can of course still argue about definitions, can also move on and talk about substance rather than form, for some postmodernists this is not so easy, as to a greater or lesser extent the form is the substance. Indeed, looking to the unpleasant extremes of left- and right-wing politics in the past century, it has not been unusual for totalitarians to update terms just to keep people on their toes; the more banal the better. Often the less something matters, the more bitter the argument.

But to impose discipline on what words one can use is an infringement of freedom of speech, and if successful, our fundamental liberty to think for ourselves. It grates against the principle of secularism that nobody has a right to impose their moral beliefs on the whole of society. To take offence when it is meant is natural, to take offence when something might easily be construed as offensive is understandable and, circumstances permitting, might warrant a clarification of whether harm was meant or not, but to take offence when clearly none is intended is an act of self-centred intolerance.

Postmodernist lack of space for objective reality has created not

HAVE WE ALL GONE MAD?

intellectual engagement with those outside but a simple pattern: there is 'us' and 'them'. Where it has gained traction in universities, the aim of academic activity is to some extent an exercise in displaying loyalty inside the group and aggression to outsiders. This in part explains how a number of spoof papers trying to show up the ridiculousness of what passes for academic enquiry have managed to get past peer review and into academic journals, including the University of Portland assistant philosophy professor Peter Boghossian's series of around seven papers, amongst them his re-writing of *Mein Kampf* with feminist terminology. Those teachers who are so wicked as to think they can say something universally true about the human condition may have to face students used to negotiating truth in place of using rational argument. The current assault on the curriculum is to impose a standard of 'political correctness' of non-exclusion and non-judgement – but within strict boundaries and with, ironically, dogmatic judgement against all critics. As argued in Chapter 3, our young (and their teachers) can rebel and are even encouraged to do so. But their rebellion is formulaic and within-group, and if anyone actually rebels by questioning central dogma, they are disciplined. Most postmodernists don't realise they are captured in its embrace. They like being in the rebellious group, the sense of joint purpose, the values of the tribe, the clarity of enemies who have to be opposed and the comfort of the clear discipline and limited need to delve past simple slogans and memes. Yet they are its slaves, working for its assault on reason.

UNIVERSITIES UNDER ATTACK

Universities' central roles are the pursuit and dissemination of knowledge, which require an appetite for intellectual challenge and debate. Yet this is coming under threat. They have long faced pressure from funders and student protests, but they are now also being pressured to provide not just physical safety for students but safety from offensive ideas, as defined (and constantly changed) by postmodern groupthink.

Research has long been captured by corporate interests. The tobacco industry's setting up of the Tobacco Industry Research Committee and funding of research to spread doubt about the negative effects of smoking is well documented.[10] The preferred outcome of research can be the suppression of knowledge through deliberate obfuscation, denial and confusion. In other cases, corporate funding has influenced decisions which have led to bad science and bad practice, even whilst there may be no clear, deliberate attempt to mislead – incompetence is more prevalent than fraud.*

Big Tech's influence is also a concern. The NYU Ad Observatory had been researching political advertising on Facebook, in particular how ads are targeted and the amplification of partisan misinformation. Its accounts and access to Facebook were disabled by the company, citing privacy concerns. This suggests the possibility of Big Tech commercial interests conflicting with democratic freedoms, but it also reflects a broader pattern of unregulated censorship by Big Tech of anything their owners can be persuaded is harmful or offensive. An issue like this is worrying not just if the balance between privacy and legitimate public interest is

---

* An example is that of suppression of heart arrhythmia. In the 1970s, the idea gained traction that because an irregular heartbeat often precedes heart attacks, one should prevent it. Widespread adoption of arrhythmia-suppressing drugs followed, tested for their effectiveness. Unfortunately, these drugs were not initially tested for, and were later found to increase, heart attack deaths.

considered wrong, but because the pattern is to reinforce existing groupthinks and squash critics.

This only adds to the problems faced by those who would challenge current dogmas. If academics are attacked for their lack of political correctness, they may find few brave enough to support them. The norm is appeasement, which was defined by Kissinger as 'the result of an inability to come to grips with a policy of unlimited objectives'. To an extent the bullying tactics, plus the moving of the battlefield outside the university and indeed (particularly in the US) to the courts, are a reflection of postmodernism having lost the battle inside the academy. However, that does not mean academics can let down their guard. The pressure is also coming from students. Speakers are no-platformed, safe spaces sought and the central role of the university as a place of research and education, and thus challenge, is being eroded in favour of safety and lack of debate. There is pressure to conform with virtue-signalling platitudes, reinforcing the growing array of insincerities and ir-rationalities. Campus politicisation is a problem, and a challenge to the traditional concept of a university. Tolerance and freedom of speech, including redefining the focus from whether someone takes offence to whether offence is intended, are paramount in a well-functioning university.

One case, quoted by David Allen and Elizabeth Reedy, concerns the well-known entomologist E. O. Wilson. His 1974 book *Sociobiology: A New Synthesis* included a thirty-page speculative final chapter on the possible relationships between genes and culture in human beings. The highly influential book is credited as having created the new discipline of sociobiology. His final chapter was not definitive but meant to start a debate, which it did, and his views on the mix between nurture and nature have since become mainstream. Yet his views were misrepresented at the time and he was attacked (including physically) and accused of racism and misogyny. He was accused of having said or implied things he neither said nor implied. The case was typical in that those making the accusations could be safe in the knowledge that they could say outrageously false things without being criticised or seriously held to account. When he was assaulted at the annual meeting of the American Association for the Advancement of Science, the police were not called and the offenders not even asked to leave the hall.[11]

Since 1974, things seem to have got worse, particularly in the US. The norm is still that freedom of speech and fair treatment of academic employees are well defended, but worrying exceptions abound. No-platforming and other efforts to prevent freedom of speech have increased as safety-ism has progressed on campus. The typical cause of no-platforming is the fear that challenging ideas may be considered offensive by some students. The search for truth by negotiation, not reason, is also, whilst rare, a retrograde step in the search for knowledge. We now have more open letters signed by academic staff denouncing and condemning peers, and there is the constant fear of unwittingly being accused of causing offence (one inappropriate sentence and your career could be over). Academics who fall out of line may be bullied, subject to aggression and constructive dismissal and denied an effective chance to defend themselves.[*]

Uniformity in adherence to various elements of political correctness and the fear of speaking out is not exclusive to universities, but it can restrict effective challenge of entrenched theories and

---

[*] Florencia Peña Saint-Martin gives us a list of academic mobbing in *Sham Dealing and Sham Peer Review in Academic Publishing.*

groupthinks. The peer review system remains generally highly effective, but it suffers if there is widespread groupthink across a whole discipline and where a small group of like-minded people police what is deemed acceptable. Independent replication or refutation of results by other academics is still the best test of new research (in those disciplines where this is possible).

Many members of the public are disillusioned with scientists if not science, just as they are disillusioned with other elements of society, like democracy. Some of this comes from its inability to provide definitive answers. Some is due to a lack of contact with scientific results. Some is due to an irrational and ideological objection to science. Some is also, however, due to scientists losing their way, not separating their desires to change the world from their role in describing it. They both withhold parts of what they know and misrepresent what they know in order to persuade. The US National Association of Scholars 2018 report 'The Irreproducibility Crisis of Modern Science' highlights a crisis across a wide range of scientific and social-scientific disciplines, from epidemiology to social psychology. 'Improper research techniques, lack of accountability, disciplinary and political groupthink, and a scientific culture biased toward producing positive results together have produced a critical state of affairs.' The report lists eight contributory factors: inherent statistical test limitations; small sample sizes; small numbers of studies; willingness to publish studies reporting small effects; fishing expeditions; flexibility in research design; prejudice and conflicts of interest; and competition to produce positive results. It goes on: 'In 2005, Dr. John Ioannidis argued, shockingly and persuasively, that most published research findings in his own field of medicine were false.'

He also warned Covid-19 modellers in the early stages of the disease about the serious deficiencies of their data, but that didn't stop anyone, or their wildly inaccurate results, being given too much credibility. Neil Ferguson's initial Covid model predicted there would be 500,000 deaths in the UK and 2.2 million in the US without measures to suppress the virus. These results were soon found to be highly exaggerated, but the modelling was released prior to peer review and weeks went by before requests to look at the coding were acceded to. When this did finally happen, problems were found. Whilst rushing in a crisis is to an extent understandable, the episode does not fill one with confidence. The remarkable thing was that such models were given the credence they were. A previous model of his predicted up to 136,000 cases of Creutzfeldt-Jakob disease in the UK, when in fact there were 178 over twenty years.[12] In 2012, the biotechnology firm Amgen attempted to reproduce the results of fifty-three landmark studies in haematology and oncology but succeeded in replicating only six. There is an urgent need to weed out bad practices. It is a scandal that there are now so many papers published with non-replicable results. Moreover, just as fake news spreads faster and more widely than real news, so it is claimed that non-replicable studies are cited more often than replicable ones.

This is mostly due to incompetence, but also fraud. Such fraud is mostly committed despite the near certainty of eventually being found out. As discussed in the review of the problem of irreproducibility of science by the US National Association of Scholars, this is often in the hope that a hypothesis will eventually be proved correct and that publication will help sustain research funding.

There is an epidemic of scientists confusing conjectures and facts. We discussed the normal curve in Chapter 4; it only exists when events are truly random, thus excluding much of its legitimate use in the social sciences. But the problem is perhaps most obvious with the use of models. The appropriate acronym is GIGO, which stands for garbage in, garbage out. Models do not constitute facts and are often no more than merely wishful thinking. Their limits are typically understood by the academics who use them but not by policy-makers or other users. That they can, like climate models, be extraordinarily complex does not change the basic problem that if the assumptions constitute guesswork – or worse, massaged inputs to obtain the desired result – then the output is meaningless. Climate models have been hopeless for thirty years, by which I mean that their predictions have not over time added any credibility to their reliability. This does not mean that some models have not arrived at the correct prediction. A common technique is to generate many models and then, when empirical data finally comes in, select the one which best fits the data. The king was hunting in the forest one day, so the story goes, and he saw an arrow in the dead centre of a bullseye painted on a tree. The young lad who fired the arrow confirmed he had fired it from a great distance, and so the king immediately recruited him into his service. Later, when asked how he managed to hit with such accuracy, the boy replied: 'Oh, it was easy. I shot the arrow into the forest and then painted the bullseye afterwards.'

A RETURN TO REASON

As in previous epochs – such as from the English Civil War through to the Restoration – rapid change in communications technology is leading to more diversity of views, many of them highly intolerant, hence the religious wars of the past and the culture wars of today. These need to be challenged through insistence on normal, tolerant rules of engagement and by ensuring all students (indeed all of us) are intellectually equipped to balance evidence and make their own decisions – i.e. they need to be taught to think critically and using the scientific method, not exclusively using essentialist reasoning from accepted authority. This may sound obvious, but in line with postmodernist philosophy, challenging dogma is often not what dominant thought leaders want students to do. Likewise, policy-makers need to be clear on how they should use scientific advice, and what decisions cannot be delegated.

There is no alternative to the scientific method that is as credible. We should not be looking for an alternative to science. We have to improve scientific ethics and practice, and in that way increase its usefulness and credibility. There is a need to re-establish that science requires a separation between motivational presumption and facts. Many scientists who know there is much uncertainty yet do not trust politicians to make policy decisions have decided to become activists. In doing so, they have abrogated their responsibility to present all the evidence; they have to an extent decided to act not as scientists but as citizens. To act as citizen in this way is fine outside their professional life, but not at work. The betrayal of trust perverts policy and misleads the public, but it also brings science into bad repute. The problem is worst in clinical and social sciences, where controlled experiments are so much more difficult than in natural sciences, but it is also particularly bad in the most emotive and political areas.

The two main immediate causes of bad science are fraud and incompetence. To reduce fraud, incentives to commit it must be challenged. Currently, groupthink can help prevent detection, lead to cover-ups and even enhance the careers of the fraudsters through higher public profiles. Although most get caught out eventually, it can take many years, some are never called out and penalties are often negligible if any. For example, whilst there is little accurate global temperature data prior to about 150 years ago, climate alarmists wanted evidence to support their claims. Michael Mann used highly questionable statistical manipulation to create the desired global temperature data. The output from his adjustments to the underlying data shows temperatures gradually declining over the past thousand years and then rising dramatically in the late twentieth century like the shape of a hockey stick. Both the Medieval Warm Period and the Little Ice Age which followed conveniently disappeared. This 'hockey stick' graph was adopted by the green lobby and the IPCC and was widely used to demonstrate the effect of rising CO_2 on temperature. Statisticians have subsequently shown that Mann's manipulations would achieve this shape almost whatever data was input.[13] It was his adjustments to the data, not the data itself, which created the shape of the graph.

There need to be clear consequences for those caught distorting, including by the sin of omission, what they know and discover.

Incompetence is much more prevalent than fraud, and measures to prevent it can also help expose the fraudsters. It can be mitigated through better statistical and data handling standards, including making data publicly available; better research practices, including standardisation and pre-registration of research protocols to prevent currently excessive flexibility;* incentives not to skew results, such as

---

* Midstream changes to procedures to avoid negative outcomes is common, yet a 2011 study showed that four degrees of researcher freedom is enough to generate a 61 per cent false-positive rate.

funding and space in journals for refutations/negative results; more effort to test reproducibility of findings, including official funding; institutionalised ways to include criticism and thoughts outside the current consensus views, including funding for paradigm challenging research; changes to peer review where groupthink might be a problem, as, if all one's peers are in the same groupthink, existing peer review strengthens it further, perhaps through publishing of (still anonymous) peer critiques of articles alongside them; and mechanisms to flag clearly conjectural research, including GIGO models, which do not add to scientific knowledge. There is also a case for better auditing of research results at the government level – e.g. through an Office of Science Quality Assurance as proposed by Peter Ridd. Further, there may be a case to be made for some training for the most senior policy-makers (and journalists) who may rely on scientific knowledge and conjectural models.

Finally, truth, even if we do not know what it is, is not simply a matter of opinion. Not everyone can be correct. We do not all have our own truths, just our own versions of events, perspectives and opinions. As discussed in Chapter 1, we should not substitute emotion for reason in order to come to decisions. To abandon reason in a world where emotions are increasingly manipulated by fear and advertising amounts to sacrificing some essence of what it is to be human.

SUMMARY

- Given what we know about human irrationality, scientific advance is not easy. Scepticism, from Socrates, is the basis of science. The scientific method relies on testable hypotheses which can be disproved but not proved. The choice is between on the one hand certainty and perceived truth, or on the other hand scepticism, science and progress.

- Of crucial importance to science is separation between facts and motives. Scientists need to present all germane evidence, not just that which fits their hypothesis. Yet many scientists now fail this basic test.

- Another important aspect of science is nominalism: words are defined to be useful shorthands for scientists, enabling them to express complex ideas in fewer words than before, not to exclude alternative interpretations or characteristics. This contrasts with essentialism: Aristotle, following Plato, believed we can visualise essences and by intuition find correct definitions. Meanings for words are thus given which exclude other possible meanings, and these meanings are used as building blocks in thought. Throughout history this has been a route to empty verbiage and scholasticism.

- As new experiments verify new facts which contradict existing theories, we have to check the reasoning and assumptions of those existing theories. Faulty reasoning may be more readily discoverable than faulty assumptions. Faulty assumptions may come from previous experiments, so those experiments may need to checked. Their assumptions in turn may then need to be verified and so on, until, unless an error is found, an assumption at the base of a paradigm previously assumed self-evident must be reassessed as faulty, casting doubt on the whole paradigm.

- Scientific advance thus experiences paradigm shifts. This differs from the approach of essentialists, who come up with partial meanings and use them as building blocks of thought.

- From Hegel through to Marx and now three phases of postmodernist philosophers, there has grown a serious attack on reason, science and history. Contradiction is not seen as disproving Hegelian theory but is embraced.

- Postmodernism thinking is essentialist, with a focus on use of words to mould thoughts. Objective reality is denied. Truth is defined by the loudest voices and is transient, with bitter infighting and no toleration for dissent.

- Postmodernism sees power relations everywhere, yet such analysis is either partial or not valid in liberal democracies, as opposed to its greater relevance in tyrannies. It is cynical, destructive, misanthropist and dogmatic.

- This anti-reason has now seeped out of universities, where it started growing after the Second World War. It is now infecting much of society in its various forms of political correctness. It has formed and spread various mass groupthinks.

- I have listed a number of ways to reduce the spread of the nonsense induced by postmodernism in universities and society.

CHAPTER 6

WE HAVE SEEN WORSE

'When troubles had once begun in the cities, those who followed carried the revolutionary spirit further and further, and determined to outdo the report of all who had preceded them by the ingenuity of the enterprises and the atrocity of their revenges. The meaning of words had no longer the same relation to things but was changed by them as they thought proper. Reckless daring was held to be loyal courage; prudent delay was the excuse of a coward; moderation was the disguise of unmanly weakness; to know everything was to do nothing. Frantic energy was the true quality of a man.'

THUCYDIDES

Following the recommendations of the 2014 Collins Report, the electoral college system for electing the leader of the UK Labour Party was changed. Voting weights had been a third each from the Parliamentary Labour Party (PLP), individual party members and trade unions. This changed to a one member, one vote system, effectively disenfranchising MPs. However, candidates had to receive a minimum 15 per cent of MP nominations. In the 2015 leadership election, this equated to thirty-five MPs. Jeremy Corbyn, representing the left wing of the party, was nominated by the lowest number of MPs ever (thirty-six), yet he won the race clearly on the first round of voting against split votes for the more moderate candidates. Corbyn benefited from a social media wave of enthusiasm. Although he would have, just, won on the first round anyway, he gained the votes of many who joined the Labour Party for the sole reason of voting him in as leader in order to render the Labour Party unelectable. He was clearly not considered the best choice by his parliamentary colleagues. The following year, in June 2016, Corbyn lost a vote of confidence from his PLP colleagues 172:40. However, he did not, and according to Labour Party rules did not need to, resign as a result. Although he oversaw a substantial recovery in the 2017 election, he went on to lead the party to major defeat in the 2019 general election.

I believe Corbyn's election as Labour leader was in a way more significant than the Brexit vote, insofar as it reflects not merely a disenchanted electorate overthrowing the status quo but the consequence of social media's power in politics as an amplifier of emotion, tribalism and myopia. Brexit was a symptom of rejection, but it was still the product of a legitimising process. Destroying the possibility of reaching sincere compromises is more profound. Social media momentum was combined with the removal of an important institutional filter – the approval of sitting Labour MPs for their leader. This filter had long been relied on to check excesses and create compromise and consensus. By emasculating the UK's parliamentary opposition, it also led to the ruling Conservative government being less accountable. Majority rule is not the same as democracy, and it can be tyrannical. The Roman mob comes to mind – the smash-it-up brigade have through history been empowered by populism.

THE TRIALS OF LIBERALISM AND DEMOCRACY

We have the Greeks, in particular Solon and other Athenians before Plato, to thank for sowing the seeds of open societies – democracies which engender both individuality and altruism. Closed societies can be destabilised by commerce and trade. Hence Athens, a sea-power, was a spreader of liberty.

Yet Plato believed that the closer one is to never-changing natural form, the less corrupted. His preference for perfection in all things is represented in his political goal of unchanging authoritarianism. He argued that the ideal state was one which suppressed change and saw political degeneration as a four-stage process from the perfect state to timarchy (the rule of worthy and competent individuals), to oligarchy (the rule of the rich), to democracy (the rule of the mob i.e. lawlessness), and lastly to tyranny. Based on his acute observations at the time, Plato equated freedom with uncooperative selfishness and so democracy with irresponsibility. This was after the over-confident democratic Athenians caused and then lost the two and half decades-long Peloponnesian Wars, waged principally against Sparta.

Plato argued that the best and noblest solution was a system of rigid class divisions and rule by the philosopher king – i.e. himself. A problem for Plato's ideal state is how to select a wise leader – the good leader, indeed the good individual, is not necessarily the most knowledgeable. The reality is that choosing a leader is a gamble. Several of Plato's own students and associates did not turn out so well on entering politics – at least nine became tyrants!* In practice, a more important question than the choice of leader is how one should constrain and balance the power of whoever is in power. The difference between those who ask the one and those who ask the other of these two questions still divides the supporters of authoritarian leadership and democracy to this day.

Plato's pessimism excludes the real possibility that, with experience and institutions to guide them, free citizens can learn to value the wider welfare of society and to appreciate how best to achieve it. Socrates was highly critical of the democratic leaders of his time, but he complied with the law and his criticisms were meant to be constructive. He was much more critical of tyranny and non-democratic politics, advocating both individualism and altruism – an impossible combination according to Plato. In Plato's defence, democracy may be easier today. With wealth also comes the easier affordability of greater altruism. Freedom and good governance are not easy bedfellows, but our modern democracies are built on their fragile co-existence.

Plato's political vision remains tempting. If only the strongman, Hobbes's Leviathan, a benign dictator, would rule in our best interests, we would not have to worry about politics. We could get on with more agreeable aspects of our lives. Unfortunately, power corrupts. Rousseau's response to Plato, that the people not the

---

* Not forgetting Plato's two uncles, Critias and Theramenes, who led the thirty tyrants who ruled Athens after the Peloponnesian Wars. Their regime managed to kill 5 per cent of the population in their eight months in power.

aristocracy should rule, whilst revolutionary, does not solve the problem that the people's choice can be equally tyrannical. History bears out that the choice of leader is not as important as having checks and balances to counter their activities. It is a myth, unfortunately, to think that we can trust important political decisions to others without the risk of our freedom being stripped from us. We fear admitting to ourselves a simple truth: we cannot escape our political responsibility. If we put our political trust in another, we are still responsible for that decision. Freedom is not, as B. F. Skinner (whom we met in Chapter 3) thought, a form of ignorance. It is, however, very easily abused or lost altogether.

Socrates, unlike Plato, did not support the suppression of thought and reason for the sake of political order. He also planted the seed of scepticism from which we can trace modern science. But whilst there were many experiences of democracy and other constitutional forms in ancient Greece, a modern political theory independent of ideals, one which objectively assessed what political actions were necessary to reach which goals, had to wait two millennia for Niccolò Machiavelli, as we briefly touched on in Chapter 1. He made a distinction between the reality of politics and the 'imaginary republics and monarchies that have never been seen nor have been known to exist'. By separating ethical and moral considerations from the consideration of political cause and effect, Machiavelli, as with modern science, separated facts from motivational presumption. He remains a controversial figure to this day because he dared to consider positively actions commonly practised by politicians but deemed immoral. He was, however, motivated by a lofty goal: the political unification of Italy.

There are many parallels today. Should one, for example, use gas power stations as a means to transition to a much lower CO_2 emission economy, if that is your goal? If one is dispassionate about the technological, economic and politically achievable options, one may conclude yes. If one sees the issue in more moral terms, then the answer may be no. Following Machiavelli's lead in assessing politics as it really is, so others did likewise in the study of human nature. Spinoza was amongst them, criticising utopian philosophers who 'conceive men not as they are but as they would like them to be'.[1] Much of social science still falls short by this measure.

Nation states have grown and transformed over time, and their constitutions have typically evolved with them or been based on pre-existing forms. The establishment of the US constitution was an exception, being constructed in a short period and substantially new, not a copy. With the Enlightenment came a rational discourse on politics and man, breaking free from the confines of religious thinking. It was understood that an individual may have countervailing passions, but it was a novel jump to believe the same may apply to the body politic and that compromise and balance might be a constitutional requirement. The three branches of government in the United States (legislative, executive and judiciary) were established to check each other, so that, according to 'Federalist 51', 'ambition must be made to counteract ambition'. Its effectiveness and longevity is a lasting credit to the thoughtfulness of its creators, as well as to George Washington's wisdom in stepping down from office when he did. It has proved a victory for Socratic over Platonic thought insofar as the question of who should rule has been supplemented by the more important one of how to hold power to account. This does not mean that the constitution has not been under threat, but it has survived those threats to date.

Concentrations of power can also occur outside formal politics. An incoming US President normally brings with him advisers from Wall Street. The two notable historical exceptions were Andrew Jackson and Theodore Roosevelt. When Roosevelt took office in 1901, the banker J. P. Morgan, who had assisted in the creation of several large national monopolies, did not get the call he expected from the new President. Large companies, with too much market power, can become anti-competitive bureaucratic rent-seekers. Although anti-trust (anti-monopoly) legislation was introduced in 1890, it was not much used initially, and by 1902 about 40 per cent of the nation's industrial capital was controlled by the top 100 firms. Roosevelt pursued an aggressive agenda to ensure better market competition, creating permanent administrative oversight and ensuring the break-up of some of the largest companies with monopoly power, including the railways, Rockefeller's Standard Oil Company and US Steel. The result was more healthy competition, which helped propel the US economy to greater prosperity. The divergence of economic performance from that of the country's southern neighbour, Mexico, which did not implement similar reforms, is clear. As with politics, so with commerce – too much concentrated power without proper checks and balances is not good. Just as people are anti-fragile, so too are our politics and our companies. Competition and challenge are good for them.

For some, the rejection of religion was essential for human progress. Stirner, echoing Socrates's lack of certainty and mirroring our current understanding that one can either have certain truth or science and progress, wrote: 'As long as you believe in the truth, you do not believe in yourself, and you are a ... servant, a ... religious man.'[2] Religion can take non-traditional forms, though. Feuerbach, the first of Hegel's students to break from him, argued that it was man who made God in his own image and not the other way round, but that the religion of humanity is still a religion. Despite the decline of religion, our ability to follow consensus blindly does seem undimmed. If we see the fascism and communism of the twentieth century as temporary aberrations from the enlightened path of our liberal democracies, not likely to be repeated, then I fear we are complacent. If so, we do not fully understand authoritarianism's rootedness in human nature, our ability to fool ourselves and well over 2,000 years of history.

Liberalism's continuous adaption and change is evidence that it is uncertain of itself and open to criticism. As with science, from doubt and scepticism comes progress. Enough people do not treat it as a religion and have been worried enough by its weaknesses to ensure its continued relevance and vibrancy. How to describe an ever-changing thing though? As Pluckrose and Lindsay put it, the easiest way to understand liberalism is as opposition to illiberalism, i.e. to totalitarian, hierarchical, censorious, feudal, patriarchal, colonial or theocratic states.

DEMOCRACY, THE STATE, THE CITIZEN

Both democracy and liberalism have developed in the context of the nation state, which has in turn been through several stages as sovereign power has been ceded to citizens. This shift of power, which has also made the state more stable, has been facilitated by developments in education and communications technology.[3] One does not have to deify the state, as Hegel does, in order to appreciate its robustness. The modern state's imminent demise has been exaggerated at least since before the First World War.

To be legitimate in a free society, the power of the central administration of the state has to be limited. John Stuart Mill set the standard for the promotion of individual liberty and the non-invasion of our private lives by the state. He argued for one very simple principle: 'The only purpose for which power can be rightfully exercised over any member of a civilized community, against his will, is to prevent harm to others.' Moreover, 'His own good, either physical or moral, is not a sufficient warrant.' Liberty of thought is absolute, and, with it, liberty of speech, essential for its own sake but also for truth, as truth requires challenge and absolute freedom of speech. No proscribed words in case they might offend others for Mill, for that would impinge too gravely on individual liberty.

Such absolute liberty can lead to people saying things which offend, and deliberately so. Different morals dictate different priorities, as discussed in Chapter 1. There are practical limits on liberty, for without them the civilised truce between those with different moral foundations may end, bringing conflict and with it a potential loss of liberty. There need to be exceptions to Mill's dictum of allowing people to do what they want as long they do not harm others, for the simple reason that people with different moral foundations define such harm differently.

Tocqueville, for example, considered religion essential for liberty, and one could argue that the religious wars of the seventeenth century support this view. Moreover, Mill was writing before we understood as much about social capital and trust, which moderates liberty in practice – there is a need for compromise and toleration in order for us to live together peacefully and constructively. Many of Mill's contemporaries and those who have written since do not go as far as him, having a list of reasoned exceptions. Kant's response was that freedom not be restricted beyond that which is necessary to ensure equal freedom for all. There is, however, more agreement that people should be able to think as they please than do as they please.

In contrast, Plato and his totalitarian followers would stamp out individuality. Liberals take this as an attack on people's humanity. Yet in order to prove Plato wrong about human nature, we have to achieve both liberty and altruism. We have to combine freedom with good governance. And this is not the same as freedom plus minimum government, which can easily alienate people from each other and erode social capital.

This is not easy. Democracy requires constant intelligent engagement to be effective and equitable. Citizens need some education so as to appreciate the value of democracy and to ensure they have a voice within it. They also have to care for democracy, believe it works (for them) and trust authority – trust which has to be earned. Legitimising compromises through participatory decision-making by political representatives is essential. Without it, destructive reactive tendencies can come to the fore. A constant problem, not least as they are more prone to groupthink, is that elites think they know best yet often don't. Failure by elites to consult sufficiently and listen and take account of what they hear is all too commonly cause for political dissatisfaction.

Necessary, constant, intelligent political engagement of citizens has nearly always been a struggle. Social media, by making people less tolerant, has caused more polarisation in politics, including amongst legislators.* Elites have neglected to spend sufficient effort to ensure their policies are understood and perceived as legitimate, instead drifting into technocratic solutions. After war there often follows disillusion – the vision of a better world can be disappointed. Without a unifying thread, numerous other disagreements come to the fore. The harmony war brings is temporary and fades, and a long period of peace can lead to complacency. These combined factors have fostered disillusion with democracy. According to a 2016 study, the share of young Americans who think it important to live in a democracy dropped to 57 per cent (from 91 per cent in the 1930s). Those who thought it would be good or very good to have military rule in the US rose from one in sixteen in 1995 to one in six in 2016.[4]

But just engaging with democratic politics is still not enough. Many people have not thought through where their own interests lie – a problem exacerbated by the lack of challenge to trite memes and by the immediate emotional gratification that many have grown used to. This problem is not without precedent. Spinoza observed: 'All men certainly seek their advantage, but seldom as sound reason dictates; in most cases appetite is their only guide, and in their desires and judgements of what is beneficial they are carried away by their passions, which take no account of the future

---

* In the UK Labour deputy leader Angela Rayner described Conservatives as 'homophobic, racist, misogynistic … scum', for which she later apologised, and Conservative Prime Minister Boris Johnson falsely smeared Sir Keir Starmer, Leader of the Opposition, accusing him of having failed to prosecute a notorious paedophile when Director of Public Prosecutions.

or of anything else.'[5] We learn to control such passions in favour of our interests. We build institutions and habits to assist us. But then social media comes along, and it seems we are back to square one.

Democracy requires a clash of ideas and thrives on challenge. Yet challenging the status quo can be difficult and dangerous. One of the most worrying things about our current deification of the precautionary motive is that by ignoring other priorities and costs it can cause major damage, and in its reckless focus can bypass not only rationality but also freedom. All too often fear is used to police its dogma. When we are told that an issue is too important to waste time on further discussion, but there clearly is time, our freedom is being demoted as a priority. Too often the objective of policy formation is seen as reaching the pre-conceived 'right' answer. If this is the objective then democracy and consultation, listening to a cacophony of views, seems like a waste of time. Yet not only is there wisdom in crowds, but democracy is also a muscle which will atrophy if not used. In other words, getting the 'right' answers is not the overriding objective when designing policy in a democracy – not least as being able to get the 'right' answer implemented so often depends on the cooperation of the public, which might not be forthcoming if the policy is viewed as technocratically imposed and illegitimate. Legitimacy matters. Electorates learn by making mistakes and so must be allowed to make them. Legislators must take electorates with them if they want their legacy to last. And this enables not prevents lasting reform.

Karl Popper said: 'Only democracy provides an institutional framework that permits reform without violence, and so the use of reason in political matters.'[6] Legal change is required to facilitate such reform. The only legal change which is not allowed is that which would threaten democracy. The rule of law protects political freedom from those in power. It protects the prejudices of the past from radical change, common law being particularly well suited to this. Tradition, institutions and norms of behaviour in turn protect us from our irrationality, especially when this is dressed up as rational. As Scruton puts it:

> The knowledge that we need in the unforeseeable circumstances of human life is neither derived from nor contained in the experience of a single person, nor can it be deduced *a priori* from universal laws. This knowledge is bequeathed to us by customs, institutions and habits of thought that have shaped themselves over generations, through the trials and errors of people many of whom have perished in the course of acquiring it.[7]

This fits with our appreciation, from Chapter 1, of how irrational we are, as well as with the theory and experience of the benefit of decentralised decision-making in politics, not least the inefficiency of its opposite, i.e. Soviet-style central planning.

As we move more to remote meetings, we should not forget that one of the most effective ways to reach compromise and decisions is through face-to-face discussion, as observed in America two centuries ago by Alexis de Tocqueville. We also mentioned the mass political party and its importance at the start of the chapter. These are important filters, brokering special interests to create compromises which people see as legitimate and will not seek to alter through violence. One reason why such filtering mechanisms are necessary is the huge diversity of political interests. The failings of authoritarian regimes is instructive, as for example in Brazil. The authoritarian rulers there, from Getulio Vargas (in power 1930–45 and then elected President again 1951–54) through to the end of military rule in 1985, still had to rule with consent. However, as the country urbanised, industrialised and became more complex, it became impossible for any set of policies to please more than a tiny minority. Hence chaos, military rule and then democracy.

AUTHORITARIANISM

Once societies reach a certain complexity, stability can only be sustained over long periods without coercion through using the filters of democracy to create consensus and compromise. The organic theory of the state, which equates the body politic to an organism, has been used to justify having a single commanding brain – a strong leader – yet the analogy is a misleading one: there is no upward striving, no class struggle, in an organism. History has shown us that entrusting power to a single individual is a gamble. Power corrupts. Moreover, words do not necessarily convey intent: they are tools of the manipulative politician. As Machiavelli inconveniently pointed out, successful leaders often show few scruples when they believe they can get away with it. Their words cannot be trusted unless they have an incentive to keep their word, as Banfield's Mezzogiorno villagers understood (discussed in Chapter 2). In short, there is no reliable way to ensure good governance if one does not possess, or gives up, sanction over those in power. Without such sanction, power is highly likely to be abused.

Long after the Athenians had lost the war against Sparta, oligarchs despised the people. Aristotle reports an oligarchic oath in vogue: 'I promise to be an enemy of the people and to do my best to give them bad advice.' Is it possible that such views are not only still held but have influence? It is not uncommon that elites think they know best. In many cases they do, but when affected by groupthink they often do not. Sometimes they fall into Plato's trap of thinking perfection on earth is somehow possible. We live in a world of inevitable compromise. To ignore this and impose supposedly correct solutions against the popular will can erode trust and support. Politicians, especially self-confident, capable, far-seeing ones, are often overcome by events. Political change cannot be arrested as Plato wished. Dreamers are, almost without exception, disappointed by reality. By trying to impose perfection too vigorously, one can create the very chaos one wishes to prevent or, worse, restrict freedom and start down the road to authoritarianism.

Hegel is, as Popper puts it, the missing link between Plato and modern totalitarians. The latter are indebted to him for his sublimation of human desires to the interest of the state and its leaders and to his sense of historical determinism. Marx's historicism is straight out of Hegel's songbook. He claimed: 'It is not the consciousness of man that determines his existence – rather it is his social existence that determines his consciousness.' In other words, Marx believed people malleable creatures whose actions and thoughts are determined by economic and historical forces. I am optimistic, but let's hope that the forces of surveillance capitalism do not prove him right. In such a world the state and its leader(s) become the font of moral wisdom and power. Freedom is taken from the people, who are cynically told that the state is working in their best interests.

Belief in a more perfect world may be a motivator for revolutionaries, but fear is the carthorse of totalitarianism. It breeds anger.

Lucretius said all political anger is bred from fear. Hence Orwell's Two Minutes Hate sessions in 1984 to release the anger which state-induced fear has caused. Hence also the need for an enemy to vent at – the other, 'Them', those outside our moral system, those whom we suspect do not accept our values. Not only is tolerance a casualty of totalitarianism, but intolerance is its clarion.

To keep fear most effective, punishment should be somewhat arbitrary. This creates more uncertainty and prevents people from trying to test limits. For example, Bergesen describes three common features of political witch hunts: they arise quickly, they involve crimes against the collective, and charges are trivial or fabricated. These characteristics describe witch hunts from the French Reign of Terror to Stalinist show trials. The innocent are often found guilty. The uncertainty of what is and what is not allowed helps breed self-censorship. Signs that this is occurring are apparent in what is not said and not reported in the media – there are common patterns in the things nobody talks about.

Willing support of the dominated is essential for totalitarianism. People's intelligence is used as a weapon against their own interests. Groupthink is manufactured, especially in the more erudite – useful idiots have always been used to spread propaganda. And they are most effective when they do not realise the unbalanced nature of their message.

The proselytising role was traditionally performed by priests. But once Marxism had spread agnosticism, the use of religion to appeal to the working classes was no longer the route to power it had been. It was replaced in the 1920s and 1930s by fascists, with a dose of historical determinism and Hegelian nationalism. When fearful people do not want political responsibility, they can be persuaded to vote for strongmen in the knowledge that they are giving up some freedom, in return, they hope, for order and a reduction of fear. Elected fascists contract with their electorate precisely this: trust me by giving me absolute power, and I will take away some freedom but I will act decisively to solve your problems. The burden of coping with life in 1930s Germany is a partial explanation for the rise of the Nazis. As alienation is now increasing, academics are warning of a democratic recession. Many liberal democracies could be moving to a more authoritarian future. Support is growing for rule by experts, by a strong leader or by the military.

Not only is technocratic rule broadly acceptable to much of the population, but it is much simpler for political leaders. The results are deliberate obfuscation and use of technical jargon, reliance on experts foisted into the public view to justify political decisions, and the explosive growth of independent agencies. Democracy is undermined when decisions are made by people who do not stand for election. Without oversight, ulterior motives come to the fore and bureaucracies create their own cancerous momentum and invent fictitious problems to solve. The public interest and original institutional goals can get lost as institutions shift from what Weber called substantive rationality to formal rationality, from focus on external goals to internal ones.

The more fear a leader can induce, the more compliance, the less dissent and so the more power they are handed. Constant vigilance is required to prevent such leaders getting into power and imposing their distorted views, their groupthink, on whole populations. Voters are responsible. To acquiesce in the election of a fascist, or worse to worship authoritarian power, is an act of irresponsible cowardice.

REVOLUTION

There is still, for many, a deep yearning for revolution, which comes from dissatisfaction with current social, economic and political conditions. Revolution may no longer be a near-term threat in the developed world, but it is worth spending a little time to consider the warning signs, or rather the lack of them. Whilst revolution is preceded by a range of dissatisfactions, there does not seem to be much pattern, though one feature is the talk of revolution. In *The Anatomy of Revolution*, Crane Brinton studied the English Civil War, French Revolution, American War of Independence and Russian Revolution. Revolution succeeds in part because it is unreasonable and has no qualms about dispensing with individual liberty. More reasonable and moderate attempts to overhaul society speedily typically end in failure, as resistance has time to organise and prevent change. As Robespierre bluntly put it: 'Virtue, without which terror is destructive; terror, without which virtue is impotent. Terror is only justice prompt, severe and inflexible; it is then an emanation of virtue.'

To commit the necessary violence, proponents of such views need to have no doubt in the moral truth of their argument, and there must be tight discipline of beliefs and actions in the revolutionary group – like religion, like groupthink. Brinton said that perhaps 'the most important uniformity in our four revolutions is that as gospels, as forms of religion, they are all universalist in aspiration and nationalist, exclusive, in ultimate fact. They end up with a God meant indeed for all mankind ... brought ... by a Chosen People'.[8] Effective revolutions, as with the most radical groupthinks facing major opposition, require total commitment by adherents, and being the chosen people on a mission from God helps them cement this.

Idealists can clearly cause a lot of problems. Kissinger said that the limitation of righteousness is the most fundamental political problem;[9] Popper that 'the attempt to make heaven on earth invariably produces hell'.[10] Revolutionaries are not, in their minds, doing anything but saving others. The enormous destruction and chaos they unleash, and the mess and damage they leave behind when they are done, are entirely inconsequential to their thinking except as means to induce fear and enforce compliance. We see the same intransigence in some of today's intolerant groupthink-infected radical activists.

Brinton lists five uniform features of his four revolutions. Firstly, echoing Plato's contention that revolution comes from dissent within the ruling class, is that all societies were on the up economically and dissention came from the relatively well-off. This, incidentally, together with the medieval struggles between popes and emperors and early kings against kings, counters Marx's overwhelming focus on class struggle. Secondly, feelings are strongest when classes are nearly equal and expectations are unmet. Liberal elites beware: in his memoirs of the French Revolution, Rivarol says it was not the taxes or lack of justice but the 'prejudice of nobility' which caused the bourgeois to instigate the revolution.[11] Thirdly, there is a transfer of allegiance of the intellectuals – i.e. groupthink in academic and media circles today is dangerous. Fourthly, government administration is inefficient – my contemporary take on this is that we should perhaps fear the possibility of inflationary chaos following years of excessive quantitative easing and absurd energy policy. Fifthly, many in the ruling class lose faith in their peers and become politically inept. The reader may notice worrying similarities with present conditions on all five counts.

The sequence of revolution also has some commonalities. Emergency centralisation of power comes first, together with suspension of individual civil rights/intrusion into normal private life. Next come changes to courts and legal procedures and suppression of dissenters, dictated by a small elite who hold a monopoly on power. Lastly, government power expands to control many more actions in society than before. I, for one, am glad I live in a country with common law, a sophisticated electorate and ancient traditions not easily dispensed with.

Just as pressure for revolution can build, so there is a limit to how much interference in their lives individuals will put up with from a revolutionary state. Most cannot sustain a life dictated by high ideals for long, which is why revolutionary fervour fades quickly. Revolutions invariably go wrong and lead to unintended consequences. This is because societies are complex and their institutions either brittle or resilient, not easily adaptable.

We should try to avoid revolution and see the warning signs. We should not be complacent. As Scruton says: 'Those who imagined, in 1989, that never again would an intellectual be caught defending the Leninist Party, or advocating the methods of Josef Stalin, had reckoned without the overwhelming power of nonsense.'[12] There are those who will support any lunatic cause in order to attack 'the system' – they support revolution for the sake of very little.

POLITICS IN THE AGE OF SOCIAL MEDIA

Alexis de Tocqueville, in a Platonic echo, warned that despotism was more to be feared in democratic ages because of the tendency to self-centredness. The recent moral shift in our leaders is noteworthy. What changed leading up to the 2016 US election was not a significant change in views of the electorate but a shift in the rhetoric of the candidates.[13] Why? We discussed in Chapter 3 the disruptive effect social media is having on society, leading to rising intolerance and mental illness in the young. Just as the printing press turned everyday folk into theologians, some of them fanatics, we now have a whole new generation of people communicating with each other without filters or compromise, which amounts to communicating without knowledge of how to do so constructively. Trust, morals and institutions are under threat, and mass groupthink, often expressed via shared values and shared views on certain charged issues, have become tribal identifiers. Barriers are being constructed, and communities within them. There is less contact with diverse opinions or tolerance of others than in a past more constrained by geography. The sense of 'us versus them' has strengthened such that both leftists and followers of Donald Trump can consider themselves victims.

Institutions are also under threat from postmodernism. The Occupy Movement may have fizzled, but it set a new pattern for activism in which emotional commitment is more important than knowledge. There has been a marked shift from peaceful demonstration within democratic norms to an intolerant anti-democratic insistence derived from moral certainty. Activists no longer respect the views of others or are even inquisitive about what they might be.

GROUP RIGHTS

Rights are seen as moral absolutes. Jeremy Bentham called them 'nonsense on stilts' in objection to their being arbitrary. He considered them designed simply to fit the prejudices and wants of those making them up. In a stable political democracy, citizens gain rights from the state in return for responsibilities. The most important responsibilities are abiding by decisions taken legitimately and electing representatives who are believed to be likely to act in the best interests of all. The problem is that identity politics can be tribal, intransigent and myopic. Moreover, from Plato through Hegel, Marx and now political correctness, individuality is seen as secondary to group identity and potentially harmful to political progress. Hence, rights are assigned to groups not just individuals. But you cannot make groups responsible in the same way as individuals; they remain fickle and may decline into destructive and self-destructive fanaticism. Freedom without responsibility results. Security diminishes. This feeds further tribalism. In practice, Plato's view on the incompatibility of individualism with altruism and responsibility rears in all its ugliness. The anti-democrats of today are those who cannot tolerate the views of others and do not accept the way decisions are made. Some use wealth and influence to lobby change. Others use disruption, violence or the threat of violence.

When rights are initially asserted, they are not created in a vacuum but also replace existing rights, rights which may have been established over generations of habit and customs. So, their replacement often leads to strong resentment and resistance. Hence, Aristotle emphasised anger as the response to status reduction. As mentioned in Chapter 5, Orwell said of socialists that they did not love the poor so much as hate the rich, and as just noted, the 'prejudice of nobility' can spur a revolution.

Radical changes to an existing arrangement of rights can have unintended and disruptive consequences, just as radical change to other institutions can. With many new rights now being made up, we also have new types of intolerance and conflict. We have moved from honour and dignity cultures to victimhood culture.

Hence though the common presumption is that more rights are always a good thing, sometimes they are not. As Collier and Kay point out,[14] from 1974 to 1984 the UK Paedophile Information Exchange advocated the rights of children to have sex with older men. Today, transgender and gender-critical groups conflict over who is entitled to use female toilets.*

Strong groupthink discipline amounts to an anti-individualist bias. Strong group adherence can be partly a reaction against the stress of personal responsibility, with rights to be provisioned by the state replacing responsibility for one's own life and decisions. We need to remind ourselves that with rights come responsibilities, for without this we all become takers from the state, giving back nothing. As Margaret Thatcher said: 'The problem with socialism is that you eventually run out of other people's money.'

Rights are not conducive to compromise. As mentioned, one person's rights can conflict with those of another. To have a right is a licence to be intolerant of anyone who does not respect it. The problem is amplified when people do not understand each other

---

* The first words from the host of an international conference I spoke at in Cambridge University recently concerned toilets, all of them unisex, he announced; some with and some without urinals, he added. Why was this top of the agenda? Our international guests took it in good grace, but I wonder what mental image of Britain they went back home with.

and, liberated from traditional geographical communities and the need for proximity in order to communicate, can shut out people with contrary views. We can have limited incentive to be tolerant, listen to strangers or be polite in public.

PRAGMATISM AND MORALITY

Nietzsche had little time for English moralists who talked of liberty but had not, in his view, escaped traditional religious morality. As social capital and trust based on religious morality was discarded, many feared selfishness would predominate to the detriment of society – many thought ethical behaviour could not survive the death of God. Perhaps, lip-service apart and echoing Machiavelli, we were never that dependent on religion. With the proviso that we master our passions to a minimum degree, and following the work of Douglass North in particular, I consider our behaviour and institutions largely determined by incentives (our interests), and more specifically our economic incentives. The only other consistently significant factor is technology, though tastes also play a role. Lack of religion does not mean lack of ethics or morality. Without religion we still need, and for the most part find, a moral compass. There has always been a minority who do not, but historically most disruptive have been conflicting moralities, not their absence.

People are rarely motivated in politics by anything but personal reasons, notably vanity. Indeed, such is the typical making of pure heroic action, not ideals. Vanity can lead to consistency. This in turn makes vain politicians understandable, if not predictable. This has the potential to engender a sense of reliability and with it trust, and so lead to effective power. In *The Coming Anarchy*,

Robert Kaplan points out the irony that it is the idealists who are often attracted to politics and who make the worst politicians. He suggests that reading Conrad, whose heroes are consistently vain, might provide a useful addition to their education.

Nietzsche perhaps takes English morality too much at face value. It was the lack of effective sanctions which helped the English to be practical without being obviously immoral by the standards of the day. A more rigid interpretation of morality may be more likely to result in obvious breaches by the dynamic and entrepreneurial. In other words, it is England's tolerance which has made it a civilised and pleasant place to live, not just English religion and philosophy, much of which has, in practice, been unconstraining.

It is this tolerance which is now under threat. With greater moral certainty, the electorate has less appetite for political hypocrisy. Yet, as David Runciman points out, due to the need for complicated compromises and different perspectives within the electorate, voters face a choice 'not between truth and lies, or sincerity and hypocrisy, but between politicians who are sincere but untruthful and those who are honest but hypocritical'.[15] The point is that hypocrisy is, at least from some people's perspective, inevitable in any politician given enough exposure. A statement made by a politician means different things to different people and comes with different contradictions with other statements and actions. Thus a politician, who can also no longer keep secrets or deliver different messages to different audiences, cannot both appear consistently sincere (non-hypocritical) and be truthful.

The divisions in society are increasingly seen by those steeped in groupthink as moral ones between the virtuous and the evil.

The more traditional and conservative see this as misguided and unnecessarily divisive. With politics becoming a moral contest, mutual trust and respect declines and compromise becomes more difficult. As Jonathan Haidt explained in *The Righteous Mind*, the moral foundation of liberals/Democrats is more focused. This makes their understanding of the conservative/Republican mind more difficult than vice versa. The widespread Democrat view that Republican voters are simply stupid is neither credible nor helpful, and indeed has been used to make the case for replacing democracy with more authoritarian rule.* Pragmatism suffers.

NATIONS AND THEIR FOREIGN POLICY

Identity politics is also blurring national loyalties. Nations, which have been more than tribes since Alexander the Great, have a long and successful history. But the nation state has evolved many times, and with it the relationship between rulers and ruled. After the Thirty Years War, the Treaty of Westphalia (1648) established the principle of non-intervention in the internal affairs of neighbouring states. This conflicts with the predisposition of countries to build empires, including interfering for 'the greater good'. President Wilson's promotion of national self-determination has also conflicted with the non-interference principle. Multiple identities and identity groups which ignore geography form the latest challenge to the state. It is fashionable in some circles to think of oneself as a citizen of the world. But dreams of a post-nation state world are still premature. There is a strong dose of fantasy about potential and actual harmony in the world. International politics is often

---

* Jason Brennan describes US voters as either hobbits (who do not want to know) or hooligans (who are fanatics).

about real disagreements, not value-neutral cases of misunder-standing. The UN is part of this fantasy, its longevity not due to its effectiveness as a source of political power but to the veto power of the permanent members of the security council. It poses little threat to existing power relations and is not a world government or decision-making body. It is, however, a beacon of hope and at its best a venue for constructive discussion.

Whilst there is an important place for multilateralism, foreign policy is still mainly between nations. It tends to be either realis-tic and in the national interest, with sacrifices sometimes being necessary and provided by citizens, or mere puff – expressions of domestic politics which, when push comes to shove, are found to be insubstantial and for which citizens are unlikely to make sacri-fices. Lord Palmerston said nations have neither perpetual friends nor enemies, only permanent interests – in other words, foreign policy is not about 'us versus them' but should be thought of as a coping mechanism amongst nations. There are those who think they know best for all concerned – we can call them imperialists. Others see the problems of foreign policy more akin to a market where each nation has different preferences but agree to numerous compromises which are mutually beneficial. The latter is a more realistic description. It puts lofty opinions about the role of interna-tional organisations and international law (a set of treaties between nation states) in perspective.

Defining the national interest is not easy. Different constituen-cies want different things. The politically tempting option is often not to have a foreign policy but just pretend – i.e. foreign policy becomes merely an expression of domestic policy. Unfortunately, this often leads to muddled thinking and disastrous results. Lack of focus is particularly common after a long period of peace. The Cold War was an extension of the Second World War. The objectives of foreign policy were clear and set within a joint memory which ensured domestic political support. Since the end of the Cold War, things have become much more confused. The strategic leadership of the US has largely failed to adapt. Extending NATO against the warnings of Kennan and others, and after a promise not to do so in exchange for the recognition of a united Germany, has proved a particularly egregious mistake. As one Russian close to power expressed their disappointment to me: 'We used to think you in the West hated communism like us, but now we realise you hate us Russians.' Whether true or not, this perception is an important cause of misunderstanding and tension.

Doing good abroad is the new missionary movement. Social media and political correctness have fed a move in foreign policy towards myopia and pleasing soundbites, and sometimes away from long-term national interests. Follow-through on the early foreign policy optimism of the Obama years in the Middle East, for example, evaporated fairly fast. Without a clear focus on the national interest, further drift towards the ineffectual, the contradictory and the damaging in relations between nations can be expected. For foreign policy to have teeth it needs the credibility that it will be adhered to in adverse situations, possibly requiring citizens to fight, pay taxes or make other sacrifices. For this, it needs to be perceived as in the national interest. Reinhold Niebuhr was influential in post-Second World War Washington, warning that power combined with pride can cause blindness. He specifically warned against the folly of foreign policy being shaped by a sense of destiny. Yet as described by Andrew Bacevich, Niebuhr's many powerful

US admirers from Presidents downwards considered this aspect of his views did not apply to them.[16] As mentioned, it is not uncommon for adherents of groupthink to believe they are a chosen people by God, be it in the form of US manifest destiny, British imperialist jingoism or the desire for world communism. From Vietnam to Afghanistan, US intervention has often lasted much longer than originally planned, been more costly than expected in lives and money and fed fear of, and antagonism towards, the US. As previously mentioned, it was the Bay of Pigs invasion of Cuba which Irving Janis referred to when he coined the term groupthink. Much foreign policy and international conflict remains rife with inflexible ideas, sustained through ignoring signs which do not fit preconceived ideas. And many voters, across the political spectrum, are getting wise to how ineffective much of what passes for foreign policy is. It does not promote the national interest and, worse, is often incompetent. That Europe did not foresee and prevent Russia's invasion of Ukraine, and moreover became dependent on Russian gas, is a case in point (which is not to criticise one way or the other the Western response since the invasion).

DYSFUNCTIONAL VISIONS

We should remind ourselves that uncertainty was always there for our ancestors, as it is for us. I do not know if uncertainty is high by historical standards – that is probably unknowable. It is not prosperity which has led to our fearfulness. Even the disruptive force of today's rapid technological change, as we saw in Chapter 3, has precedents in past communications revolutions. I don't think an intelligent ancestor of 200 years ago would necessarily lack comprehension of some of the issues we worry about today, though the history behind current debates would need to be adequately explained. So, maybe we can learn from history, at least from what appear to be warning signals and huge mistakes. The irresponsible idea that we are now beyond history – i.e. that now is a special time in which we can no longer learn from the past – has no foundation, though it does have precedents in totalitarian regimes.

The word totalitarianism only came into existence in the twentieth century, but authoritarianism has threatened freedom throughout history. Totalitarianism in the twentieth century ruthlessly aimed to reengineer the human soul, destroy individualism and dominate all political power at the centre. The imagined threat of a totalitarian future is perhaps best captured by George Orwell's *1984*. Today's would-be controllers of human minds are not as similarly willing to commit genocide but try to achieve their objectives more through psychological than physical methods. There are also now two sources of power vying to achieve a hold on people's behaviour. Governments use fear, 'emergencies' and behavioural manipulation as well as, perhaps less intentionally, moral suasion and groupthink. But we also have commercial interests, the new Big Tech companies, which wish to manipulate individual behaviour and programme consumers to be more compliant and predictable. They wish to maintain the ability to steal personal data and then exploit it. To reduce the risk from legislators – who if they tried could do a lot more to uphold privacy and freedom and so seriously damage the Big Tech business model – they employ several strategies. As mentioned in Chapter 3, they engage in heavy lobbying, research funding and the revolving door. Increasingly, they also use the threat of ostracism from their networks. They also offer potential reward for political allies through the ability not merely to predict but to influence electoral politics. What they and authoritarian governments share amounts to an attack on dissent, liberty, privacy and individualism.

Two centuries ago, the balance was being debated between on the one hand the desire for political power and influence and on the other hand material gain. If the interests were to become the overwhelming focus of the population (they get hooked on hedonism), the concern was that this may leave the way clear for tyranny. Insofar as this is now happening, Aldous Huxley's *Brave New World* is perhaps a more likely dystopian vision of the future than Orwell's *1984*. In Huxley's vision, people are genetically and emotionally controlled from birth. They are unaware of being manipulated. A modern version of the same vision is the film *The Matrix*, in which machines have taken over the world and are using human beings as batteries. People are kept compliant through feeds into their brains which make them believe they inhabit an entirely fictitious simulated reality.

For the past seventy-five years, the majority in the US and Western Europe have been able safely to ignore much of what passes for intellectual and political debate. They have done so in the knowledge that they cannot influence events and thus need not worry themselves unduly. This may now be changing. New communications technology has given us more political voice. Increasingly, we feel we have to use it, if only to counter waves of nonsense. Others simply disengage from politics. There have always been visionaries/doomsayers. Now we are not only being told ever more loudly to worry about things beyond our control, but many of us are listening. People are being seduced by the emotional pull of the urgent existential threat. And there is nothing historically unusual about vast masses being led by ideology and dogma in more authoritarian and religious times. Hence, we should not be surprised by the existence of some massive irrationalities in politics and society today.

Those of us fortunate enough to live in the developed world have been spared much collective oppression, pain and angst in recent decades. But the fear of disagreement has started to rise again. We like to convince ourselves that we value freedom of expression, yet the number of taboo topics and words is increasing. Since the end of the Cold War and the reduced (but still not negligible) risk of nuclear holocaust, we have not faced the same imminent existential threat. But with global warming we are being told that we do once again face such a threat. We are expected to believe, yet there is something very unconvincing about this new collective fear. It remains every citizen's responsibility, in order to guard against the loss of freedom, to think critically. It has become increasingly difficult to do so.

A more important question than 'Why obey the machine?' is 'Why support it?' Trite memes and cliches are the traps which Orwell's Newspeak was designed to create for us. As we limit our vocabulary, avoid politically incorrect words and thoughts, so we become more controllable, but also less human. We need spaces where we can express our thoughts freely, yet new communications technology increasingly does not provide this.

THE CASE FOR OPTIMISM

Thanks to liberalism and science, we are doing much better than commonly perceived. However, democracy requires active citizen participation if it is to remain vigorous. It is constantly under threat from many in our elites who think they know better. For those who subscribe to Churchill's famous quote that democracy is the worst form of government except for all those other forms that have been tried from time to time, and so think it worth saving, we have a task ahead. We must counter the tendency of social media to pander to our immediate hedonistic desires and emotions. We should prove wrong Plato's belief that individual legal entitlements undermine moral responsibilities. We should build social capital and trust, including a focus on support for geographical communities. We should limit the use of fear by government, for its own sake but also to preserve trust in government and social capital. Rights were seen by Franklin Roosevelt, who embedded them in his New Deal, as an equaliser which gives us protection from envy. Social media, certain features of which, as discussed, we are still learning to adapt to and control, has clearly been of huge benefit in allowing rights to be exercised and has greatly empowered many previously unempowered. For example, it took the #MeToo movement to reassert the right not to be sexually harassed.

We can legislate to ensure Big Tech continues to bring benefits but does not unreasonably infringe on our privacy and freedom, mainly through more effective restrictions on its use of personal data. We can also stop its promotion of propaganda. To achieve this we need not more top-down censorship (which will inevitably arbitrarily discriminate against some and buttress groupthink) but a better attempt to help internet and social media users avoid harm to themselves and others. We should also clearly segregate and label partisan interference in electoral politics as we attempt to do in other media.

It is disappointing that measures to help us overcome current threats to democracy have not been taken, but it is a cause for optimism that such measures are available. One of the aspects of groupthink is that it affects the elite more than others. Hence, it is a source of hope that many of us are not part of the political and media elites and do not suffer their illusions. We do not buy the fear and various nonsenses propagated. We know that elites often simply do not know best, despite their adamant view that they do.

At some point it is to be hoped that all supporters of democracy will appreciate that it is in their interests to dial down the fear. Only then will rational debate have a chance to reassert itself. Politicians need to reconnect with electorates, listen, rebuild trust. Local geographical communities should be supported and nurtured, enabling interaction with and tolerance for people met randomly with diverse views and values. This is all achievable but requires a complete change from the current direction of travel. It requires leadership not currently visible.

As societies become more complex and diverse, the challenge of democracy is not the ever more futile goal of control but the nurturing of institutions which enable political participation. This requires the means to create legitimate compromises. We come back to the Labour Party and the sense it would make to give MPs back more say in electing their leader. The mass membership political party is worth saving. But we also perhaps need additional fora to help generate compromises and assist policy-makers in the manufacture of policies which are both legitimate and practical. A reformed Big Tech sector could help us with this. What we need less of is succour to people viewing politics through the pre-modern, pre-Machiavellian eyes of good versus evil.

Finally, Brazilian political history offers another lesson. Even after the fall of the military in 1985, politicians were still wedded to local state political identities. Luiz Inácio Lula da Silva was the first candidate with truly national appeal. In becoming a national figure, he also constantly mentioned the poor, and in so doing he empowered them. Electorates learn by making mistakes, so an energised big category of newly active voters was disruptive. The newly empowered had to make many of the same mistakes that those long politically active had already made and learned from. Whilst looking like a step backwards, this was more a hysteresis or ratcheting. In a similar way, social media is leading to a Great Enfranchisement, which is initially chaotic and will continue to be until people learn how to behave – largely, unfortunately, through making and then learning from mistakes. However, so long as our leaders learn to accommodate new voices, which means listening to them better, and so long as democratic institutions survive, then things will calm down as they have in the past. Our goal should be to minimise the disruption and risks during this transformation – hoping for a bright future in which responsibility catches up with our new capacities to communicate. We can start with what has worked and still works – courage, reason, science, tolerance and an appreciation of history.

SUMMARY

- The struggle between authoritarianism and democracy has a long history. Plato was preoccupied with who should rule – he thought the wise. Yet a more important question is whether there are effective measures to hold power to account. Competition in politics is good for us, as it is in business.

- John Stuart Mill argued against interference with individual liberty except where an individual's actions hurt others. However, defining what hurts others is a moral question, and different moral systems give different answers. It is the coexistence of different moral systems, not the absence of religion per se, which causes most conflict.

- Democratic responsibility cannot be ignored. Delegating it to our leaders, trusting them without means to hold them to account, most obviously through electing a fascist leader, is not only a gamble but an act of irresponsible cowardice.

- Yet authoritarian rule is seen by many as an attractive alternative to democracy. This is in the context of increased moral conflict in politics and less tolerance, both functions of new communication technology and patterns. Not only is tolerance a casualty of totalitarianism but intolerance is its clarion.

- Revolution often gives few warnings, but signs of anti-democratic tendencies and fanaticism have increased. There is no shortage of people prepared to believe in dangerous nonsense and who support revolution for the sake of very little.

- Rights are transferred, not created. They can reduce envy but are often arbitrary, designed simply to fit the prejudices and wants of those lobbying for and establishing them. One can have too much of a good thing, and group as opposed to individual rights can lead to irresponsibility.

- Political elites often think they know best and that the aim of policy is to attain the 'right' solution. Fear is used to manipulate behaviour at the cost of social capital and trust in our governments. The precautionary motive sidelines rationality but also freedom. Yet democracy is a muscle which atrophies if not used, and voters learn most through making mistakes. Taking that option away with a drift to technocracy is a threat to democracy and freedom.

- The nation state is still robust and useful. However, poor or non-existent foreign policy is increasingly a derivative of domestic groupthink and a sign of irrationality and incompetence in government.
- The changes in communications technology mean we in the West are now being drawn into political debate and conflict more than we have been for seventy-five years. Both governments and Big Tech are trying to manipulate our behaviour, and this requires conscious responses if we wish to preserve our freedoms.

CHAPTER 7

MEDIA AND ELITE BUBBLES

'The essential English leadership secret does not depend on particular intelligence. Rather, it depends on a remarkably stupid thick-headedness. The English follow the principle that when one lies, one should lie big, and stick to it. They keep up their lies, even at the risk of looking ridiculous.'

JOSEPH GOEBBELS

In the early 1990s, I worked in the Strategic Planning Office of the Inter-American Development Bank (IDB), two thirds the size of the World Bank and the main official lender for Latin America. The office was housed within the plans and programs department, which was amongst other things in charge of fast-disbursing loans amounting to about a quarter of the bank's lending. The department's manager was a former US Treasury official. Some of the loans were politically sensitive, for example money to rehouse soldiers in Central America. They were directed through the IDB instead of through the US's official aid administration (AID) or the World Bank, in part, one suspects, to avoid close outside scrutiny.

In a sense the department I was in was a bank within a bank – the US-controlled part of the IDB.

At this time, the 'Washington Consensus' had hardened from a collection of ten policies which Latin American countries had found useful into a dogma.* One of these ten policies was privatisation. Yet there was also a reaction against privatisation in parts of Latin America – a referendum against the sale of a publicly owned water company had just won in Uruguay, for example. The IDB's research department had done a lot of work on the issue. However, when I wrote a technical guide on when and how to privatise – an effort to take some of the ideology out of the debate and preserve what was useful – my paper was banned from distribution. Specifically, it was banned by the department manager, not from distribution outside the bank but from distribution outside the department.

One of his deputies invited me to his office, where it was explained to me that there was nothing wrong with the content of the paper. However, whilst other areas of the bank had published numerous studies of the topic, and that was all fine and well, our department, in contrast, could not be seen to question any aspect of privatisation. The parallel which occurred to me shortly afterwards was that of Umberto Eco's book (and film starring Sean Connery) *The Name of Rose*. Set in a monastery in the Middle Ages, there is a secret Aristotelian text in the library considered contrary to contemporary religious dogma. After a number of mysterious murders, the library is burnt down to prevent such sinful knowledge

---

* As related by Frances Stewart in *Comment on John Williamson and the Washington Consensus Revisited*, in 1997, the 'Washington Consensus' was initially a Latin American, not a US, consensus coming out of a 1989 conference but cleverly coined to garner US support.

being disseminated. I was similarly being told that knowledge was sin.*

PROPAGANDA VERSUS NEWS

As discussed in Chapter 1, much of our thinking is less reasoned than we imagine, and with greater intelligence and education often comes not more rationality but a greater ability to convince ourselves that we are rational when we are not. It is thus understandable if states (and companies) try to channel our thoughts. Certain messages, if repeated enough and not otherwise contradicted, can pass unquestioned. These can include advertising slogans, political soundbites and gossip, and range from the idea that bulls get angry when they see red to the idea that we fully understand the science of climate change, to that breakfast is the most important meal of the day. Another way to channel thoughts is for certain concepts and words to be off limits, and the most effective form of censorship is self-censorship, with fear the tool of choice for ensuring discipline.

Propaganda is defined as the unbalanced dissemination of half-facts and lies intended to deceive. Importantly, it does not require

---

* Unfortunately for the manager, an earlier draft of my paper had gone to someone at the World Bank for comment. Without my knowledge, photocopiers were soon employed across Washington, copying the draft: the fact it had been banned meant everybody wanted to read it. Sir William Ryrie, head of the IFC (the private lending arm of the World Bank), who had not seen eye to eye with Mrs Thatcher on privatisation when a senior British civil servant, immediately invited me to lunch. The paper was translated and published in Brazil, again without my knowledge, and I am told was used as teaching material at Johns Hopkins University. All this did me no harm. I had also passed a test inside the IDB as far as many senior Latin American figures were concerned (many of whom had been Finance Ministers or had held other senior ministerial positions previously back home). They subsequently took me into their confidences a little more than they might otherwise have done, which helped me understand a great deal more about Latin American politics.

unambiguous falsehoods. If one defines a lie in a narrow sense of saying something one knows to be untrue, then they are not essential for propaganda. Lawyers typically take such a narrow approach, and careful wordsmithing is often used as a way to mislead and cheat in many contexts. A clearer ethical division is whether there is intent to deceive. If we define a lie as any deliberate attempt to mislead, including through the biased selection of facts, then propaganda does require lies.

So, propaganda does require the intention to deceive and we can say it is a form of lying. One may also unwittingly be used to distribute others' propaganda. In the case of journalists, this can result from sloppiness – such as, not seeking alternative views to see if an interpretation stands up to scrutiny. However, it is the ethical responsibility of the journalist to consider if their sources are biased and to try to ensure impartiality. The reason is, as with science, that without a separation between facts and motives, reason is abandoned in favour of emotions, morals and the noisiness of those making a case. The result is all too often deception and misrepresentation. Another way of putting it is to say that journalists, similar to scientists, are entrusted to search out the truth in an objective, impartial manner.

As an example of when propaganda does not require a factual error, suppose that within the context of the prospects for global sea level changes, there are two highly relevant facts known to scientists about the changing mass of ice in the Antarctic. The first is that the continent's glaciers are calving at an increased rate, with more ice floating into the ocean. The second is that precipitation has increased across the continent, adding on average an extra 1.7cm to the icecap every year (this mass of extra ice amounting to more than that being lost through calving). If one's propaganda purpose is to scare people into thinking that the Antarctic ice cap (constituting about 90 per cent of the world's ice) is melting at an alarming rate one could present the first fact and ignore the second. In doing so, one would not be making a factually incorrect statement, but one could easily be accused of presenting a misleading picture. If one does this deliberately, knowing both facts to be true, then one is creating propaganda.

There are some other aspects of propaganda which may seem familiar. A rule of thumb for the propagandist is to have a clear, simple message and repeat it constantly, to saturation. The emotions should be played to, and moral messaging should be ever present. This makes it easier to avoid any contrary arguments, but these can occasionally be presented in a simplistic and negative way so as to be discounted. This helps maintain the pretence of impartiality and so gives credibility. Also, opponents should continuously be attacked, and particular adversaries picked out for vilification.

Not all persuasion is propaganda. Advertising and branding are seen as largely inevitable, if not always acceptable. The purpose of advertising is not simply to make associations which speak to our inner elephant but to signal a company's commitment to their product. To be effective, propaganda and advertising both use psychological manipulation to get people to do things they otherwise wouldn't, and they work best when repeated many times.

One of the features of mass groupthink is the reassurance of being in a large group of people who all think the same. It makes it easy to assume one is not in error. That confidence leads to us not bothering to check. We trust the crowd even when another part of our brain tells us they can be disastrously wrong. We just don't think it applies to us. Add to that the severe cost of stepping out of line, such as being 'cancelled' – the discipline of the group – and many people, even if they are slightly uneasy in the groupthink, will not publicly speak against it.

Some form of indoctrination, like other lies, may also be justified by the greater good. In wartime, it may even be expected, though to be most effective people will still need to be unaware of exactly what part of what they are told is propaganda and what is not. During war, people are most willing to suspend their freedoms, including thinking for themselves, in the interests of the greater group. Consistent and repetitive lying, and even the creation of false facts, are key components, as is emotional manipulation. All of this was apparent during the Second World War. It was understood that state broadcasts were designed to contribute to the war effort, and this for some if not all countries included not just careful selection of news but unbalanced interpretation and falsification.

Propaganda works best, however, if people are not aware of it at all, and this is a key distinction from a lot of commercial branding and advertising. Those doing the manipulation may also consider it acceptable for the greater good, so long as people do not perceive it. The ethically dubious idea is that if people are hoodwinked but don't know it, then they are no worse off. Aside from ethical objections, there are several practical problems to this view. Firstly, propaganda is anti-democratic and perverts and dilutes the checks and balances on our leaders. Dumbing down is a recipe for more groupthink and more dubious decisions, as well as more abuse of power. Secondly, people may suspect they are being lied to, even if they cannot definitely pinpoint propaganda. They may reasonably perceive it as an infringement of their liberty. Once you learn you are being unjustly lied to, it is difficult to unlearn it. Thirdly, this in turn can erode trust in government and undermine social capital, which can reduce cooperation with future government policies. It can also radicalise. Fourthly, knowing one can manipulate people and get away with it is not good for the manipulators. It dehumanises them, possibly making them feel superior, despising and intolerant of the manipulated. It can reinforce the often false perception of knowing what is best for others better than they do themselves.

However, the most entrenched groupthink is so well established that even those propagating it are unaware they are doing so. Brainwashing eventually reaches a point where the ideology is so internalised that people have no idea they are captured by groupthink. This can be true for those in the business of pushing ideological messages in the media even more than for those on the receiving end, not least as discipline is severe if one steps out of line.

Today's versions of media groupthink are a great deal more subtle than in the totalitarian states of the twentieth century. There is freedom to think, and robust debate is mimicked, but always within the constraints of well-established certainties which cannot be questioned – as we have seen, a lot of what looks like rebellion also occurs within groupthink boundaries. To best hide propaganda, one must mimic balanced debate. It is essential to present certain permitted forms of dissent and disagreement, so these can be examined and appropriately discounted. This is indeed a skill, typically involving substantial distraction. An issue will be raised, skirted round, but not addressed. Straw men will be set up to be knocked down in a predictable way. The entertainment of professional wrestling comes to mind – is it all just theatre? One suspects it is largely fixed, but we are not entirely sure. It looks real, with plenty of people going along with it. This is important, not least to preserve the motivation of those working within propaganda administrations.

Quite distinctive and revelatory is that when the mask drops, for whatever reason, the reaction is to ignore it and quickly move on. Explanations can be found to explain any breach. Facts which are contrary to the propaganda are ignored, even when proven, accepted and obvious. The flexibility of dialectic and other forms of bogus reasoning is that contradiction can be insufficient to break an argument; it is simply assimilated, discounted and ignored. Even if there is a series of scandals or failures, they can all be described as one-off events. Debate of inconvenient events and facts soon shuts down.

Why use propaganda in a democracy? Its presumption is that the public is better off with than without it, prefers it or cannot be trusted with the truth. Central is the arrogance of those in power who believe they know best. Plato not only thought the wise – himself – best qualified to rule but also saw the merit in leaders themselves believing in their own propaganda. He saw it as the best way to arrest all further political change. So, being the giant of philosophy he unquestionably was, not only did he consider he knew best how to manage a country, but he thought no one in the future would have anything useful to add. This is consistent with his concept of perfection and the gradual corruption of all earthly things. His political task was to try to preserve the pure for as long as possible against inevitable decay. There is no overall progress in his conception, only an effort to stem decline. Most people do not today share this depressing view of history, not least given the impressive progress of mankind over the past few hundred years.

Yet we still have arrogant leaders, not remotely in Plato's intellectual league, who believe they know best what others should do and think.

Plato's view that people cannot be trusted with freedom of action or thought is still with us. In Chapter 6, we discussed the importance of filtering mechanisms to help reach consensus. Another approach is to create unanimity by channelling thought. Orwell's Newspeak redefines words to mean their opposite, so, for example, the Ministry of Peace wages war. Today, words have also been morphed into new meanings. One could describe postmodernism, and much else in modern philosophy, as an effort to confuse, to destroy reason. Those who would uphold and defend democracy we now call 'populists' and 'nationalists' as terms of abuse. Those who would question the new green dogma are denigrated as 'sceptics' or even 'deniers', when in fact scepticism is the basis of all science.

JOURNALISM VERSUS ACTIVISM

In Chapter 3, we mentioned the challenges facing journalism from Big Tech. Two additional problems face newspapers and television news today. The first is a slide away from objectivity. People have different definitional interpretations, but one can think of three types of writing, all of which pass for journalism, which I shall call reporting, impartial journalism, and opinion forming or activism. A reporter simply writes down facts in as dispassionate a way as possible, adding some explanation and background maybe to aid comprehension. An impartial journalist will add more interpretation to help the reader/viewer understand the implications of a story. An opinion former or activist does not attempt to present an impartial case though may include opposing arguments so as to discount them.* They have a view and want to influence the audience. The line between what I have called impartial journalism and activism is a matter of semantics and degree, but a simple test is whether the reader/viewer can ascertain what the view of the writer/presenter is. If so, then there is at least some activism. We have moved from the role of journalism being to make sense of the world from examination of third-party sources to being a matter of advocacy. With such advocacy, the individual becomes a public personality separate from the profession of journalist. This is attractive to their ego, as it panders to the inner guru. Significantly, an associated shift is from trusting the reader/viewer to make their own mind up given the evidence, to not doing so.

Activism in practice is often revealed by the sequence in which arguments are assembled. An objective approach will try to find all evidence, not simply the easily to hand. It may take considerable effort to source and think through opposing views. Then conclusions are drawn. An activist approach is much less time consuming – deciding what spin or conclusion one wants and then finding the evidence to support it. The reasons this leads to lack of impartiality are, I hope, obvious, but one way of clarifying the issue is by using our definition of a lie as anything which deliberately misleads, and that includes selective provision of information and selective exclusion of contrary information. In other words, the defence that everything written or said is true is not enough; for seeing through efforts to mislead in a law court one does not only listen to a prosecutor. There is also a defence and then a judge, the reader/viewer being the ultimate judge in the case of journalistic offerings.

---

* Impartiality should be distinguished from balance, which is just the giving of space or airtime to opposing views.

Some might argue over definitions, saying I have just described the line between reportage and journalism, not between journalism and activism, but the simple test remains a valid one. Unfortunately, one could argue that activism is now the norm, impartial journalism the exception. A tiny fraction of articles present alternative views in an impartial way. They do often present two sides, but they then give the reader a clear steer by countering and discounting the non-preferred view, which may thus appear incorrect, morally wrong or outweighed by other factors. Even the attempt to achieve real balance, let alone impartiality, is but a distant memory for some.

A second, related, problem with journalism is the increase in groupthink. A lot are cynics, but many activists believe they are impartial. The natural tendency of most who have discovered a truth is to think they have reached it carefully and reasonably, having considered the alternatives. The tendency is to think this whether it is the case or not. Many activists believe themselves to be journalists. But activism can be thought of as the opposite of impartial journalism. It is intended to push a particular view, propaganda, whereas journalism should aid independent thought and consideration and respect the audience's capacity to form their own conclusions. Significantly, activism turns a lot of customers away who can see the difference – another reason why much of mainstream media is in trouble when one can get reaffirmation of one's existing views elsewhere.

Objectivity is difficult when one's audience is already within a single group. Some readers/viewers want the assurance of apparent objectivity but do not want challenges to their views. Being objective can lose a journalist their job. In such a working environment, no more than a cursory effort is made to speak to or convert opponents, few of whom will anyway pay attention to the arguments. However, the better newspapers are a broader church than social media networks. Political blogs may lie somewhere in between, though liberal and conservative political blogs in the US have been shown to form two clearly separate groups with few links between them. As William Blake said: 'When I tell any truth it is not for the sake of convincing those who do not know it, but for the sake of defending those that do.'

A further facet of journalism in the presence of groupthink is that repeated arguments fuel themselves and can lead to major distortions in perception, as well as media hysteria. Hans Rosling's book *Factfulness* is a catalogue of systematic pessimism and distorted views on global health, well-being and development. This pessimism is largely due to our lack of balance and impartiality in media articles, but also ridiculous imbalance in what is covered.[1] As a small example, getting fed up with the exaggerated coverage over swine flu in 2009, Rosling worked out that in a two-week period, thirty-one people had died of it, but a Google search brought up 253,442 related articles. Meanwhile, about 63,000 had died of tuberculosis. This distortion and pessimism in worldviews is fairly ubiquitous. A survey of multiple-choice questions Rosling presents at the start of his book has been answered in a similar way by thousands of people with different backgrounds and education, yet the results are consistently distorted. People are unaware of enormous progress and are especially full of the prejudice against developing countries, which in a financial sector context I coined 'Core/Periphery disease' in my first book. It is one thing to think one has discounted the normal bias of editors that comes with their objective of selling newspapers, but most of us still massively underestimate progress and good news. I suspect that the gulf between reality and perception is now growing faster than ever.* If we are all so incapable of adjusting for media bias in something as well documented and evident as global social and economic development, what else are we unwarrantedly pessimistic and misinformed about?

We should not forget that the goal of a newspaper is to sell newspapers and please advertisers. The media often lacks the ability to drag its focus away from the immediate present, which it sensationalises. It has no sense of shame in its inconsistency. It tries to jump onto moral bandwagons and motivate readers/viewers by appealing to their emotions and morals. It backbites but lacks irony. Moreover, in a society at peace, less accountability is required from the media than in wartime, when there is more at stake.

A government which wishes to use fear to mould the population to its designs – i.e. one which has less than full respect for its citizens' abilities to make informed choices and thinks it knows better – may find a groupthink-riddled media well used to pushing propaganda a boon. This is so long as the media is not wedded to constantly attacking the government too fiercely. Once there is a common goal, or at least an understanding, the media may be counted on to be cooperative/complicit.

There are good examples where most people would agree government persuasion, if not propaganda, is justified – campaigns for vaccination or against smoking, poor diet or unsafe driving,

---

* I believe it is possible to compensate for the bias, but as someone who has spent years trying to do this (and although I cannot completely discount the possibility that I am becoming more prejudiced), I find newspapers less and less useful. Television news is much worse, almost entirely pointless except as a form of entertainment.

for example. However, there is a point beyond which government nudging and media support for it become excessively deleterious to individual liberty and even infringe on electoral choices. It is difficult to gauge where that line is, but there is a clear difference between making a strong case following a full, balanced assessment of the costs and benefits, and widespread distortion of facts to achieve a controversial, contentious and hidden goal.

There is also something fundamentally objectionable to attempts to inflict fear of catastrophe on a whole population. We should be focusing on hope, not fear. As Martha C. Nussbaum says:

> Fear is connected to the monarchical desire to control others rather than to trust them to be independent and themselves … Martin Luther King Jr. understood that a fearful approach to the future of race relations would play into the hands of those who sought to manage things by violence … His emphasis on hope was an attempt to flip the switch, getting people to dwell mentally on good outcomes that could come about through peaceful work and cooperation.[2]

How opposite this attitude appears to much of current activism on race issues. Likewise Churchill motivated Britain to fight on in the darkest days of the Second World War not by hiding the arduous task ahead but with talk of blood, toil, tears and sweat. He did employ judicious use of propaganda, yes, but he did not predict catastrophe or spread pessimism. His effect was not to damage but to improve people's mental health in order to motivate them. The overall message was one of defiance, hope and optimism. Only a moment's reflection is needed to see that that approach was valid, indeed winning. Yet this approach is not the norm today. The German philosopher Hans Jonas, for example, has argued for a 'heuristic of fear' in order to motivate people. Maybe that is because he has found using reason hasn't worked? And maybe reason hasn't worked because what he has in mind is not reasonable and would never be acceptable to a well-informed electorate?

Unfortunately, this outrageously undemocratic and damaging view has become worryingly acceptable. As Furedi observes: 'Astonishingly, his [Jonas's] promotion of the principle of fear, his elitist contempt for people, and his advocacy of deception and tyranny, are rarely held to account.' He goes on to comment on Jonas's supporters: 'Their lack of concern with [his] politics of fear and promotion of the noble lie indicates that they, too, accept the view that politization of the principle of fear constitutes an exercise in moral responsibility.'[3]

Such a system of excessive use of fear and manipulation has been coined a 'psychocracy'. Once the right national mood of fear and urgency is attained, technocratic policy and the use of pseudo-scientific argument – perhaps most topically, the pretence that models which are highly dependent on uncertain assumptions are consistent with the scientific method – is often enough to stop further probing.* This may be aided by widescale scientific ignorance amongst legislators and the media, the lack of clarity of scientific findings, and an ongoing attack on scientific objectivity – a reflection of skewed funding, institutional biases, and groupthink.

---

* This includes probing by MPs: in 2020, seventy UK MPs asked for, and did not get before the vote, a full cost–benefit analysis of the three-tiered system planned to follow lockdown.

THE BBC

If one wanted to create a modern propaganda machine in Britain, it would look worryingly similar to the current BBC News. Reform is not a new topic. There is a long history of criticism – of politicisation and lack of impartiality, though perhaps the biggest problem is what the BBC chooses to exclude from coverage: its agenda is focused on concerns of the metropolitan elite. Also, its comment programmes are a constant source of moral imperatives, activism is rife, and conflict with politicians is often a substitute for constructive engagement on topics of public interest.

Many of the criticisms levelled against it are also valid for other news media (television and print), but the BBC has market dominance, is publicly funded and is accountable to Parliament and the public. The case for public sector broadcasting is real, but it is strongest for those activities which can boost competition of ideas and provide coverage otherwise absent. The BBC currently squeezes out commercially viable competition. There may be a case for coverage of parliamentary debates, and serious investigative journalism, and indeed for more competition for global news agencies, of which there are currently only three. There is less of a case for services already adequately provided by the private sector.

The BBC was charged with generating propaganda during the Second World War. Nicknamed Auntie, it has a culture of thinking it knows best. Under John Birt's leadership in the 1990s, content was successfully renewed and the corporation revitalised, though arguably at the cost of standards and the staff's sense of public service and morale. In the process, changes were introduced into the way journalism was conducted. The pattern of deciding what

MEDIA AND ELITE BUBBLES

the storyline was going to be before interviewing guests was more clearly established. I have experienced the result myself, being asked to come onto a programme but then disinvited once I made clear I was not going to toe a particular line.* News is too often staged. The purpose of guests and interviews is not to discover truth or facts but merely to communicate most convincingly the view already decided. The purpose of guests, it would seem, is to give the impression of debate and agreement outside the BBC with the BBC's views, hiding the truth that the storyline is decided beforehand.

We discussed in Chapter 5 the importance for science and reason that motivational presumption be separated from facts. Good journalism, as explored, also requires this. Just as a good scientist can be proud to give a lecture on a disputed issue and have a student come up afterwards and ask: 'Yes, but what is your view?', so a good journalist should be proud if their readers/audience cannot work out their own personal view on a controversial topic. One gets the impression that BBC News has a pre-defined view on nearly every topic, and as news comes in it sees its job to select and present it in a way which will support its existing line and contradict opposite views. In other words, it does not engage in journalism but in activism. It uses a whole range of techniques to do this. The selection of what is deemed comedy and the use of fear and smear techniques are all telling, but the main tool is perhaps simply what gets airtime, and how much, and what does not.

People whose views are contrary but cannot be easily discounted

---

* Specifically, I was asked to criticise the International Monetary Fund on *Newsnight* in a way I thought unjustified. Instead of trying to understand my viewpoint, the BBC editor, apparently having next to zero understanding of the IMF, simply said that they wanted a particular line. Mine was not what they were looking for.

are simply not given airtime.* Anyone who has lived in the UK through lockdown may have got the sense that when it comes to Covid-19 there is plenty of fearmongering but not much balanced critical debate. There has been lots of hypothetical discussion about worst-case scenarios (which do not later transpire) and very little on anything else.

This is quite subjective, but one clue as to whether BBC News (and other news sources the impartiality of which one has doubts about) has a pre-existing line on a topic is whether, given a particular piece of news, their spin is or is not predictable. Gaps, i.e. what is not covered or is quickly pushed into the background, are, with a little reflection, also discernible. Topic introductions (as habitually for newspaper headlines) are often leading and distortionary, even contradictory to the subsequent content.

Another telling sign is that the BBC does not appear to be open to the possibility of groupthink inside the organisation. If it were, I would expect red teams† and governance processes, which do not exist. Above all, I would expect to see more display of informed debate and intelligence in news content. Yet the trend is in the other direction: dumbing down.

---

* Mrs Thatcher's longest serving Chancellor of the Exchequer, Nigel Lawson, is one example. Lord Lawson's first Cabinet post was Energy, and he has for the past decade and a half been highly critical of UK energy policy. But his views are morally repugnant to those who see catastrophe coming soon if we do not cut CO_2 emissions at any cost. The BBC does not want an impartial debate on the issue, indeed any debate, and appears to lack confidence that they could counter Lord Lawson's persuasive and knowledgeable presence on television, so they simply no longer invite him on. The same fate has been meted out to many others, including those within the BBC who have had the temerity to question the corporation's dogma. David Bellamy (who, unlike David Attenborough, was a scientist) claimed his television career ended over the same issue.
† A red team is a group assigned the task of simulating an opposing view or strategy to test defences and robustness.

DUMBING DOWN...

Even the pinnacle of BBC News, the *Today* programme on Radio 4, bans words which it considers too complex.* This is consistent with pandering to the audience's perceived ignorance, glossing over issues rather than trying to elucidate and educate. Huxley's vision is one of dumbing down.

Both dumbing down and distortion can be amplified in a time of perceived crisis, fear and guilt tapped into to motivate the desired response. An emergency can help governments bypass normal scrutiny – think of the 'War on Terror'. The 9/11 attacks in the US were used as propaganda to justify the Iraq War, ostensibly because of weapons of mass destruction, which never materialised after the event. We are told there is a timebomb. We have only a few minutes to midnight. Such metaphors, far from being worn out, gain more strength the more they are repeated. Like the word emergency, they are calls to action and signals to stop critical thought. Anxiety can in response overwhelm rationality. We are appealed to urgently to save the lives of those less fortunate than ourselves and to save the planet. Visual images are often employed for greatest impact, such as the recent British National Health Service posters of Covid patients with the words 'Look her in the eyes and tell her you never bend the rules'. We are constantly reminded that some great catastrophe is just around the corner.

In his advice to rhetoricians who wish to induce fear, Aristotle recommends emphasising an impending event's closeness, its significant impact on well-being and even survival, and that things are out of control. However, he also advises that the source must be

---

* I was asked once, when being interviewed on the *Today* programme in a segment on finance, not to use the word 'bond'.

trusted. The BBC and other news media, captured by groupthink and believing their own propaganda, are no longer trusted sources for a growing number of people. Just as a cascade of thought can work for the propagandists, so it can also work against them, and surprisingly quickly. The BBC seems not to understand this or know what to do about it.

Propaganda aims to distort meaning. Orwell goes so far in 1984 as to invert word meanings, defining them as their exact opposite. Today, similar irony is no better demonstrated than by the so-called precautionary motive, which amounts, as discussed, to reckless disregard for other risks. Similarly, investors are encouraged to invest in risk-free assets when there can be no such thing. Concepts are often simplified and dumbed down to aid our comprehension, and whilst this is mostly helpful it can also enable intellectual laziness and stunt inquisitiveness. As society mitigates more risks for us, we do not need to be quite as much on our toes and are more easily guided to think in certain ways.

...AND DUMBING OF ELITES

Dumbing down is to an extent unplanned, but if governments and companies and elites try to dumb down the masses they can also make themselves dumb. We might call this process elite dumbing down, or perhaps dumbing up.

When many misguidedly trust the authority of others, significant exaggeration and distortion can easily result and come full circle, just as with a game of Chinese Whispers (called 'telephone' in the US) in which a message is distorted as it passes from one person to the next. In line with Plato's preference, people do often believe their own propaganda. They also often think it relatively harmless to exaggerate or simplify the message a bit, maybe dropping some of the qualifications and provisos around statements. Yet this can lead to significant distortion. So whilst the IPCC estimates sea levels may rise by 47cm by the end of the century, there are activists who believe major coastal floods will become a threat across much of the world in as little as a dozen years. It is easy to blame broadcasters of bias, but they are no less prone to be swayed by distorted messages than anyone else. One might suppose they had greater responsibility for checking, but when groupthink, and its discipline, is strong this checking may only occur with reference to sources of authority within the limits of the groupthink. Journalists, a hardened cynical lot, should know better than to consider BBC News an authoritative source, yet too often need to keep up in a competitive space and consider they have limited liability if they use the BBC as a source. However, using the words 'according to...' is often just a cop-out.

One of the necessities for the dominance of groupthink is that people affected do not believe they are captured by it. Some go so far as to deny the very existence of groupthink as a phenomenon despite overwhelming evidence over decades that the psychology and conditions leading to it are very real, and plenty of case studies, including organised religion. Conversely, after the Bay of Pigs disaster, President Kennedy could see there was a problem and acted on it. A groupthink identified as such is a groupthink at risk of ending shortly.

When an idea becomes challenging, the first reaction is to ignore it. If it cannot be ignored, and the source cannot be discredited, then one may come up with arguments as to why it cannot affect you or the things you believe in. If, however, we accept the existence of groupthink and that groupthink adherents may be unaware of it, then how does one test for it? In a susceptible institution, do tests and processes to identify and counter groupthink exist? If, like BBC News, there is plenty of reason to believe groupthink a possibility, then the lack of governance- and management-level challenge may indicate resistance and the suspicion there may be something to hide.

One's prejudice is part of one's identity and is defended much more vigorously than one's ignorance. It is those people who know something to be true (or not true) who are hardest to convince otherwise. Such people are deliberately shutting themselves off from thought. They do this through perfunctory discounting of opposing views, through shortcuts in thinking and reference to trite memes. They doublethink and prefer to comply. We become what we mimic, and that is precisely the intention. But much worse, some of us do this to ourselves, without being forced, willingly, knowingly. We do this even though we do have a choice. To protect prejudices some of us metaphorically place our fingers in our ears. We dumb ourselves down or 'dumb up'.

MEDIA FOR A NEW AGE

How can media be reformed to cope better in the new world of the internet and social media? One change would be to ensure Big Tech companies have to choose between either being platforms without their current ability to alter, exclude or edit content, or assuming responsibility (and associated liabilities) for the content on their platforms. This means they would have to agree to the same editorial standards as others. They should also make a better effort, and if necessary be regulated, to reduce the most harmful effects of social media overuse, most particularly by teenage girls.

To cope with fake news, fact-checkers have emerged, but these are just as capable of pushing a particular interpretation of facts as those they are trying to constrain. They can be mind guards. Progress in science does not come from finding the truth and then shutting up everybody else. We are all human and nobody has a monopoly on truth. Likewise, appointing a more official news czar seems to me a dangerous path. That does not mean I am in favour of a free-for-all. Just as in other markets, being laissez-faire in information may lead to undesirable collusion and monopoly rather than the desired competition of ideas. But I am against censorship. Fear of information and mis-speaking is, like other fears, a risk to the democratic process itself. Censorship requires power, which, especially if it is arbitrary, is corruptible. Who would check the censors? A censor could in any event do little to halt the flood without significant harm to freedom. Information is the hardest thing to control without draconian measures. So I do not think that fact-checkers are the answer. Indeed, they can further bolster existing groupthink and are a poor substitute for users learning how to make up their own minds.

I prefer the risk of offending people in a democracy than not offending them at the cost of freedom of thought and expression. Yet the legislation and police practice concerning 'hate crime' is moving in the opposite direction. If offence is not meant, then it should not be a crime. Is 'thought crime' next? If someone means to cause hurt through their choice of words, it may constitute ethically unacceptable behaviour (a hate crime), but it may also be a constructive challenge. Both may cause some discomfort and it may be difficult to differentiate between the two. The word of an accuser may be taken into account, but it cannot constitute independent evidence. The law until recently focused not on whether a form of words caused offence to an individual but whether it constituted a threat of crime or violence or could incite crime or violence. This is in stark contrast to the situation increasingly prevalent in society, if not yet in the courts, where it is the listener's interpretation of slights which seems to be given priority over the intent of the speaker. Describing some use of words as offensive or as hate crimes when no offence was meant is to rob us all of our individual right to choose words. It robs us of free speech and in proscribing words reduces our freedom to think. In the battle for dominance of different moral principles it all too often (for my comfort at least) seems that equality trumps freedom. Moreover, if a legal or other authority makes it known that this is to be so, then this in itself may encourage offence to be taken at the most trivial opportunity. Nonsense ensues and victim culture is strengthened, as is self-censorship. Our ability to challenge each other is muzzled.

We should try harder to identify and compensate for some of the fake news. But we should mostly ignore it, deprive it of the oxygen it needs to replicate. We should try to reduce manipulation and the use of fear and secretive overly intrusive algorithms. We appear not to be trying much, if at all, at present. But that will not be enough. We should focus on enabling people to identify, and themselves cope with, the challenges we have identified from social media and the internet. That means empowering people to think clearly and create their own balance and impartiality in their information sources. It means giving them the means to find and explore alternative views – ones which are not just straw men. This may eventually prove much more effective than so-called fact-checkers and other efforts to limit content on the web and in social media, precisely because it does not require heavy-handed Big Tech or government intervention. It means going in the opposite direction of current policy, which appears to be ever more control and ever more use of nudging and fear to ensure predictable patterns of behaviour. We need to learn from the likes of Hayek that trying to control everyone's actions and thoughts is an unobtainable and ugly fantasy. We should encourage competition of ideas instead. Audiences should be encouraged to think and probe and consider motives and sources. We need more scepticism, not less; more courage, less fear; more reasoning, less dependence on authority for key knowledge.

This is not such an impossible thing to achieve. If leaders were more Socratic (humble), they might understand this better. People can see through nonsense, the attempts to manipulate them and trite memes. It is a common mistake to think one's opponents simply stupid and not acting in their own interests. A better explanation is that many of our elites are in a collection of bubbles.

Moreover, the further away from the elite people are, the less they may have to lose from being politically incorrect and thinking outside the box. They only lack motivation to do so. But that often soon comes if government does something to inconvenience them, like costing them money. Otherwise, they only seem to be swayed and manipulated on unimportant issues. Brand loyalty works primarily because people cannot be bothered to think about choices, but this changes if the choice is highly consequential for them. People are not more stupid than elites, merely bored and distracted.

Legislators and regulators can work with the news media to nurture better and clearer standards of journalism. Better in the sense that there should be less activism and more objectivity. Clearer in the sense of what is and what is not editorial and opinion. The difficult and complex should be explained, not dumbed down.

ELITE BUBBLES

To counter groupthink, and thus reach better decisions, one needs a diversity of views to be heard. This is particularly challenging with ambitious, like-minded people anxious of what their peers, the media and the public think of them. Fear of stepping out of line, including fear of offending, can significantly stifle proper challenge and debate. And fear can spread where there is neither tolerance nor courage to resist it.

Modern elites are bred primarily in universities. One of the effects of higher education is to help the young identify which ideas are useful and important, and that includes values and modes of expression most likely to signal elite group membership. This can improve social mobility and empower individuals to reach their potential. Unfortunately, a sense of moral superiority can arise from a belief in intellectual superiority. Belief that one knows better can be nurtured and strengthened in universities. This can combine with excluding other perspectives and can feed a sense of entitlement. Ambitious young egos can be very focused, self-confident and dismissive of contrary people and ideas. I remember being teased when I was a young professional with three degrees that I had been very efficient in my education – i.e. at the expense of other knowledge. Add in a dose of moral purpose (or even outrage) and the result can be self-deception, intolerance and noble-cause corruption.

For example, a dogmatic approach to diversity, one based on quotas and rigid moral categorisation and generally intolerant of other moral systems (for instance, following Martin Luther King's dictum, that we should not judge anyone by the colour of their skin), is one often not conducive to outspokenness, challenge or stimulating new ideas. It is very difficult to resist joining in when everyone around you is on a bandwagon of intolerance. One needn't promote diversity in such a dogmatic way, but it is too seductive for some and too painful to resist for others.

Rather, advancement in the media and politics, as in other fields, is reserved for those who stay within tribal, group and moral boundaries. Speaking against the groupthink is to risk being considered unreliable, to risk ostracism. Heresies are policed by fears of guilt by association and reputational damage. Are they like us? Can they be trusted? Do they share our values?

The great benefit of democratic elections, in contrast to other systems of leadership selection, is that a candidate who opposes an elite groupthink can be elected and challenge accepted ideas. However, candidates still normally have to work within party or other group structures. As there are only a very limited number of political parties capable of controlling government (sometimes only two), there is often a consensus of views on certain topics across all major parties. The mainstream media may also be unwilling to give column inches or airtime to heretics. Hence, it may be difficult to have any reasoned debate in the mainstream public sphere. Further, although groupthink is widespread and affects politicians and the media, we still have politicians who are oblivious to this.

Some appear to think that listening to voters and listening to the mainstream media are equivalent.

Selfless people prepared to challenge untruths and nonsense for the greater good are not feted to rise in politics as much as those who hanker after power and are prepared to cut corners to get it. There are now perhaps too many career politicians and too few who enter politics late in life from a sense of public service after success elsewhere. Having an open mind is valuable in many walks of life, and when the facts change one should be prepared to change one's mind. But few do. To do so can be embarrassing if one has already pronounced a strong view. There should be a balance between, on the one hand, thinking independently and challenging dominant ideas and, on the other hand, the pragmatic need to cooperate and win trust and support. Too much stubbornness can lead to stalemate; too little challenge can aid groupthink. Without clear and justified convictions, one worries that many politicians follow the whip when they ought not to and change their minds simply for expediency. There are even those who, to increase their chances of attaining power, choose which values to signal and even which political party to join. As the much-quoted adage goes, sincerity is the key to success. Once you can fake that, you've got it made.

There are those whose political career strategy is to do what it takes to get into a position of power and then do what they really want. However, you probably have to get to be Prime Minister or President for this strategy to really work. Justifying the bad in order to attain the power to be good later amounts to deception and probably also self-deception. A parallel might be taking up drug use in order to gain experience and advise others not to – neither a successful nor a credible strategy. One suspects it is not really a strategy at all but just a self-justification for not having any principles, an explanation of the dishonourable behaviour of one's elephant.

With a lack of anchoring from experience, politicians move herdlike in the shifting currents of groupthink. This makes them consistent and uniform much of the time. Their political leadership likes this. But there may be occasional dramatic changes in political consensus. The parallel in science is the paradigm shift; the need to cling close to power is similar to the incentive of scientists to believe in theories they have invested a lot of time and effort in. But it does mean that when minds change in such an environment, they can swing a long way. A paradigm shift can occur. When the little boy shouts that the Emperor is wearing no clothes, many others can quickly find themselves agreeing – they always thought that too, of course. More than a few may indeed be able to find an ancient and obscure record of it being their idea in the first place.

Paradigm shift dynamics are also aided by some intense knots of stubbornness. It is not surprising that, also faced with fake news, a confusing choice of information and contrary interpretations of facts, electors have a low view of politicians. Faced with perceived political herd-mentality there has been a reaction to the other extreme of stubborn moral dogmatism. Voters often decide who to vote for – or more typically who to vote against – by looking at character, not just manifesto promises. They are looking for candidates who can be trusted to make complex choices on their behalf. Sound judgement, ability to communicate clearly and persuasively and personal ethics have always been important. But, reflecting less society-wide tolerance, more and more voters are also looking for tribal markers, signs of similar belief in absolute moral certainties.

Intolerant voters beget politicians who display more explicitly moral characteristics. Such characteristics may or may not be genuine, and they may or may not coincide with pragmatic political sense, but it does make for politicians sensitive to being portrayed in a bad moral light. This, together with the prospect of social media campaigns against them, reduces their ability to compromise once elected. At the extreme of character dominance in politics, blatant lying can not only be excused but seen as a sign of authenticity – Donald Trump being a good example. Both the expedient and the dogmatic are affected by changes in communications technology. They both look myopically more at social and other mass media than in the past. This is increasingly an environment supportive of groupthink – one inimical to open, intellectually honest and challenging debate.

CONSPIRACY VERSUS COCK-UP

The study of human psychology has taught us how irrational we are. The study of history reveals how poor many political choices are. The study of human organisations reveals how difficult it is to keep complicated deceptions secret for long. Nevertheless, one of the ways to denigrate an opponent is to say that they believe in a conspiracy theory. The meaning of this is ambiguous. Insofar as it denotes a different view to that of the majority it may be benign, perhaps indicating a person who is misguided. But insofar as a conspiracy is meant to denote an organised cabal of the intentionally evil, believing in a conspiracy theory is also evil. Either way the phrase is derogatory and designed to warn off further enquiry. Contrasting with groupthink as an explanation for the objectionable, a conspiracy denotes a more fully rational purposefulness from its source, more evil than just misguided irrationality. There are no doubt conspiracists in this sense, but I am not convinced they are anything like as important in moulding history as groupthink.

Joseph Conrad's secret agent, whose efforts managed only to blow up one of his own, is a story of the ineffectiveness of much of what passes for conspiracy. In other cases, such as the assassination of Archduke Franz Ferdinand in 1914, the impact of conspiracies can be at the other extreme – beyond expectations – because they act as a spark in a highly inflammatory context. Either way, whilst I do believe there are very real threats from extremists and terrorist cells, I do not think mass groupthink is typically just a result of an underlying conspiracy, nor that conspiracy is much of an explanation for beliefs contrary to a dominant groupthink. There are activists, commercial and other vested interests, as well as some very determined, focused individuals with radical agendas, but most of those who subscribe to groupthink do so fairly blindly, from a lack of thoughtfulness. Likewise, calling something a conspiracy just because you disagree with it lacks credibility and is intellectually dishonest.

The truth is that human beings are highly prone to groupthink, which often leads large numbers of people to make very bad choices. No great conspiracy is required to explain such behaviour, although this does not preclude there being some conspirators in the mix. More necessary than the existence of conspirators for so many to be so wrong is groupthink discipline – strong incentives not to speak up against the predominant view, the shutting out of dissenters, and the refusal to engage in debate outside the limits of the groupthink. This is often a good indicator of groupthink.

Key to maintaining such discipline is a strong moral element.

The most successful groupthinks are ones where members of the group have to atone for their sins. Only through some sacrifice or suffering can they truly feel that they are making a positive contribution, even if such sacrifice is completely superficial – another indicator of groupthink.

Let us assume that Western elites are not capable of a huge conspiracy, and certainly not for very long. Let us also assume that mere incompetence is not sufficient to explain gaps and distorted patterns in collectively accepted knowledge. Into such a mix, mass groupthink can help explain what is going on. However, the insight that there is a mass groupthink, in particular one affecting the elite more than others, is a radical departure from our traditional view of our own individual and collective rationality. But ironically it is the seeming absurdity that elites can be more misguided than others which makes it all the more likely – a Big Lie, in other words, but one which grows and is sustained by groupthink rather than being consciously pre-designed in all its detail.

THE BIG LIE

To believe that the whole media and political elite have been totally taken in by a series of massive distortions, even if there is no conspiracy, raises several questions. The first question is how is it possible that no one has actually checked the underlying details and assumptions properly? Yet this appearance, if not the reality, of not checking is actually quite normal. Often, checking has occurred, but the results, and those who have done the verifying, have been silenced by groupthink; it only appears that no one has checked. For years, foreign visitors to Soviet Russia were deceived by the enormous efforts Soviet authorities extended to fool them.

But that does not mean there was no contrary evidence, nor that a few well-informed people were not fully aware of it. It may seem an implausible revelation that so many have totally neglected to check their sources, but, as Sherlock Holmes would say, when one has excluded all the other explanations, whatever remains, however improbable, must be true.* Similarly, as Kuhn explained, when we meet facts which contradict our theory, and providing that our reasoning is not faulty, then one or more of our assumptions must be in error. Working backwards through the theories from which those assumptions came and the beliefs they in turn were based on and so on, we may eventually come to the unpleasant inevitability that one of our deeply held self-evident truths, which we have been using as a building block for our entire edifice of beliefs, is incorrect. So, scientific paradigms fail. So, groupthink fails when it comes into contact with hard evidence and unassailable logic.

The second question which a fatal crack in mass groupthink raises is: if this, what else? If the elite have been so collectively stupid about one thing, what else have they got wrong? Can a whole establishment seriously believe in weapons of mass destruction in Iraq when there were none? Can eleven jurors in *12 Angry Men* all be wrong? Can burning witches have been so common? Can democracies elect a fascist dictator like Hitler? The answers to all the above questions would appear to be 'Yes.' It would be wrong to conclude that just because elites can get one thing very, very wrong, they must also be wrong about other things – but they might be,

---

* It is a pedantic point, but consistent with the arguments in Chapter 5 it is worth noting that Conan Doyle's use of language is not entirely watertight. He implicitly assumes that there exists a limited and known number of possible explanations. Yet, except in special circumstances where we can disprove the opposite, we cannot normally verify such statements. Hence what 'remains' should be considered our working hypothesis rather than the truth.

and often are. It would be as well to check the evidence and make up one's own mind as far as possible.

Thirdly, does this mean we really have to take responsibility for checking the good sense of those acting in our name? Yes. We have to remain vigilant and constantly ask for the reasoning and evidence behind decisions, especially if others are not doing this for us. We should remember (from Socrates) that the checks and balances on power are more important than the choice of leader, so at the least we should ask ourselves if these are working.

Thinking all this through can be very difficult, but we should not be bamboozled. Doublethink may be Hegel's idea of knowledge, but it represents a method to suppress inconvenient evidence. Such evidence may cause us stress until such point as it can be accepted, with all its implications of rejection of other beliefs, or discounted. We should be careful that we have not closed our mind to it. It can be very painful to accept, and it is a lot easier not to, and save a lot of effort. This is because once we believe we have considered contrary evidence and discounted it, then we will probably move on and ignore any similar evidence we encounter in the future. Likewise with people: once we have decided that someone is a flat-earther, we may ignore everything they say in the future as wrong-headed. But we might be totally wrong to do so.

SUMMARY

- Propaganda is defined as the unbalanced dissemination of half-facts and lies intended to deceive. It does not require unambiguous falsehoods, though false facts may be deliberately created.

It is most effective when not explicit, and propagandists themselves, captured by groupthink, do not recognise it. Contrary
arguments can occasionally be presented in a simplistic and negative way to then be discounted. Opponents should continuously
be attacked and particular opponents picked out for vilification.

- There are good examples where most people would agree government persuasion is justified. But there is a clear difference between making a strong case following a full, balanced assessment
of the costs and benefits and the widespread distortion of facts to
achieve a controversial, contentious and hidden goal.

- There is something fundamentally objectionable about attempts
to inflict fear of catastrophe on a whole population. We should
be focusing on hope, not fear. Widespread official propaganda is
not justified in a democracy in peacetime. Its presence is a result
of some key decision-makers thinking they know better, and the
belief that the public are incapable of reaching 'correct' conclusions on their own.

- One can think of three types of writing, all of which pass for
journalism: reporting, impartial journalism and activism. A
reporter simply writes down facts in as dispassionate a way as
possible, adding some explanation and background to aid comprehension. An impartial journalist will add more interpretation
to help the reader/viewer understand the implications of a story.
An activist tries to influence and push particular views – propaganda. Much of what passes for journalism today is activism.

- With widespread groupthink, repeated arguments fuel themselves and can lead to major distortions in perception, as well as
media hysteria.

- The BBC News output shares many characteristics of what one would expect from a propaganda organisation.

- We observe both dumbing down of audiences and dumbing up of elites (self-dumbing down). Institutions susceptible to group-think do not test for it. It is those people who know something as true (but which isn't) who are hardest to convince. They discount opposing views, take mental shortcuts, doublethink and prefer to comply. They dumb themselves up without being forced, will-ingly, knowingly.

- Big Tech companies should choose between either being plat-forms without their current abilities to alter, exclude or edit con-tent, or assume responsibility for that content.

- Better the risk of offending people in a democracy than not of-fending them at the cost of freedom of thought and expression.

- We should identify and compensate for fake news but try to ignore it rather than suppress it, and reduce the use of fear and intrusive algorithms. Rather than create fact-checkers who can turn out to be mind guards for groupthink, we should focus on enabling people to cope with new aspects of how we communi-cate. Trying to control everyone's actions and thoughts is an ugly and unobtainable fantasy. We should encourage competition of ideas instead.

- Advancement in the media and politics, as in other fields, is reserved for those who stay within tribal, group and moral boundaries. Intolerant voters beget politicians who display more explicitly moral characteristics, reducing their ability to com-promise once elected. Both the expedient and the dogmatic look more at social and mainstream media than in the past. It is an environment supportive of groupthink and inimical to open, intellectually honest and challenging debate.

- As an explanation for much society-wide idiocy, mass groupthink is better than either widespread individual incompetence or the existence of conspiracies. Human beings are highly prone to groupthink, which often leads large numbers of people to make very bad choices. A moral element is important, and the most successful groupthinks are ones where members of the group have to atone for their sins. Only through some sacrifice or suffering can they truly feel that they are making a positive contribution, even if such sacrifice is completely superficial.
- It would be wrong to conclude that just because elites can get one thing very, very wrong, they must also be wrong about other things – but they might be. It would be as well to check the evidence and make up one's own mind as far as possible.

CHAPTER 8

ESCAPING FROM GROUPTHINK

'In today's complex 21st-century world we are all faced with a subtle challenge: we can either be mastered by our mental and structural silos or we can try to master them instead. The choice lies with us. And the first step to mastering our silos is the most basic one of all: to think how we all unthinkingly classify the world around us each day. And then try to imagine an alternative.'

GILLIAN TETT *THE SILO EFFECT*[1]

Fear and pessimism have flourished during lockdown. I recently attended a charity event at which the guest speaker spent most of her time explaining why, using tired and predictable arguments, everything was terrible. She said there is too much destruction of the environment, too much industry, too many people, even too much rationality (a postmodernist misanthropist statement). Her charitable role is dealing with child mental health problems, but I hope she exudes more optimism when with children. I felt sorry for her. Her understanding of the world seems far more pessimistic than justified. What I found even more worrying was the rapturous applause of the audience, with whom her dystopian vision clearly resonated. For many of them, a read of Hans Rosling's *Fact-fulness* or Matt Ridley's *The Rational Optimist* might prove a stress-reducing antidote.

When those subject to groupthink experience doubt, a bit of effort to re-emphasise what they have in common helps re-energise commitment. When doubt persists, it is very difficult to break free, but otherwise mental stress remains. Group members acquiesce to bubble thinking when the bubble is too big for them to challenge. The enormity of dealing with doubts and inconsistencies head on is prohibitive. Just as scientists work within a Kuhnian paradigm, so policy-makers, journalists and many others operate only within the range of what is in full accord with their group thinking. Only very occasionally, where they see a realistic chance of major change in the views of all around them, will the doubtful be prepared to change their mind. They do not waste time and effort on trying to change or even think about what seems most solid. And perception of what is and is not immovable is determined by interactions inside the group, not outside evidence. This only starts to change when the inconsistencies act against in-group interests. Until then, opposing voices are dismissed as noises off by 'nutters', who are even considered the real victims of groupthink, in denial about the revealed truth. In this way, groupthink can be a cradle for intolerance, hatred and waste. The role of my charity event speaker was to reduce dissent from the dominant catastrophic view of her group. For those familiar with the charity sector, it may come as no surprise that morals can dominate over reason a bit more than in many other walks of life.

Contrary to doom warnings, the world is in pretty good shape. It is richer, greener and happier than a few decades ago. Nevertheless, this is not to argue that we should ever be complacent. The key to further progress is to allow our reason and interests to dominate and not be sidetracked by scaremongers, authoritarians or commercial interests trying to manipulate behaviour.

Despite us thinking ourselves rational, we rarely are. Groupthink is an attribute of the human brain, which has evolved to cope with historic environments in which rationality has a place but our emotions and moral systems largely determine our actions. We all benefit from constantly taking shortcuts in thinking, but this can lead to a group of people all failing to challenge an emerging or existing consensus. Groupthink was originally coined by Irving Janis in the context of small groups of decision-makers. This book has looked at the phenomenon of large-scale, society-wide instances of groupthink – something which has been with us for as long as we have lived in large societies.

Each time there is a major change in communications technology, it is both liberating and disruptive, and it has taken humanity a while to adjust. Such changes are empowering, but when combined with lack of tolerance have often led to conflict. As previously mentioned, the Thirty Years War in Europe followed the invention of the printing press and more common access to the Bible. Far more people than before had the ability to think through theological issues for themselves, and this led to strong disagreements to add to the normal conflict for territory between sovereign rulers. Groupthink can be unhelpful in such periods, as it sets tribal boundaries, 'the us and the them', those who share our values and those who do not. Today's new technology has given voice to many more people than before, which is wonderful in many ways but also associated with increased manipulation and intolerance.

The freedom to communicate more widely leads to the destruction of previous moral constraints on thought and action. It can be argued that without religion morality can be up for grabs and result in reactionary forces. As societal norms break down, anxiety, stress and revolution can follow. Our focus on virtues has shifted to values, our new tribal boundaries. Our perceptions of our interests are manipulated by companies, by their algorithms and by governments. Governments, moreover, have found control of populations easiest when they can induce fear. Anomie rises, the desire to think issues through decreases, the desire to be part of a group which instead gives comfort increases. As evidence about the world seems increasingly contradictory to groupthink and mental models, so mental health problems arise. As fear and self-doubt go up, so identity becomes complex, multiple, attracted to groups. More societal fear also panders to the authoritarian tendencies of leaders. We forget Socrates's wisdom in favour of trusting someone we consider wise. Magical, tribal or collectivist societies are described by Popper as closed societies, as opposed to open societies in which individuals have to make personal decisions. The shift from open to closed is the risk we face.

We will learn to cope better with time. The purpose of this book is to help us understand where we need to be faster. There is one big concern, however: to avoid an erosion of liberalism and reason, and with it a decline into non-democratic politics. What I suggest we need is better self-awareness and more courage, but also some government action, particularly in education, media, community-building and in how policy decisions are made.

I see almost no need to conjure up conspiracies to explain how things are. The best route out of our muddled thinking is via reason and tolerance. Of course, there are a few misanthropists out there, including some organised in dangerous networks. Their actions are in turn amplified by an even larger number of the well-meaning but confused. However, the vast majority of people are simply complacent. They have lacked incentive to behave any differently. It is through waking up the complacent that we can preserve liberal democracy and the gains we have made since the Enlightenment.

Not that I want to engage in scaremongering – it is comedic fiction after all – but as Douglas Adams's Prostetnic Vogon Jeltz in *The Hitchhiker's Guide to the Galaxy* rather aptly pointed out, the consequence of not paying attention to local affairs can be catastrophic:

> People of Earth, your attention please … As you will no doubt be aware, the plans for development of the outlying regions of the Galaxy require the building of a hyperspatial express route through your star system, and regrettably your planet is one of those scheduled for demolition. The process will take slightly less than two of your Earth minutes. Thank you.

We really do need to wake up to the risks to democracy. We always have a choice to think carefully or not, and in liberal democracies the responsibility is, and should remain, with every individual voter. The one authoritarian act which Socrates endorsed was waking up the uneducated to self-criticism, but no more than that. The teacher's authority should come only from their knowledge of how little they know. And fortunately, we do have more than two minutes.

WHAT TO ASK OF OURSELVES

Being rational is a moral decision. We should make the effort. There are many signs of irrationality, including not reflecting on your assumptions, not asking yourself why you are doing or believing in something and not considering consequences. As Daniel Kahneman recommends in *Thinking, Fast and Slow*, when there are signs of error, slow down and ask for reinforcements from the more rational part of your brain. If unsure, sleep on it.

First, we have to target our own fears, as well as the fear of fear itself, as Franklin Roosevelt said, which unless confronted will not go away on its own. Society has become estranged from courage, judgement, reasoning and responsibility, all necessary for the management of fear. We have to have the courage to move on from group identity, for to do otherwise is to be for ever constrained by the wisdom of others, notably that of contemporary and dead charismatics.

Although wrenching and difficult, we can break free from groupthink. The lone thinker, who may care less than many what others think of them, does us all a favour by leading the way. Sometimes an individual's adherence to groupthink can fall away after one decisive thought, but this is normally preceded by a lot of confusion and inner struggle. Leading up to this moment, our perception of a contrary idea can change from evil to formidable, from inadmissible and dangerous to maybe, eventually, credible and persuasive. We have to start by really having an open mind and confidence in our own ability to reason, which comes with practice. But just as with the five stages of grief, so breaking free from groupthink is confronted by denial and then anger, bargaining and maybe depression before possible acceptance of a different explanation.

Second, we need to be sceptical. To think independently and not be swayed by seemingly universal opinion, it helps to maintain the belief that our own views of ourselves matter more than anyone else's, and no one else can help as much in thinking things through. As Feynman indicated, science should be explained so as to be accessible to anyone willing to look at the evidence and use reason. Indeed, science starts with scepticism, including of the views extolled by experts. The call of those, expert or not, who desire to close debate down should be resisted. Also, whilst experts in one field might know more than non-experts, specialists in closely related fields should not be trusted any more than laypeople – sometimes less. Rosling relates how at the sixty-fourth Lindau Nobel Laureate meeting a large group of scientists and Nobel Laureates in physiology and medicine scored worse than any public polls on his standard question on child vaccinations (the percentage of the world's one-year-olds who had received some vaccination). He likewise observed how only 8 per cent of women's rights activists at a women's rights conference he attended knew that thirty-year-old women have spent on average only one year less in school than thirty-year-old men. To put this in context, all his questions were multiple choice with three possible answers. In such cases, groupthink has made the judgement of those typically assumed knowledgeable worse than that of the general population.[2]

Third, we have to be careful with our sources of information and how we weigh them. We need to take control of our own sources of information and not let algorithms do that for us. We need to be aware of the bias that is directed at us and realise that we have probably massively underestimated it – as Hans Rosling's work has illustrated quantitatively with regard to global development and health issues, and as my own career has demonstrated to me with regard to investor bias against developing countries. For those disillusioned with the mainstream media, finding a non-biased alternative is not at all easy. We can easily reject one set of nonsense for another. The independent, fact-based, well-thought-out view which challenges the consensus may also at first glance seem far from independent – we should reach our conclusion after having looked into the detail, not before.

As the media has played a large part in feeding our anxieties and repeating the images and memes which sustain them, we need to create some space in our thoughts between the messages we receive and our critical thinking. We need to make an effort to process information we receive from the internet and social media in particular, discounting it when necessary. We should very especially consider the motives of those curating and editing the content. We should challenge their arguments and motives, which, however, we may not know and about which we may speculate incorrectly.

We should ensure we are challenged by thoughtful, not just different views. We should resist the myopia of social media and even of television news in favour of more reflective ideas and discussion – there really is no good substitute for reading insightful books and listening to and participating in challenging debates. And we should remember that for reasoned debate to occur, we need to be polite to those who disagree with us. Literature often reveals truth about a society earlier than news, news and conversation being shy from both taboo and sensitive issues, and effort needs to go into seeking out and carefully considering all the available evidence, not just the easy to hand.

Fourth, we should try to know ourselves and understand our inner elephants, as well as what our interests are. We should remind ourselves that we are not normally rational and that we are largely ignorant. If we can recognise our own habits and biases, we will have a head start in detecting flaws and gaps in our reasoning when it comes to specific issues. Or put another way, we will be clear on those views we hold with strong conviction and distinguish them from those which happen to be important.

We should be able to recognise differences between our views and those of others, but perhaps these differences can help us identify what the architecture, assumptions and moral bases of our mental models are. Problems with our mental models can in part be mitigated through self-recognition of leaps of abstraction from observation to generalisation; through articulation of key assumptions normally left unstated; and through balanced enquiry and advocacy of different points of view. We can also learn to recognise the difference between theories we use to explain our actions and revealed theories-in-use, implied from what we actually do – i.e. we should recognise the difference between what we tell ourselves the motives of our elephants are and what they actually are.

Prejudice is very difficult to displace, much more so than ignorance. I argued in my first book against the deeply ingrained prejudice against emerging markets, which I coined Core/Periphery disease. Without dislodging prejudices, new useful knowledge may be simply rejected. When staff at the international company Shell invented scenario planning in the early 1970s (subsequently copied by many other companies globally), they initially realised that senior staff were largely ignoring their output. In response they changed their goal not only to describe possible alternative futures but to sow doubt into their colleagues' minds about their own mental models, in order that they might be prepared to change their views when necessary.

Fifth, when we encounter a particular issue, we need to challenge our own reasoning. As public rhetoric deteriorates to a pre-Socratic form, perverting the nature of truth and replacing it with sophistry (even including guides to debunk and discipline thought), we have to make an effort to recover reason. The scientific method remains our most reliable way of debunking misinformation and fake news, not listening to some new authority which simply replaces our preceding one. Unfortunately, appeals to conventional leadership are capable of strengthening as well as debunking nonsense. The current trend is in the wrong direction. Propaganda is rife. Nudge theory is being used more and more to manipulate people's choices without them realising or being able to opt out. Recent government efforts to manipulate behaviour in lockdown using fear seem to have occurred without serious consideration given to ethics or any exit plan.

Do we fall into Aristotle's trap of essentialist definitions, whereby words become building blocks of thought rather than simply the scientist's aids to reduce the length of sentences? In their book *The Stupidity Paradox*, Mats Alvesson and André Spicer identify various ways we can battle our functional stupidity in the workplace, including by getting into the habit of regularly challenging the routine way of thinking and doing things; by playing devil's advocate; by conducting post-mortems and pre-mortems; by listening to newcomers and outsiders who often have a fresh or different perspective; by engaging with critics; and by welcoming challenge through competitions and games.[3]

SIGNS OF GROUPTHINK

We should be on the look-out for groupthink. The moral is created, post-God, by pressure groups, groupthink and algorithms. Are moral arguments being manufactured and used in place of reason and evidence? Are appeals to authority dominant over explanations, and are they used as a way to stop further discussion? Are trite memes and such enquiry-stopping phrases such as 'the science is settled' used? Are there undisputed ideas which appear to be considered self-evident, and if so, are they really so self-evident? Is there open debate, or is there an effort to close debate down? Are inconvenient facts met with denial, mental distress and anger? Are people emotional, intolerant, impolite? Is an argument capable of being disproved should certain evidence come to light? When caught out on a point of fact or reason, are values or the greater good appealed to as justification for ignoring such inconveniencies? Is a moral argument used to justify exaggerations or selective truth? Are words or arguments used to indicate that it is morally wrong, evil even, to think or question certain things? Has satire, which uncovers moral baseness and irrationality, become taboo and retreated from certain topics?

Also, where are the gaps or questions which cannot be answered? Doris Lessing relates her father asking a difficult question on a visit to the USSR in 1952:

Always, in every society, even in the most rigid, new ideas appear, are usually regarded as reprehensible or even seditious, but then become accepted, only to be swept aside in their turn by ideas at first considered heretical. How does the Soviet Union allow for this inevitable process, which prevents cultures going rotten, or stultifying?

The minder had to consult, and next day came back with the answer: 'The Soviet Union under the guidance of the great leader Comrade Joseph Stalin will always make the correct decisions, based on Marxist principles.'[4] It is not difficult to find groupthink if you ask the right questions. It is when there is refusal to answer or engage or accept the validity of a question that one should suspect its presence.

The peer review system for academic papers gives reassurance that ideas have been challenged, but what if there is no effective challenge because a whole discipline, or at least those invited to review papers, are of one mind and share the same confirmation biases or groupthink? This is now a serious problem with some issues in some disciplines. Likewise, parliamentary debate is meant to provide challenge to new legislation, but if there is little debate or challenge even to major legislation, this may also be a sign of groupthink.

Also, when suspected, is it possible to work out the history of a groupthink? What were the incentives for its generation and why has it met little effective challenge? Christopher Booker's *Global Warming: A Case Study in Groupthink* explains the growth of current groupthink on global warming for example. He explains the media's use of propaganda, activists' hounding and bullying of those with contrary views, politicians' perversion of the underlying scientific consensus from IPCC panels, unethical manipulation of data, and the non-existence of meaningful debate in public or parliament. In doing so he gives credibility to the existence of groupthink.

Groupthink is identified by the past behaviour of its mind guards and its discipline in stopping debate and thought – it is revealed by the intellectual holes it leaves behind. This is often apparent in government policy: Is there a lack of linkage between ostensible goals and policy prescriptions? Is there something missing in the basic logic of what is proposed? What are the likely consequences, are they expected to actually happen or is there a gulf between likely and stated consequences? The utter mess of the UK's energy policy is a good sign that groupthink has stopped system-level critical thinking. Whilst rationality is evident in parts, people have shirked the responsibility of considering the system as a whole.

BE TOLERANT, COURAGEOUS, BALANCED

Toleration is essential for rational debate, and we explored in Chapter 2 how trust and social capital are important for well-being and democracy. The keys to sustaining trust are making and keeping promises, but also forgiveness when actions have irreversible consequences. To be tolerant, we need to understand and forgive human failings. Good and evil exists in all people. It is not the case that some are good (us) and some bad (them).

So much subtlety in human interactions and the building of mutual trust is lost when relationships shift from being interpersonal to that between citizen and state. The state has to design simple rules which apply to many different situations and which are thus not tailored well for many. The focus on rights, as discussed, can give a needed security to all but can also create a sense of entitlement. Rights may not be matched by reciprocal responsibilities, especially where groups, rather than individuals, are seen to possess rights. Entitlements, if not met, can foster resentment and the negative emotions of division, anger and hate.

To avoid this, they need to be part of a relationship with a local community or state which includes social capital, political engagement and mutual trust. Without responsibility and balance, rights for one group can come at the cost of rights of another.

Being tolerant is not the same as avoiding a fuss. One should control urges and ill-thought-through emotional responses and try to understand moral differences. But one should also listen critically, by which I mean one should challenge, politely, rather than let intolerance or nonsense pass unchallenged.

Humans are anti-fragile, and being a bit offended can be stimulating and better than excessive coddling. Courage is needed to confront our fears, and by courage I mean, as the Greeks did, a bravery linked to a noble goal. Without purpose, courage is a display of potential but is not necessarily useful, and at worst it is an egotistical distraction. Churchill referred to courage as the first of human qualities because it guarantees all the others. From courage we gain confidence in ourselves and can laugh at ourselves. We gain confidence in our judgement and in the future. We dare to trust others, to be open and to escape the narrow-mindedness and myopia of precaution, instead engaging in probabilistic thinking.

Our thinking about risk needs root and branch reform to replace the unthinking precautionary motive. Even when our morality demands absolutism, which takes the form of the precautionary, we should still look at the costs of different ways to achieve our objectives. Emergencies should be real, not imagined, and only in personal emergencies where split-second decisions are required should they be an excuse to abandon critical thought, and even then only in the moment.

WHAT TO ASK OF OUR LEADERS

Tackling groupthink in an age of increasing intolerance is not going to be easy. It will take nothing less than the actions of many individuals to combat current nonsense, and it will take time. However, aside from personal self-reflection, as discussed above, there are a number of things which can be addressed politically and through policy change.

DEMOCRATIC INSTITUTIONS

Not everything is political, and we need to learn to appreciate that. Contrary to the extreme-left postmodernist rhetoric, life is not a constant struggle between different groups or classes. It is possible to be optimistic and cooperative, to do away with corrosive nonsense and embrace reason. We should be open to compromises, build consensus on rules of rational engagement and then conduct meaningful political debate. When this doesn't work, we should resist resorting to excessively disruptive protests and violence. Within the constraints of civil discourse, we should also not fear (or be intimidated to fear) challenging others. This may offend them unintentionally, but honesty and challenge are needed to identify exactly where disagreement lies and to find common ground.

We should also try to preserve and build institutions which engender compromise and consensus. The mass membership political party may continue to dwindle, so we need to complement it with other, perhaps more local, forms of organisation and engagement. Public service broadcasting may have a role to play in this, as may efforts to support local communities, and both may help support universal values.

Citizens need to trust government to participate in civic and political life. This is difficult when government is thought to be manipulating the electorate through fear. Excessive reliance on focus groups and polling can be described as followership, a poor substitute for leadership. Focus groups can be almost perfect crucibles for nurturing groupthink and can often be misleading as to likely future reactions to policy decisions. They are a poor and myopic substitute for more individual conversations, let alone in-depth policy research, transparency and legitimacy. A vibrant, healthy democracy requires fundamental understanding, by the electorate as well as by policy-makers, not simply of what is popular now but of what issues matter and are in the national interest, as well as of the choice of possible solutions. To use focus groups is to signal lack of leadership.

Civil servants need to be professionally impartial and dedicated to serving our democracy, which does not mean lobbying ministers or trying to manipulate politics or electorates. The increase in the UK of special advisers and the massive increase of independent agencies outside the scrutiny of Parliament are retrograde steps. Electorates need a direct relationship with politicians, who should not hide behind experts or technocratic policies. To provide ministers with high-quality, impartial advice on policy options, reform of the UK's public sector is overdue. This includes not just those functions and staff currently designated as in the civil service, but independent agencies too. There should be procedural and governance changes to identify and mitigate the negative effects of groupthink.

TRADITIONAL MEDIA

As discussed in Chapter 7, public broadcasters should either identify and challenge their own groupthink or be regulated to do so. Public broadcasters, especially the BBC, should complement, not compete with and crowd out, private providers. The BBC should promote impartial journalism, reduce activism (and clearly flag subjective opinions) and have the highest standards of public service. It should not be an agent of propaganda in peacetime. It should not have fixed positions on issues itself and should dispense with its unjustified attitude of knowing best.

This will require major organisational and cultural change in the organisation. Many of the senior staff are oblivious to their ideological biases and abandonment of impartiality. Indeed, it may not be possible to change the internal culture of an organisation so inculcated with groupthink and unrepresentative views. In that case, BBC News should perhaps be disbanded.

EDUCATION

Matt Ridley makes the distinction between 'science as philosophy', also known as the scientific method, and 'science as an institution', which is erratic and often captured by activists and political agendas. In many people's minds, science is a body of factual knowledge, but there are different interpretations of this source of authority, and so we have disputes between those with different concepts of what 'the science' tells us. Science is never settled, and scepticism is at its heart. Scientists have too often strayed into activism, and the separation between facts and motives has been severely compromised, as evidenced by the irreproducibility crisis, particularly in medicine and social science. Speculative models have been passed off as scientific knowledge when they are not. Scientists have consequently been losing the public's trust.

Competing for authority, and as described in Chapter 5, is what can be called anti-science, the collection of postmodernist nonsense which is not destroyed by contradictions but thrives on them, denies an objective reality and corrodes reason, science and history. This cancer has infected large areas of academia and needs to be challenged effectively. One of the great strengths of the Anglo-Saxon world has been its pragmatism dominating over theoretical ideas. We have had a healthy disregard for philosophers and theorists of all kinds, often much to the annoyance of those same theorists, but it has helped to keep them honest and relevant. To re-establish trust in science as philosophy, we have to doubt more and look to Socrates's understanding of wisdom.

We also need to protect freedom of speech in universities. And we should defend the primary purpose of a university to advance knowledge, which requires challenge, not constant coddling. Research funding should be available outside main paradigms of thought, to uncover and challenge groupthink.

An inquisitive mind can be trained to spot poor reasoning and lack of impartiality in dealing with facts, and hence signs of groupthink. The teacher has a difficult task in stimulating the young mind's ability to reason, and they should introduce ideas but not try to impose higher values. Once motivated to learn, children become hungry for more understanding. It may only need one teacher to transform a child's motivation in school. Hence, it is important that teachers inspire, for which they need sufficient time in the classroom. Sports can build teamwork and trust, and the arts are particularly important in engendering trust, love and purpose.

There is no simple interpretation of history, and successive generations interpret it differently. There is, however, an argument that all subjects in school should in part be taught as history, so students may learn that knowledge is not fixed but an evolving set of ideas to explain the world.[5] The history of ideas gives context and can challenge the student to understand that in the past people had different moralities, norms and incentives. History should support Socratic doubt about our moral universe, not just our physical one.

Currently, children are not sufficiently encouraged to be independent but see problems as ones of mental health. They have been taught helplessness. In *The Coddling of the American Mind*, Greg Lukianoff and Jonathan Haidt identified six interacting trends of concern for American's young students: rising political polarisation; growing adolescent depression and anxiety; more fearful, intensive protective parenting; play and risk deprivation; over-protective campus administrations; and a postmodernist fixation on inequality and equal outcomes.

Students need to challenge and be challenged. This means putting a stop to endless positivity. It means promoting uncertainty and doubt which can lead to new thoughts and understanding (termed by the poet John Keats 'negative capability'). One needs to observe carefully, interpret, but then question initial thoughts further. Semantics is thus important – including the habit of constantly asking 'Why?' – as this not only improves reading and writing skills but helps students question assumptions and truth, uncover purpose and appreciate the capacity of language to distort. It can teach habits of precise critical thinking. We need to combat the Aristotelian essentialist use of words as building blocks, which has distracted us from scientific advance. Throughout history this has been a route to empty verbiage and scholasticism.

BIG TECH

The Great Indian Phone Book by Robin Jeffrey and Assa Doron[6] is a catalogue of how mobile phones have transformed business, social life and politics in India. Almost everything is positive, from increasing the efficiency of fish markets – as fishermen out at sea can now work out the best ports to land their fish in – to tempering local corruption through the ability to record fraudulent officials in action. But there are exceptions, such as the habit of mothers-in-law to confiscate the phones of their new daughters-in-law. New technology can liberate and enable, but it can also help entrench existing power relations. Social media, the internet and the mobile phone have had many major impacts, and by focusing on some of the negative aspects I don't want to belittle the huge benefits. However, the initial utopian optimism that greater connectivity would be good for democracy has been brought down to earth by the reality that communication has become more a public performance, enabled emotional bullying and intolerance and fostered divisions in society. It has reduced opportunities to build trust.

Social media has been a factor in increased mental illness and fed increased intolerance and political extremism. We are tool-making animals unused yet to new communication media, which are altering our behaviour, thoughts and morals. The business model employed by Big Tech is based on destroying privacy and stealing personal data without permission, and then experimenting on people and manipulating them so as to make them more predictable. Existing and new privacy laws have made little dent in this system to date – indeed the EU's general data protection regulation (GDPR) appears to have both stifled innovation and reduced competition.

Providers need to be more responsible. To reduce harm, both they and regulators need intelligent observation of behaviour to inform change. I argued in my first book that in order to reduce systemic risks in financial markets, regulators should map investor types and behaviour better and not just focus on financial instruments. Similarly, regulators should try to understand the contours and subtleties of new media's impact on people. Provision of alternatives for socialising and reduced time spent on social media is needed for some children. Some monopolies and oligopolies should be broken up. Networks may have natural economies of scale and be difficult to break up, but competition should be increased through insistence of interoperability. The benefits of this are illustrated by the contrast between the oligopoly in mobile phone services in the US, where there are three main providers, and the greater competition in the EU, where there are over a hundred. This is the result of interoperability legislation. User costs are consequently two to three times higher in the US.

Social media platforms employ tens of thousands to police content, but the rules for such censorship are under the control of the handful of shareholders who operate these companies, and they are, like other mortals, prone to groupthink. The result is reduced freedom of expression for those they disagree with, as they and their employees decide what is true and what is conspiracy. News platforms in particular should either not edit content to the extent they do or take legal responsibility for it. Without legislation to enforce this, Big Tech companies will probably, eventually, either moderate their partisan political outlooks or face more competition, but it may take a long time.

Insofar as morality becomes increasingly moulded by profit-seeking algorithms, we risk a dumbing down and gradual loss of freedom. The future could bear some resemblance to Huxley's *Brave New World*, with rising political apathy and dysfunction. Insofar as government works with commercial interests or takes over behavioural manipulation, we will be giving up our liberty. And insofar as manipulation increasingly comes from many sources, including extremists, activists and foreign powers, a more chaotic future lies in store. More authoritarian tendencies will only be kept at bay so long as voters still take enough interest in politics and are well enough informed to hold those in office to account.

There are ways social media could (be made to) reduce its negative impact on mental illness and intolerance: catering to the need for more small-group interaction and preservation of privacy, for example providing more options for limited group sizes and limiting algorithmic analysis of some types of data; reducing unverified accounts (maybe by dropping anonymity in many contexts); and slowing down reply/reaction times to aid more prior reflection. In *The Age of Surveillance Capitalism*, Shoshana Zuboff argues that we should use our resources of friction, courage and bearings to claim the digital future as a human place and that this new power must be tamed by democracy, for which we need shared trust.[7] I do not share the more radical proposals to control Big Tech, though I do approve of recent efforts to tax in the geographies where they generate profits. We cannot turn the clock back. Policy-makers should, however, try to reduce oligopolistic power and work with firms to reduce the negative effects on behaviour.

BUILDING LOCAL TRUST AND COMMUNITIES

We don't want to live in a world as described by Edward Banfield in his 1950s study of the Mezzogiorno in which you trust nobody outside your immediate family and would only take an orphaned nephew into your home if you need domestic help. We need to build trust and social capital to sustain a healthy democratic participation, and we are going to need that more than ever. There are many people who have few, if any, personal contacts and live in loneliness. Others are increasingly living lives on social media, too much in the public domain.

Complementing existing interactions with more personal repeated contacts, face to face, can be encouraged through efforts to engender more community activity. Local geography and mobility matter. Less self-selection, i.e. a bit of randomness, in who we encounter within boundaries which encourage well-mannered interaction can help reduce the current trends towards divergence of opinion and intolerance. It challenges us to consider the views of others and appreciate better the range of what others consider reasonable. It socialises us.

Planning better local communities has been haphazard in the past, but we now have the potential for plans to be informed by much better data. For example, more coordination between charities and arms of the public sector, both national and local, may be possible. Artificial intelligence (AI) could be used to seek out large, meaningful agglomerations of currently very disjointed data sets from charities and public sector bodies. These could then, using standard statistical analysis, be used to ascertain the best combinations and sequencing of interventions affecting people's multiple complex and time-dependent needs. Results could then be measured in three ways: by well-being measures, by public sector cost savings (expected to be very large) and through measures of social capital. The best combinations according to these measures, once discovered, could then be replicated nationally.

Better infrastructure, housing and local media can help build trust and social capital, as Robert Putnam showed was possible in his study of Italy. Architecture and urban design have significant roles to play, as Jane Jacobs showed in her ground-breaking work on what engenders trust and communities in cities. However, appropriate ways to intervene will vary from place to place. And again, exactly how to do this could be based on much better data than in the past.

Delegation of political power may also be appropriate, not least as at local levels it can be easier than at higher levels to engender a sense that one's views can make a difference. However, political power should align with legitimacy, which in some cases may be difficult to achieve at a local level. There is also the problem that the centre loathes relinquishing power. Subsidiarity – the idea that power should devolve to the level of greatest policy effectiveness – has in practice been invoked as justification for centralisation of power in the EU, not the other way round. However, to be consistent with a vibrant democracy, subsidiarity should include not just a technical dimension but a legitimacy one. Swiss-style democracy, in which cantons have relatively more power than the central government, certainly seems a credible alternative to the ever-centralising state. I suspect that new media may also in time significantly help boost local democracy.

What we need is not another idealist philosopher to follow in the footsteps of Marx, but piecemeal social engineering, for which nudging is an important toolset. Using behavioural science to nudge behaviour in certain ways can be both a buttress of groupthink and a solution.[8] Some of the best examples of beneficial nudging come from government, where policies can be designed to help people make better choices.[9] However, as we have seen, nudging can also be used by governments to pursue agendas which are hidden from the electorate and which are highly reliant on fear and a reduction of self-reflection. Thus, an appropriate governance framework to ensure ethical standards and that the public interest is served is needed (and currently lacking). In the UK, an inquiry into the use of nudge techniques during lockdown would be a start. Nudging can help citizens make better decisions, and this could be extended to helping them take more responsibility. However, most of this is possible because citizens trust policy-makers to act in the public interest. Abuse this, and it fails to work as well without the use of fear and coercion.

RECKLESS PRECAUTION

After the Second World War, food rationing in Britain only ended fully in July 1954 – nine years after the war! An earlier move back to a market-based allocation of goods would have been better for consumers, although several weeks of severe supply and price disruption would no doubt have accompanied a full and sudden lifting. Leaders lacked the courage to face angry segments of the population and instead favoured sub-optimal gradualism. Bureaucrats held on to power too long. It was also a time, after enormous state intervention in the economy, when support for the use of market forces was at a low.

Expectations need to change regarding risk. Use of the precautionary motive to incite fear and stop rational consideration is a threat to democracy. Its replacement of cost–benefit analysis is reckless.

The costs of the precautionary motive can be seen in many examples. Matt Ridley says: 'Since 2005 Canada has approved seventy different transgenic varieties of crops whilst the European Union has approved just one, and that took thirteen years, by which time the crop was outdated.' Following protests by a small group of extremists, there then followed an EU moratorium on all new GM crops. This excessive and costly caution contrasts with the continued use of copper sulphate – which is toxic and bio-accumulates – as fungicide by organic farmers on human food crops. This is still allowed because there is no alternative available for organic farmers. They refuse to use newer safer ones. Such lack of consistency and hypocrisy is a sign of irrationality and reflects mass moral thinking – otherwise known as groupthink.

Though not meeting all the criteria, and so not as pure a case of groupthink, there is plenty of rigid prejudice and herd mentality in financial markets. To a large extent, it stems from excessive faith in certain economic theories, the simplification and misunderstanding of risk and uncertainty, excessive extrapolation from past patterns and the tendency to focus most on what is easily quantifiable. Systemic risk remains substantial as a result.

In part, we put up with nonsense because we have been un-taught that what does not kill you makes you stronger. The safety culture stifles risk, adventure, initiative, experience and learning. It leads to atrophy. Our fear and our stunted approach to risk is central to understanding our cowardice.

LEADERSHIP

The best societal governance models which mankind has found allow competition of ideas and freedom to act, subject to limits to protect others. Attempts to restrict freedom tend to reduce our stock of happiness and well-being, not increase them. The best political leaders are typically those who face effective checks and balances and have constant challenges to their policy ideas. If lead-ers think they have important information requiring drastic action, they should share it and subject possible responses to challenge before acting, not presume to know better than everyone else.

Truth in history is multi-faceted and open to different interpre-tations. One can be appreciative of past progress and achievements without being complacent or arrogant. I consider the determinism and preponderant focus on power and class of Karl Marx and his followers overdone and misleading. There is plenty of evidence that key individuals, and not just historical socio-economic forces, have shaped history. Leadership matters. The idea that Alexander or Napoleon did not change history is preposterous. We should, moreover, be proud of and revere many of our great leaders of the past. The British anti-slavers – Wilberforce and many others – changed history by helping to abolish the Atlantic slave trade at great economic cost to Britain and against significant domestic and international vested interests. Their moral leadership was made possible by British global power and succeeded where economic incentives were absent.

In an age of untruth and multiple conflicting truths, of competing morals and increasing intolerance, wise leadership is needed more than ever to protect democracy from the angry reactions of the resentful and hateful. For this, as argued at various points in this book, we need strong checks and balances on power, effective opposition, challenge and widespread political participation. We also need leaders who can see beyond tribal groupthink-defined divisions and unite us in hope.

Janis's famous example of groupthink was how the Kennedy Cabinet failed to challenge the groupthink which led to the Bay of Pigs disaster, and then Kennedy's alternative solution in reaching a way to solve the Cuban Missile Crisis. Policy-makers have learned from this and do try to search for novel ideas, but often not enough. Sometimes they lack political capital, and sometimes they lack the courage to counter pernicious groupthink. Too often we only search hard from within the bubble, not outside.

Worse, for a not insignificant segment of the elite, there is no desire to understand opponents or to learn from them. They have no desire to exit their groupthink. For some, there is no significant shared national identity or universal value to strive for, only the struggle for power. The us versus them mentality for some leads to a (clandestine) rejection of democracy as simply too difficult and impractical. Some cover this up with anti-nationalism and globalism; many are simply cynical. It emerges in the form of technocratic arguments for independent agencies, the consideration of legitimacy as afterthought (if that) and the wish to minimise all but basic communication with voters. This is combined with hubris, status and ambition – in short, ego. The wounds of Brexit run deep, as it was in large part a rejection of this aspect of the status quo.

Reflecting Socrates's views on democracy, and in contrast to the currently more dominant views of Plato, there needs to be a rebalancing between leadership and legitimacy. Our leaders need to reconnect with the electorate and break away from their addiction to comfortable slogans and propaganda. We need to counter dumbing up. Government needs to stop hiding behind technocratic delegation and stop trying to manipulate using fear. Ethical guidelines should be established for nudge policies. We need to establish mechanisms to counter groupthink and other poor practices in policy decision-making, including red-team expert panels. We should support national universalistic values. In addition to changes in schools and the health service, better mental health can be encouraged through national leadership which challenges our fears. Our greatest leaders in the past have been able to do this.

Leadership requires responsibility. And the range of things politicians need to be responsible for has recently increased substantially. This is especially true in the UK because of Brexit and the recovery of decision-making from Brussels. But it is also true for another reason. In *Unelected Power*, Paul Tucker lays out the criteria for delegation to independent agencies, one of which is stable electoral preferences.* However, new mass communication technology, and its effects on morals and behaviour, is shaking up electoral preferences. This means leaders may have to better hold to account or delegate less

---

* Others include having a specified goal, stable societal preferences, the existence of a credibility problem in committing to a settled policy regime, confidence in the efficacy of policy instruments, the lack of big distributional trade-off decisions, legislative ability to oversee the IA, and enough prestige for the IA's policy-makers to keep them focused on the goal.

control over public sector functions, previously considered below the radar, non-controversial and technical but increasingly seen as political and partisan. With the fiscal impact of monetary policy now highly significant, this includes the central bank.

Having leaders trying to manipulate us as much as they can get away with because they think they know better is an anti-democratic recipe. Democracy requires leaders who can be trusted, and trust has to be earned. What we need is thinking and challenging by example. We need courage and far-sightedness from our leaders, not fear and myopia. We need hope, the opposite of fear.*

CONCLUSION

People are irrational, and groupthink can be dominant in large populations. Groupthink leads to in-group focus but also the danger of being seriously wrong for a long time. Changes in communications technology have combined with a post-Second World War philosophical cancer which has grown into an attack, no longer confined to university campuses, on reason, science and history. These have fed intolerance and misanthropy. Instead of mounting a robust defence of liberal democracy and reason, our mainstream media and political elites, more prone than average to groupthink, have acquiesced and appeased. The result is dysfunctional policy choices, technocratic government, huge mental health and other societal costs, loss of legitimacy and a slide towards authoritarianism.

We need to stop the most damaging groupthink. When it comes

---

* Hope shares with fear the following characteristics: they do not depend on probabilities; are linked to actions to further a good outcome; are connected to an important outcome; and involve powerlessness.

to psychology and politics, human nature has not changed much in the past 2,000 years, even though communications technology and wealth are totally different. After the Bay of Pigs disaster, ex-President Eisenhower asked J. F. Kennedy: 'Mr President, before you approved this plan, did you have everybody in front of you debating the thing so you got pros and cons yourself and then made your decision?' Obviously, he had not. Kennedy's subsequent approach to the Cuban Missile Crisis, as documented by Irving Janis, is the quintessential way to battle groupthink. There is plenty which can be learned from the past, so it is a pity this often doesn't happen.

The race to save democracy is on. One possible set of futures echo Huxley's dystopia. This is a world which may maintain some vestiges of current democratic institutions but may be anarchic except for dominant economic interests: a world in which our thoughts, morals and actions are increasingly shaped by algorithms for profit; a world in which we are dumbed down, predictable and complacent. On the other side lies a version of Orwell's *1984*, in which fear, emanating from a central authoritarian political source, is overwhelming.

Crane Brinton showed that one of the few common warning signs of revolution was talk of revolution. That does not mean that the planet is going to end shortly, any more than King Canute could stop the sea. Fanatical opinions cannot, thankfully, change the laws of physics. However, it does mean that we are headed for turbulent political times, given the increased dissatisfaction with current political leadership and democracy.

I am an optimist and believe that electorates will awaken. I hope this book can be part of that process. Plato needs putting back in his box. I am with Socrates in wanting voters to become more self-aware and wake up to the threat facing them. As Popper put it: 'We must plan for freedom, and not only for security, if for no other reason than that only freedom can make security secure.'

Those societies most complacent, most comfortable, most asleep, will find it more difficult to adjust. Wealthy people and countries can afford to pander to groupthink for much longer than poorer people and countries. Their elites have educated themselves more thoroughly in nonsense, and they are stubborn in their sense of superiority. Developing countries are also closer to recent memories of political trauma and catastrophic economic policy – they may be poorer, but their electorates are more familiar with bad policies. I think they are going to cope better with the coming transition.

Current geopolitical conflicts largely emanate from political agendas in advanced economies for control beyond national boundaries. This inevitably includes occasional imposition of illegitimate policies on nations and peoples. Modern empires, like those which have gone before, are driven by a combination of economic and moral factors, but it is the moral element which makes them most vicious and dangerous, less rational or capable of compromise. As we discussed in Chapter 6, such agendas reflect not national interests but domestic politics, including those driven by groupthink. Power corrupts. Well-meaning power corrupts sanctimoniously. Western countries need to do better at understanding their national interests and designing foreign policies to further them. A brief look at UK and EU energy policy is enough to determine that this is currently not happening.

It takes a lot of effort to counter prejudice, and it is much better to avoid developing it in the first place. Trying to change media content is near to impossible, hence we have to focus on filtering and discounting its content and on an education for children which teaches reason and how to identify and cope with groupthink.

It is in the best interest of all of us to tackle groupthink better. To political conservatives, this may seem obvious. Yet the mainstream left has most to lose from the growth of fear in our societies. This is because it can both encourage their extremists and move the reactionary electorate more to the right. Just as Jonathan Haidt explained how Republicans seem to understand Democrats more than vice versa, the left has most to gain from understanding what is going on.

So, have we all gone mad? It is human nature to be a bit mad. We have the habit of irrationally hanging on to moral interpretations in the face of contrary evidence, and we have an array of techniques to allow us to do this. In extremis, this leads to mental illness. Those of us better able to believe in six impossible things before breakfast, as Lewis Carroll put it, cope better but are more prone to be enslaved by groupthink. Some of those in our elite are madder than others, and we (voters) need to steer them back to sanity. So yes, we are definitely mad, and getting madder, in both senses of the word, English and American.

But I am optimistic things will get better. We need to trust ourselves and each other. I have a greater faith in liberal democracy than in our elites. Just so long as we can wake up sufficiently to head off current authoritarian tendencies, which I believe we shall, we can emerge stronger. Yet I also believe that if our elites can be made better aware of the traps of groupthink, they will be more able and willing to identify and counter instances of it. Then the Great Enfranchisement brought about by new technology heralds a bright future of enhanced social capital, stronger local communities and vigorous democracy.

NOTES

INTRODUCTION

1   I. Janis, *Victims of Groupthink* (Boston: Houghton Mifflin, 1973).

CHAPTER 1: FOOLING OURSELVES AND OTHERS

1   Quoted in R. D. Kaplan, *The Coming Anarchy: Shattering the Dreams of the Post Cold War* (New York: Vintage, 2000), p. 152.

2   Quoted in D. Robson, *The Intelligence Trap* (London: Hodder & Stoughton, 2019), p. 40.

3   H. Melville, *Moby-Dick* (London: Richard Bentley, 1851).

4   M. Alvesson and A. Spicer, *The Stupidity Paradox: The Power and Pitfalls of Functional Stupidity at Work* (London: Profile, 2016).

5   G. Klein, *Sources of Power: How People Make Decisions* (Cambridge, MA: MIT Press, 1999).

6   M. Polanyi, *Personal Knowledge* (Chicago: Chicago University Press, 1958).

7   D. Kahneman, *Thinking, Fast and Slow* (London: Allen Lane, 2011), p. 24.

8   Robson, *The Intelligence Trap*, p. 84.

9   J. Haidt, *The Righteous Mind: Why Good People are Divided by Politics and Religion* (London: Penguin, 2012), p. 52.

10 A. O. Hirschman, *The Passions and the Interests: Political Arguments for Capitalism before Its Triumph* (New Jersey: Princeton University Press, 1977), p. 110.

11 Quoted in F. Furedi, *How Fear Works: Culture of Fear in the Twenty-First Century* (London: Bloomsbury Continuum, 2019), p. 25.

12 D. Riesman, *The Lonely Crowd* (New York: Yale University Press, 1961).

13 P. Bruckner, *The Fanaticism of the Apocalypse* (Cambridge: Polity, 2013).

14 See G. Lukianoff and J. Haidt, *The Coddling of the American Mind: How Good Intentions and Bad Ideas are Setting Up a Generation for Failure* (London: Penguin, 2018), p. 100.

15 M. Bond, *The Power of Others: Peer Pressure, Groupthink, and How the People Around Us Shape Everything We Do* (London: Oneworld, 2014), p. 119.

16 Haidt, *The Righteous Mind*, p. 31.

17 G. Himmelfarb, *The De-Moralization of Society* (New York: Vintage, 1994).

18 J. Henrich, S. Heine and A. Norenzayan, 'The Weirdest People in the World?', *Behavioural and Brain Sciences* (2010), vol. 33, pp. 61–83.

19 D. Kahneman and A. Tversky, 'Prospect Theory: An Analysis of Decision Under Risk', *Econometrica* (1979), vol. 47, no. 2, pp. 263–91.

20 See Kahneman, *Thinking, Fast and Slow*, p. 144.

21 Furedi, *How Fear Works*, p. 158.
22 See A. King and I. Crewe, *The Blunders of our Governments* (London: Oneworld, 2013).
23 See Lukianoff and Haidt, *The Coddling of the American Mind*, p. 208.

CHAPTER 2: GETTING ALONG TOGETHER
1 E. C. Banfield, *The Moral Basis of a Backward Society* (New York: Free Press, 1958).
2 R. Axelrod, *The Evolution of Cooperation* (New York: Basic Books, 1984).
3 R. Putnam, *Making Democracy Work: Civic Traditions in Modern Italy* (New Jersey: Princeton University Press, 1993).
4 L. Dodsworth, *A State of Fear: How the UK Government Weaponised Fear During the Covid-19 Pandemic* (London: Pinter & Martin, 2021).
5 J. Burnham, *The Managerial Revolution* (London: Penguin, 1941).
6 P. Tucker, *Unelected Power: The Quest for Legitimacy in Central Banking and the Regulatory State* (Oxon: Princeton University Press, 2018).

CHAPTER 3: SOCIAL MEDIA
1 S. Fry, J. Peterson, M. E. Dyson and M. Goldberg, *Political Correctness Gone Mad?* (London: Oneworld, 2018), p. 26.
2 Riesman, *The Lonely Crowd*, p. 176.
3 S. Zuboff, *The Age of Surveillance Capitalism* (London: Profile, 2019), p. 457.
4 M. Gladwell, *The Tipping Point* (London: Little, Brown, 2000).
5 N. Christakis and J. Fowler, *Connected: The Amazing Power of Social Networks and How They Shape Our Lives* (London: Harper, 2009), p. 133.
6 G. Henriques, 'Groupthink and the Evolution of Reason', in D. M. Allen and J. W. Howell (eds), *Groupthink in Science* (Switzerland: Springer, 2020).
7 According to Zuboff, *The Age of Surveillance Capitalism*, p. 456.
8 Quoted in Lukianoff and Haidt, *The Coddling of the American Mind*, p. 48.

CHAPTER 4: FROM ONE CRISIS TO THE NEXT
1 J. Jacobs, *The Nature of Economies* (New York: Modern Library, 2000).
2 M. Ridley, *How Innovation Works* (London: Fourth Estate, 2020).
3 Per Bak, Chao Tang and Kurt Wiesenfeld, 'Self-Organized Criticality', *Physical Review A* (1988), vol. 38, p. 364.
4 K. Hopper and W. Hopper, *The Puritan Gift: Reclaiming the American Dream Amidst Global Financial Chaos* (London: I. B. Tauris, 2009).
5 R. G. Rajan, *Fault Lines: How Hidden Fractures Still Threaten the World Economy* (Oxon: Princeton University Press, 2010).
6 'Oral Evidence: Coronavirus: Lessons Learnt', Health and Social Care Committee and Science and Technology Committee, HC 95, 26 May 2021.
7 M. King, *The End of Alchemy: Money, Banking and the Future of the Global Economy* (London: Little, Brown, 2016).

CHAPTER 5: SCIENCE AND ANTI-SCIENCE
1 J. E. H. Smith, *Irrationality: A History of the Dark Side of Reason* (Oxon: Princeton University Press, 2019), p. 295.
2 K. Popper, *The Open Society and Its Enemies*, 5th edn (Oxon: Routledge, 1945).
3 Ibid., p. 229.
4 A. Bloom, *The Closing of the American Mind* (New York: Touchstone, 1987), p. 21.
5 L. Breuning, 'The Neurochemistry of Science Bias', in Allen and Howell, *Groupthink in Science*, p. 11.
6 R. Scruton, *Fools, Frauds and Firebrands: Thinkers of the New Left* (London: Bloomsbury Continuum, 2015), p. 159.

7   For further details see H. Pluckrose and J. Lindsay, *Cynical Theories: How Universities Made Everything about Race, Gender, and Identity – And Why This Harms Everybody* (London: Swift, 2020).

8   Ibid., p. 209.

9   Both examples from D. Murray, *The Madness of Crowds: Gender, Race and Identity* (London: Bloomsbury Continuum, 2019).

10 See for example A. Brannigan, 'Conflict Between Public Health Science and Markets: The Case of Tobacco Research – Illustrations from Tobacco and CO_2', in Allen and Howell, *Groupthink in Science*.

11 D. M. Allen and E. A. Reedy, 'Seven Cases: Examples of How Important Ideas Were Initially Attacked or Ridiculed by the Professions', in Allen and Howell, *Groupthink in Science*, pp. 51–3.

12 Dodsworth, *A State of Fear*, p. 151.

13 See A. Montford, *The Hockey Stick Illusion* (London: Anglosphere, 2010) and Chapter 4 in C. Booker, *The Real Global Warming Disaster* (London: Continuum, 2009).

CHAPTER 6: WE HAVE SEEN WORSE

1   Hirschman, *The Passions and the Interests*, p. 13.

2   Quoted in Himmelfarb, *The De-Moralization of Society*, p. 60.

3   See for example P. Bobbitt, *The Shield of Achilles: War, Peace and the Course of History* (London: Penguin, 2002).

4   Y. Mounk, 'Yes, American Democracy Could Break Down', Politico, 22 October 2016, and quoted in I. Bremmer, *Us vs Them: The Failure of Globalism* (London: Portfolio Penguin, 2018), p. 163.

5   Hirschman, *The Passions and the Interests*, p. 44.

6   Popper, *The Open Society and Its Enemies*, p. xxxviii.

7   Scruton, *Fools, Frauds and Firebrands: Thinkers of the New Left*, p. 57.

8   C. Brinton, *The Anatomy of Revolution: Revised and Expanded Edition* (New York: Vintage, 1965).

9   See Kaplan, *The Coming Anarchy*, p. 135.

10 Popper, *The Open Society and Its Enemies*, p. 442.

11 Brinton, *The Anatomy of Revolution*, p. 58.

12 Scruton, *Fools, Frauds and Firebrands*, p. 271.

13 See J. Sides, M. Tesler and L. Vavreck, *Identity Crisis: The 2016 Presidential Campaign and the Battle for the Meaning of America* (Oxon: Princeton University Press, 2018).

14 P. Collier and J. Kay, *Greed is Dead: Politics After Individualism* (London: Allen Lane, 2020), pp. 38–9.

15 D. Runciman, *Political Hypocrisy: The Mask of Power, from Hobbes to Orwell and Beyond* (Oxon: Princeton University Press, 2008), p. 205.

16 A. Bacevich, *After the Apocalypse: America's Role in a World Transformed* (New York: Metropolitan Books, 2021), p. 27.

CHAPTER 7: MEDIA AND ELITE BUBBLES

1   H. Rosling, *Factfulness* (London: Sceptre, 2018).

2   M. C. Nussbaum, *The Monarchy of Fear: A Philosopher Looks at Our Political Crisis* (New York: Simon & Schuster, 2018) pp. 211–12.

3   Furedi, *How Fear Works*, p. 167.

CHAPTER 8: ESCAPING FROM GROUPTHINK

1   G. Tett, *The Silo Effect* (London: Little, Brown, 2015), p. 254.

2   Rosling, *Factfulness*, p. 188.

3   Alvesson and Spicer, *The Stupidity Paradox*, p. 229.

4 Martin Kettle, *The Guardian*, 24 June 2021.

5 As argued in N. Postman, *Technopoly: The Surrender of Culture to Technology* (New York: Vintage, 1993).

6 R. Jeffrey and A. Doron, *The Great Indian Phone Book: How Cheap Mobile Phones Change Business, Politics and Daily Life* (London: C. Hurst, 2013).

7 Zuboff, *The Age of Surveillance Capitalism*, p. 524.

8 See for example B. Frischmann and E. Sellinger, *Re-Engineering Humanity* (Cambridge: Cambridge University Press, 2018).

9 See R. H. Thaler and C. R. Sunstein, *Nudge: Improving Decisions About Health, Wealth, and Happiness* (London: Yale, 2008).

ACKNOWLEDGEMENTS

This book is a product of lockdown. I ran out of distractions and excuses not to write it. It is also thanks to regular long Saturday morning walks with my neighbour and friend Liam Halligan, who not only encouraged me to write the book but on whom I tested many of my thoughts. I would also like to thank those friends and family members who read and gave me comments on earlier drafts, including Jolyon Booth, Nicolas and Jeanne Lynch-Aird, James Plummer, John Sandham, Hector Luisi, Peter Lilley, Sara Varey and Francis Lambert. Special thanks also to the team at Biteback, particularly Olivia Beattie, whose intelligent editing has greatly improved the book.